For internal use

Enclosures code(s)

Copies: In 1
No. of Parcels 1

1

Total weight .622kgs

Delivery arranged by WDS Ltd.

Great Britain Pounds

Initiator: SWESTBY
CSCOMBEOD PRTINVR QPGMR 22/03/23 19:30:35 JWINV3F

WILEY

Publishing Offices and Accounts

John Wiley & Sons Limited
The Atrium, Southern Gate
Chichester, West Sussex
PO19 8SQ, UK

VAT No   GB   376 766987
Telephone +44 (0) 1243 779777
SAN   GB   001 2279

Service, Distribution and Returns

John Wiley & Sons Limited
European Distribution Centre
New Era Estate, Oldlands Way
Bognor Regis, West Sussex
PO22 9NQ, UK

Telephone +44 (0) 1243 843291
E-Mail   cs-books@wiley.com
www.wiley.com

Bill to

Princeton University Press
Review Account
99 Banbury Road
Oxford
OX2 6JX

Ship to

Victoria Addis
Academic Chatter AC Rev ofBook
50 Grosvenor Drive
Derby
DE23 3UQ

REVIEW COPY No.   2297246

Tax Point Date	22/03/23
Account No.	0009173 /0000
Wiley EORI No.	GB37676698 7000
Page No. 1	
Run No.	925
Order Type	53

Carrier   DPD - Standard

Special Instructions ***

Customer Notes

Order Reference/ Stg Locn	Quantity	Author/ Title	Binding	ISBN/ EAN	Price
19170416	1	Bartels Democracy Erodes from the Top	CLOTH	0691244502 9780691244501	25.00

REVIEW COPIES

Free of charge.

DEMOCRACY ERODES FROM THE TOP

PRINCETON STUDIES IN
Political Behavior

Tali Mendelberg, Series Editor

Democracy Erodes from the Top

LEADERS, CITIZENS, AND THE
CHALLENGE OF POPULISM IN EUROPE

LARRY M. BARTELS

PRINCETON UNIVERSITY PRESS

PRINCETON & OXFORD

Published by Princeton University Press
41 William Street, Princeton, New Jersey 08540
99 Banbury Road, Oxford OX2 6JX

press.princeton.edu

Library of Congress Cataloging-in-Publication Data

Names: Bartels, Larry M., 1956– author.
Title: Democracy erodes from the top : leaders, citizens, and the challenges
    of populism in Europe / Larry M. Bartels.
Description: Princeton : Princeton University Press, [2023] | Series: Princeton
    studies in political behavior | Includes bibliographical references and index.
Identifiers: LCCN 2022037339 (print) | LCCN 2022037340 (ebook) |
    ISBN 9780691244501 (hardback) | ISBN 9780691244518 (ebook)
Subjects: LCSH: Populism—Europe. | Democracy—Europe. | Europe—Politics and
    government. | BISAC: POLITICAL SCIENCE / Political Ideologies / Democracy |
    POLITICAL SCIENCE / Civics & Citizenship
Classification: LCC JN40 .B356 2023 (print) | LCC JN40 (ebook) |
    DDC 320.56/62094—dc23/eng/20220915
LC record available at https://lccn.loc.gov/2022037339
LC ebook record available at https://lccn.loc.gov/2022037340

British Library Cataloging-in-Publication Data is available

Editorial: Bridget Flannery-McCoy and Alena Chekanov
Production Editorial: Nathan Carr
Jacket/Cover Design: Karl Spurzem
Production: Lauren Reese
Publicity: James Schneider and Kathryn Stevens
Copyeditor: Hank Southgate

Jacket/Cover Credit: Vladimir Polikarpov / Alamy Stock Photo

This book has been composed in Arno

There are, I believe, immense confusions in the current theory of democracy which frustrate and pervert its action. I have attacked certain of the confusions with no conviction except that a false philosophy tends to stereotype thought against the lessons of experience. I do not know what the lessons will be when we have learned to think of public opinion as it is, and not as the fictitious power we have assumed it to be.

—WALTER LIPPMANN, *THE PHANTOM PUBLIC* (1925)

CONTENTS

DEMOCRACY ERODES FROM THE TOP

1

A Crisis of Democracy?

THERE IS A PALPABLE sense of crisis in Western democracies. The rise of right-wing populist parties in several parts of Europe, the erosion of constitutional checks and balances in Hungary and Poland, the 2016 Brexit vote in the United Kingdom, the election of Donald Trump as US president, and the antidemocratic turn of the Republican Party under his leadership have all stirred significant alarm regarding the present state of democracy and prospects for its future.

Political leaders and would-be leaders have not hesitated to stoke perceptions of crisis in pursuit of their own ends. The then-vice-president of France's right-wing National Front greeted Trump's election with a triumphal tweet: "Their world is collapsing. Ours is being built." Even more ominously, Hungarian Prime Minister Viktor Orbán declared that "the era of liberal democracy is over."[1]

The notion that democracy is in crisis provides a compelling hook for much recent political writing. In the opening pages of his book *Fractured Continent: Europe's Crises and the Fate of the West*, a former chief European correspondent of the *Washington Post* warned, "Just a quarter century after the liberal international order of open markets, free speech, and democratic elections had triumphed over the forces of communism, the Western democracies now seem in danger of collapsing, as a backlash against globalization arouses angry opponents of immigration, free trade, and cultural tolerance."[2]

---

1. Josh Lowe, Owen Matthews, and Matt McAllester, "Why Europe's Populist Revolt Is Spreading," *Newsweek*, 23 November 2016. Marc Santora and Helene Bienvenu, "Secure in Hungary, Orban Readies for Battle with Brussels," *New York Times*, 11 May 2018.

2. Drozdiak (2017: xii).

Some academic observers have echoed this apocalyptic tone. One's attention-getting book began,

> There are long decades in which history seems to slow to a crawl. Elections are won and lost, laws adopted and repealed, new stars born and legends carried to their graves. But for all the ordinary business of time passing, the lodestars of culture, society, and politics remain the same.
>
> Then there are those short years in which everything changes all at once. Political newcomers storm the stage. Voters clamor for policies that were unthinkable until yesterday. Social tensions that had long simmered under the surface erupt into terrifying explosions. A system of government that had seemed immutable looks as though it might come apart.
>
> This is the kind of moment in which we now find ourselves.[3]

One of the world's most eminent scholars of comparative politics began his book *Crises of Democracy* with less purple prose, but many of the same empirical premises. "Something is happening," he wrote. "'Anti-establishment,' 'anti-system,' 'anti-elite,' 'populist' sentiments are exploding in many mature democracies. . . . Confidence in politicians, parties, parliaments, and governments is falling. Even the support for democracy as a system of government has weakened."[4]

All of this does sound portentous. But, at least insofar as the attitudes and preferences of ordinary Europeans are concerned, *virtually none of it is true.* On the whole, Europeans were just as satisfied with the working of democracy in 2019 as they had been 15 years earlier. Trust in national parliaments and politicians remained virtually unchanged. They were just as enthusiastic as they had been about the project of European integration. While "angry opponents of immigration" dominated the headlines, most Europeans' attitudes toward immigrants and immigration were becoming significantly warmer, not more hostile. In these and other respects, the conventional wisdom about a "crisis of democracy" in contemporary Europe is strikingly at odds with evidence from public opinion surveys.

One aim of this book is to document the gulf between the alarming portrait of democracy in crisis and the more prosaic reality of contemporary European public opinion. The point of this debunking is *not* to suggest that all is well with European democracy—though, for what it is worth, I do think the "dan-

---

3. Mounk (2018: 1).
4. Przeworski (2019: 1).

ger of collapsing" is greatly overblown. The deeper issue here is that the focus on public opinion as a barometer of democratic functioning is itself fundamentally misguided.

The "folk theory" of democracy, as Christopher Achen and I have called it, exalts "government of the people, by the people, for the people," in Abraham Lincoln's famous formulation. Even when citizens' preferences do not directly determine policy, they are, somehow, supposed to be the primary force animating democratic politics. The myth of rule by the people implies that bad attitudes, rash choices, or insufficient diligence in fulfilling the obligations of citizenship must constitute a crisis of democracy. And conversely, if democracy falters, its erosion or breakdown must somehow be traceable to faults of public opinion. Regardless of whether the reasoning goes forward, from vagaries of public opinion to their presumed consequences, or backward, from failures of democratic institutions to their presumed causes, the logical glue connecting public opinion and crises of democracy is supplied by the "folk theory."[5]

The alternative view propounded here might be termed an *elitist* account of democratic crisis. "Elitist" has become a scornful term in modern discourse, especially in the context of discussions of democracy.[6] My aim in employing it here is not to wade into complex normative debates regarding the appropriate roles of leaders and citizens in democratic politics. It is simply to underscore the remarkable disconnection of ordinary public opinion from the developments that are commonly taken as indicative of a "crisis of democracy" in contemporary Europe, and the crucial role of political leadership in preserving or dismantling democratic institutions and procedures.

At first glance, it may seem preposterous to suggest that ordinary citizens are bit players in Europe's political troubles. However, the notion has a good

---

5. Achen and Bartels (2016). The "folk theory" undergirds a good deal of scholarly writing as well as popular thinking about democracy. For example, one of the most influential scholars of contemporary democracy, James Stimson (2015: xix), described shifts in public opinion as "the most important factor in American politics" and "the drive wheel" of policy change; "the public governs," he wrote, "much more than most realize."

6. See, for example, the 1966 exchange in the *American Political Science Review* between Jack Walker and Robert Dahl regarding "the elitist theory of democracy." In a letter to the editor, Walker (1966: 391) wrote, "After reading Professor Dahl's rejoinder, I am convinced that it was a mistake to use the label 'The Elitist Theory of Democracy'. . . . The word 'elitist' apparently carries, at least in Dahl's view, some objectionable anti-democratic connotations." Despite Walker's misgivings, a Google search for the exact phrase "elitist theory of democracy" returns more than 10,000 results.

deal of both tacit and explicit support in scholarship on breakdowns of democracy. One of the most striking, but little-remarked-upon, features of Steven Levitsky and Daniel Ziblatt's scholarly best-seller, *How Democracies Die*, is the scant attention the authors felt compelled to devote to public opinion. "Institutional guardrails," "unwritten rules," "fateful alliances"—these are the constraints and choices facing political leaders, not their followers. The same might be said of much scholarship on democratic instability over the preceding 40 years. One scholar who did pay unusually close attention to the role of "ordinary people" in more than a dozen full-blown breakdowns of democracy in 20th-century Europe and Latin America, Nancy Bermeo, concluded that "in the vast majority of our cases, voters did not choose dictatorship at the ballot box," and that "the culpability for democracy's demise lay overwhelmingly with political elites."[7]

A key implication of the evidence presented in this book is that the culpability for Europe's current political troubles likewise lies overwhelmingly with political elites rather than ordinary citizens. That is not to say that public opinion is necessarily wise or highly principled. We will see plenty of instances of ordinary Europeans exhibiting foibles common to humans in all realms of life, including short-sightedness, scapegoating, and aversion to change. But their failings have generally not been decisive in accounting for toxic politics, policy failures, or democratic backsliding.

Of course, recognizing the decisive importance of political elites in the democratic process will not, in itself, explain why they behave the way they do, much less provide a blueprint for curing the ills of democracy. In that sense, the present work is merely a *preface* to democratic theory rather than a fully developed account of how and why democracies succeed or fail. Nonetheless, given the distorting impact of the "folk theory" on thinking about democracy, being clear about what Europe's crisis of democracy is *not* may be an indispensable first step toward better understanding what it *is*.

"Something Is Happening"

Perceived crises of democracy are hardly rare. A Google search turns up almost 300 million results for the phrase "crisis of democracy," ranging widely through time and space, from "The Present Crisis in Democracy" by former Harvard

---

7. Levitsky and Ziblatt (2018); Linz and Stepan (1978); Mainwaring and Pérez-Liñán (2013); Bermeo (2003: 222, 221).

University president A. Lawrence Lowell in *Foreign Affairs* in 1934 to "The Crisis of Democracy" report prepared for the Trilateral Commission by three prominent social scientists in 1975, to the recent survey "Democracy in Crisis" from the global research and advocacy organization Freedom House.[8]

On the *New York Times* op-ed page, legendary columnist James Reston pondered "The Crisis of Democracy" in 1974, and again in 1975. A generation later, in 2012, the distinguished economist Amartya Sen addressed "The Crisis of European Democracy," warning that "drastic cuts in public services with very little general discussion of their necessity, efficacy or balance have been revolting to a large section of the European population and have played into the hands of extremists on both ends of the political spectrum." In 2018, political researcher David Adler amped up the alarmism, writing, "The warning signs are flashing red: Democracy is under threat. Across Europe and North America, candidates are more authoritarian, party systems are more volatile, and citizens are more hostile to the norms and institutions of liberal democracy." The following year, not to be outdone by op-ed writers, the *Times* Berlin bureau chief capped off a five-part podcast on "The Battle for Europe" with an episode asking ominously, "Can Liberal Democracy Survive in Europe?"[9]

A few writers have swum against this strong tide of alarmism. For example, a leading scholar of populism, Cas Mudde, provocatively characterized populist radical right parties as "a relatively minor nuisance in West European democracies," pointing to

> the relatively modest electoral support that these parties generate in parliamentary elections. With an average support of less than 10 per cent of the electorate, few PRRPs are major players in their national political system. Moreover, even fewer make it into government, majority or minority, and most are shunned by the other parties in parliament. Hence, direct policy

8. Muliro (2017); Lowell (1934); Crozier, Huntington, and Watanuki (1975). Michael J. Abramowitz, "Democracy in Crisis," Freedom House, https://freedomhouse.org/report /freedom-world/2018/democracy-crisis.

9. James Reston, "The Crisis of Democracy," *New York Times*, 3 March 1974. James Reston, "The Crisis of Democracy," *New York Times*, 29 June 1975. Amartya Sen, "The Crisis of European Democracy," *New York Times*, 22 May 2012. David Adler, "Centrists Are the Most Hostile to Democracy, Not Extremists," *New York Times*, 23 May 2018. Katrin Bennhold, "Can Liberal Democracy Survive in Europe?," *New York Times*, 14 June 2019.

influence is already quite rare. And even when PRRPs make it into power, they are dogs that bark loud, but hardly ever bite.[10]

Unfortunately, many observers are not as clear-eyed as Mudde—and even if they were, "a relatively minor nuisance" would stand little chance of capturing the popular imagination when pitted against a "crisis of democracy" in which "everything changes all at once." Journalists, especially, are partial to dogs that bark loud, even if they hardly ever bite.

In this book, I summarize broad trends in European public opinion from 2002 through 2019, focusing particularly on attitudes commonly taken as symptomatic of a "crisis of democracy," including economic disaffection, antipathy to immigration and European integration, ideological polarization, distrust of political elites, and dissatisfaction with the workings of democracy itself. I examine the impact of these attitudes on support for right-wing populist parties, which turns out to be substantial. I also explore their role in precipitating significant erosions of democracy in Hungary and Poland, which turns out to be remarkably modest.

My data on European public opinion come primarily from the European Social Survey (ESS), an academic collaboration that has tracked political and social views in most European countries since 2002. I focus on 23 countries, each of which has been surveyed at least four times; 15 are represented in all nine rounds of the survey, providing roughly biannual readings of opinion from 2002 through 2019.[11] Table 1.1 shows the countries represented in each wave of the survey as well as the sample size in each country-round; the total sample includes 354,829 survey respondents.[12]

A major virtue of the ESS project is that the survey content has been admirably consistent across countries and rounds, providing hundreds of thousands of responses for most key indicators—an unparalleled record of con-

---

10. Mudde (2013: 14).

11. Data, documentation, and background information appear on the ESS website, https://www.europeansocialsurvey.org/. My analysis generally includes EU countries as of 2006 and those in the Schengen area. It excludes countries admitted to the EU after 2006 (Bulgaria, Croatia, and Romania), some small countries with little or no ESS data (Cyprus, Iceland, Latvia, Luxembourg, and Malta), and several other countries represented sporadically in the ESS dataset (Albania, Israel, Kosovo, Montenegro, Russia, Serbia, Turkey, and Ukraine).

12. The 354,829 respondents represent 183 country-rounds; the country-round sample sizes range from 985 to 3,142 and average 1,939. Surveys were not conducted in the remaining 24 country-rounds (11.6%).

TABLE 1.1. Countries Represented in European Social Surveys, 2002–2019

	1	2	3	4	5	6	7	8	9	Total
Austria (AT)	2,257	2,256	2,459	0	0	0	1,825	2,010	2,503	13,310
Belgium (BE)	1,899	1,778	1,798	1,760	1,704	1,869	1,769	1,766	1,769	16,112
Czechia (CZ)	1,360	3,142	0	2,394	2,518	2,076	2,148	2,269	2,398	18,305
Denmark (DK)	1,506	1,487	1,505	1,610	1,576	1,650	1,502	0	0	10,836
Estonia (EE)	0	1,989	1,517	1,954	1,935	2,452	2,111	2,019	1,905	15,882
Finland (FI)	2,000	2,039	1,921	2,340	1,878	2,197	2,087	1,925	1,755	18,142
France (FR)	1,503	1,806	1,986	2,073	1,820	2,021	1,977	2,070	2,010	17,266
Germany (DE)	2,919	2,870	2,916	2,751	3,031	2,958	3,045	2,852	2,360	25,702
Great Britain (GB)	2,052	1,897	2,394	2,352	2,422	2,286	2,264	1,959	2,211	19,837
Greece (GR)	2,566	2,406	0	2,249	2,811	0	0	0	0	10,032
Hungary (HU)	1,685	1,498	1,518	1,544	1,561	2,014	1,733	1,624	1,661	14,838
Ireland (IE)	2,069	2,304	1,814	1,764	2,576	2,628	2,433	2,757	2,216	20,561
Italy (IT)	1,207	0	0	0	0	985	0	2,653	2,746	7,591
Lithuania (LT)	0	0	0	0	1,677	2,109	2,250	2,122	1,836	9,994
Netherlands (NL)	2,364	1,881	1,889	1,778	1,829	1,845	1,969	1,681	1,673	16,909
Norway (NO)	2,036	1,760	1,750	1,760	1,653	1,666	1,451	1,545	1,406	15,027
Poland (PL)	2,110	1,716	1,750	1,759	1,852	1,999	1,728	1,705	1,500	16,119
Portugal (PT)	1,511	2,052	2,222	2,642	2,296	2,229	1,265	1,270	1,055	16,542
Slovakia (SK)	0	1,512	1,766	1,810	1,856	1,847	0	0	1,083	9,874
Slovenia (SI)	1,519	1,442	1,476	1,477	1,403	1,257	1,224	1,307	1,318	12,423
Spain (ES)	1,729	1,664	1,876	2,828	2,021	1,967	1,975	1,958	1,668	17,686
Sweden (SE)	1,999	1,948	1,927	1,830	1,497	1,898	1,829	1,551	1,541	16,020
Switzerland (CH)	2,084	2,141	1,804	2,005	1,583	1,555	1,582	1,525	1,542	15,821
Total	38,375	41,588	36,288	40,680	41,499	41,508	38,167	38,568	38,156	354,829

Note: Sample size by country and ESS round

temporary European public opinion.[13] In analyzing these data, I focus on both broad patterns and cross-country variation in attitudes and trends. The adult populations of the 23 countries represented in my analyses vary widely, from just over one million in Estonia to more than 70 million in Germany. To provide trustworthy summaries of public opinion in Europe as a whole, I generally weight the data from each country in each round of the survey in proportion to its population.[14] In analyses characterizing trends or comparing time periods, I employ statistical adjustments designed to compensate for changes in the set of countries participating in each ESS round.[15] Additional information regarding my data and analyses—including details of survey question wording and coding, descriptive statistics for key indicators, comparisons of trends based on weighted and unweighted data, and discussion of statistical methods and assumptions—appears in the Appendix.

Economic Crisis, Political Crisis?

Much of what has been written about the "crisis of democracy" in contemporary Europe posits a key role for the political ramifications of the global economic crisis triggered by the Wall Street meltdown of 2008. The magnitude of the economic crisis and its resonant echoes of the Great Depression led many observers to draw parallels between contemporary political developments and those of the 1930s, including the rise of populism in the US and fascism in Europe. For example, Matt O'Brien of the *Washington Post* argued that "it shouldn't be too surprising that the worst economic crisis since the 1930s has led to the worst political crisis within liberal democracies since the 1930s." The thesis of John Judis's popular book *The Populist Explosion* was conveyed by its subtitle: *How the Great Recession Transformed*

---

13. There are at least 330,000 nonmissing observations for 16 of the 22 key ESS variables listed in Appendix Table A1.

14. Appendix Table A3 details the composition of the weighted sample. Table A4 provides a comparison of overall trends in the weighted and unweighted data. My substantive conclusions remain essentially unchanged when each country-round is weighted equally.

15. Unless otherwise indicated, all analyses of data from Europe as a whole include indicators ("fixed effects") for countries. To the extent that cross-country differences in opinion are consistent over time, this approach will provide reliable estimates of shifts and trends in opinion despite missing country-rounds. To allow for statistical uncertainty due to idiosyncrasies in the timing and administration of each survey, most analyses allow for arbitrary correlation among the statistical disturbances in each country-round ("clustered standard errors").

American and European Politics. A scholarly guide *The Global Rise of Populism* reported that "a prolonged global financial downturn, rising unemployment in a number of areas and a loss of faith in perceived elite projects like the European Union are helping fuel the flames" of populism, threatening "a crisis of faith in democracy" in which citizens are "more and more disillusioned with mainstream politics."[16]

Despite this alarmism, as we shall see, Europe's "worst political crisis" since the 1930s turned out to be milder, briefer, much more localized, and different in kind from the rise of fascism. European politics was altered, but hardly transformed—and even the alterations were often quite temporary. This is particularly true for shifts in public opinion. The timing of the economic crisis roughly divides the period covered by my analyses into three distinct subperiods: a pre-crisis period (from 2002 through 2007), a crisis period (from 2008 through 2013), and a post-crisis period (from 2014 through 2019). Thus, in many cases it will be fruitful to characterize stability or change in public opinion, or in the bases of public opinion, across these three periods, with due allowance for the roughness of the division and for differences in the precise timing and duration of the economic crisis in different parts of Europe.[17] Applying this periodization, we shall generally find that public opinion shifted somewhat during the crisis, but subsequently reverted to pre-crisis patterns.

In Chapter 2, I briefly review the economic and political developments that constituted "the worst economic crisis since the 1930s," including the collapse of financial arrangements built on subprime mortgage lending, the resulting global recession, the sovereign debt crisis stemming from the impact of that recession on the balance sheets of governments and financial institutions, and the struggles of European political leaders to respond to those economic blows. Despite the severity of the economic downturn, Europeans' economic mood was surprisingly resilient. By 2014–2015, average satisfaction with the economy was higher than it had been before the crisis began, and it continued

---

16. Matt O'Brien, "Why Liberal Democracy Only Dies When Conservatives Help," *Washington Post*, 17 May 2017. Judis (2016); Moffitt (2016: 159–160, 1).

17. In other cases, this periodization will be less helpful. For example, in considering attitudes toward immigrants and immigration, the salience of the asylum crisis of 2015 argues against the assumption of consistency in the nature and bases of opinion from 2013 to 2019, so I focus considerable attention on stability and change *within* the post-(economic) crisis period.

to improve substantially until the onset of the Covid-19 pandemic in 2020. There were pockets of severe, prolonged economic pain; but for most Europeans, the crisis was successfully contained.

Many observers viewed the Euro-crisis as a failure, first and foremost, of the European Union. Ashoka Mody, an international economist with experience at the International Monetary Fund (IMF) and the World Bank, castigated European leaders' "hesitant monetary and fiscal policy response to the global financial crisis" and "disastrous policy errors in dealing with the eurozone's own rolling crises between late 2009 and early 2014." According to political scientist Sheri Berman, "The EU's technocratic rather than democratic nature generated a backlash against the EU as it became associated with economic problems rather than prosperity."[18] Here, too, however, public opinion surveys reveal remarkably little evidence of crisis. Overall support for European integration dipped only modestly in the wake of the Euro-crisis, and by 2019 it was higher than at any point since at least 2004. Moreover, the places where enthusiasm for European integration did decline significantly— Slovakia, Czechia, Poland, and Hungary—were places that experienced unusually *high* levels of economic growth, suggesting that the most important challenges facing the EU were not rooted in "economic problems," but in cultural and political frictions.

The Euro-crisis also magnified long-standing concerns about the viability of the European welfare state. Even before the crisis, scholars were writing of "the beleaguered welfare states" of Western Europe. In 1998, the managing director of the IMF announced a "Worldwide Crisis in the Welfare State," warning ominously that "reforms will be necessary." The Euro-crisis was a massive additional shock to the system, driving up public debt and generating demands for austerity from bondholders and the so-called Troika—the European Commission, the European Central Bank, and the IMF. "As the financial crisis puts strains on national budgets," an analyst writing in the midst of the crisis anticipated, "the dissatisfaction with the way democracy works is likely to be exacerbated. High deficits and huge public debt will force governments to curb spending, shrink the public sector, and look for further revenues from privatization for years to come . . . and citizens' faith in democratic politics is likely to erode further as a result."[19]

18. Mody (2018: 391, 458); Berman (2019: 402).
19. Esping-Andersen (1996: ix, 1); Michel Camdessus, "Worldwide Crisis in the Welfare State: What Next in the Context of Globalization?" International Monetary Fund, 15 Octo-

In Chapter 3, I explore the implications of the economic crisis for the contemporary European welfare state. I assess the impact of the crisis on patterns of social spending, focusing especially on the austerity policies imposed or inspired by the Troika in Greece, Spain, and Ireland. I also explore the impact of the Euro-crisis on citizens' perceptions of the quality of social services and on overall satisfaction with their lives. Surprisingly, Europeans were significantly more satisfied with the quality of health services, education, and life as a whole in the years after the Euro-crisis than they had been before it began. These improvements in subjective well-being seem to have been due, at least in part, to a gradual increase in real social spending, notwithstanding the strains put on national budgets by the financial crisis.

In light of these improvements in subjective well-being, it should perhaps not be surprising that public support for the welfare state remained steadfast. The Euro-crisis produced no perceptible shift in overall left-right ideology or in support for income redistribution. More detailed questions regarding specific government social responsibilities and spending programs produced virtually identical readings of public opinion in 2016 as in 2006. The largest—still modest—shift in opinion over the course of this tumultuous decade was a decline in public support for *cutting* government spending as a means of bolstering the economy. Both functionally and politically, the European welfare state emerged from the Euro-crisis in remarkably good shape.

Not-So-Bad Attitudes

The resilience of public support for the European welfare state and for the project of European integration are just two significant examples of a broader pattern in European public opinion. Time and again, readers primed to expect a political terrain in which "everything changes all at once" will instead find that, with respect to public opinion, not much changed at all—and certainly not for the worse.

In Chapter 4, I document another instance of this pattern, public opinion regarding immigrants and immigration. Europe has experienced a steady inflow of immigrants in recent decades, and in 2015–2016 faced a massive influx of asylum-seekers, mostly from war-torn Syria, Afghanistan, and Iraq. Observers trumpeted an "immigration crisis," with headlines warning that "The

---

ber 1998, https://www.imf.org/en/News/Articles/2015/09/28/04/53/sp101598; Schäfer (2013: 192).

Immigration Crisis Is Tearing Europe Apart" and that "Europe's Immigration Crisis Is Just Beginning."[20] But while "angry opponents of immigration" have dominated media portrayals, there is remarkably little evidence that these surges in immigration and asylum-seeking produced any significant erosion in public attitudes toward immigrants. In Sweden, which experienced substantial net immigration over the past two decades and one of Europe's largest influxes of asylum-seekers in 2015, attitudes toward immigrants and immigration remained more positive than anywhere else in Europe. In Germany, where Chancellor Angela Merkel's determination to open borders to refugees was hailed as an act of remarkable political courage, public support for immigration remained unwavering throughout the asylum crisis, even in the wake of a deadly terrorist attack by a foreigner denied asylum.

Overall, European public opinion toward immigrants became gradually but significantly more positive in the face of these developments, largely due to generational replacement of older cohorts by young people with more welcoming attitudes. The few places where anti-immigrant sentiment increased were mostly conservative, highly religious countries in which prominent nationalist political leaders mounted vigorous anti-immigrant campaigns—most notably, Orbán's Hungary. And even in those places, the same process of generational replacement seemed to be at work, making it likely that anti-immigrant sentiment will fade with time, as it already has in other parts of Europe.

In Chapter 5, I turn to a variety of specifically political attitudes, including ideological polarization, trust in political leaders and institutions, and satisfaction with the workings of democracy itself. Here, too, the conventional wisdom is that the Euro-crisis has reshaped public opinion for the worse. For example, the editors of the scholarly volume *Politics in the Age of Austerity* argued that the "vast deterioration in public finances" stemming from the crisis put "pressure on government to make unpopular choices," producing popular frustration with democracy. "In parallel with the faltering capacity for discretionary spending," they wrote, "public fatigue with democratic practice and core institutions has grown."[21]

But here, too, the reality seems rather less dire. Europeans' trust in parliaments and politicians, having dipped modestly during the Euro-crisis, rebounded completely once it ended. So, too, did satisfaction with incumbent

20. Bruce Stokes, "The Immigration Crisis Is Tearing Europe Apart," *Foreign Policy*, 22 July 2016, http://foreignpolicy.com/2016/07/22/the-immigration-crisis-is-tearing-europe-apart/. Max Ehrenfreund, "Europe's Immigration Crisis Is Just Beginning," *Washington Post*, 1 July 2016.

21. Schäfer and Streeck (2013: 2).

governments. Overall satisfaction with the workings of democracy remained robust even through the crisis. In times and places where these attitudes did deteriorate, they shifted in close parallel with assessments of the economy, suggesting that democratic frustrations often reflected economic dissatisfaction rather than specifically political grievances.

Populism and Democratic Backsliding

If Europe is experiencing a crisis of democracy, most Europeans seem not to have gotten the message. Over the past two decades, the key discontents that are supposed to be "exploding in many mature democracies" have, in fact, hardly budged. In Europe as a whole and in most countries considered separately, attitudes toward immigration and European integration, trust in parliament and politicians, and satisfaction with democracy turn out to be largely unchanged since the turn of the century.

In Chapter 6, I consider the implications of this stability for our understanding of the "populist explosion" that is supposedly rocking contemporary Europe. First, I examine the bases of support for sixteen prominent right-wing populist parties. In most cases, that support is indeed strongly related to attitudes figuring centrally in discussions of populism, including antipathy toward immigrants and immigration, opposition to further European integration, and political distrust. But that fact presents a considerable puzzle. If the attitudes conducive to right-wing populism have been essentially constant over the past two decades, what explains the surge in support for right-wing populist parties?

One answer, as Mudde's characterization of "a relatively minor nuisance" implied, is that the surge in support for these parties is commonly exaggerated. While several countries have seen flare-ups in voting for populist parties in recent years, the overall increase has been very modest—by my tabulation, amounting to just a few percentage points over two decades.[22] Insofar as there *has* been an increase in support for right-wing populist parties, it seems to be driven much more by the "supply" of populist mobilization, conditioned by institutional rules that facilitate or inhibit that mobilization, than by citizens'

---

22. Figure 6.1 in Chapter 6 shows a secular increase in the average vote share of 16 European right-wing populist parties from 12.6% in 2001 to 16% in 2021. Norris and Inglehart's (2019: 9) tabulation of support for "populist" parties in 32 Western democracies produced an even less dramatic trend; these parties' average vote share increased from 10.9% in the 1980s and 9.9% in the 1990s to 11.4% in the 2000s and 12.4% in the 2010s.

"demand" for populism. Contrary to the familiar image of a *wave* of populism in the wake of the Euro-crisis, European public opinion has long provided a *reservoir* of right-wing populist sentiment that political entrepreneurs have drawn on with varying degrees of success at different times in different places.

This reservoir of right-wing populist sentiment is by no means inconsiderable. As Mudde has observed, "The public attitudes of many Europeans were already in line with the basic tenets of the populist radical right ideology (even if in a more moderate form)" long before the current "populist explosion." The prevalence of attitudes conducive to populist mobilization represents a significant resource for would-be populist leaders, and a significant challenge for mainstream politicians, in every democracy. On the other hand, the success of contemporary European populists in exploiting this sentiment has, so far, been rather limited. As a result, the relationship between the extent of populist sentiment in specific times and places and support for populist parties at the polls has been remarkably hit-or-miss. Of the nine European countries with the highest levels of right-wing populist sentiment in 2014–2019, only three (Hungary, Italy, and Slovenia) had right-wing populist parties attracting as much as 15% of the vote. On the other hand, right-wing populist parties flourished in Switzerland, Sweden, Norway, and Denmark, all of which were among the half-dozen European countries with the *lowest* levels of right-wing populist sentiment. In these cases, as political scientist Cristóbal Rovira Kaltwasser put it, "populist radical right parties have shown a great success precisely in those regions of Europe where the structural prerequisites for their rise were hardly existent."[23]

I explore this paradox by examining the rise of some key right-wing populist parties in recent years, including Vox in Spain, Lega in Italy, and the United Kingdom Independence Party (UKIP). My analyses suggest that none of these parties owed their rise to a significant increase in right-wing populist sentiment; indeed, in some cases, their electoral support grew even as the prevalence of right-wing populist sentiment in their societies declined significantly. Their successes seem to be due mostly, in varying degrees, to charismatic leadership, over-the-top media coverage, and the stumbles and scandals of mainstream competitors. Nonetheless, political observers have not hesitated to interpret these electoral gains as evidence of fundamental shifts in public attitudes and values.

While support for right-wing populist parties in Western Europe has provoked consternation, the most concrete and alarming evidence that "democracy is under threat" in contemporary Europe comes from Hungary and Poland,

23. Mudde (2013: 7); Kaltwasser (2012: 188).

where nationalist leaders have gone some way toward dismantling democratic institutions, curbing the power of the judiciary, muzzling independent media, and rewriting electoral laws in efforts to entrench themselves in power. In Chapter 7, I examine these two crucial instances of democratic backsliding, tracing the bases of popular support for Fidesz in Hungary before and after its rise to power in 2010 and for the Law and Justice party in Poland before and after its rise to power in 2015.

I find surprisingly little support for the notion that these parties were swept into office by popular waves of right-wing populism, much less a hankering for authoritarian rule. Indeed, most of the factors contributing to support for right-wing populist parties elsewhere in Europe were unrelated to support for both Fidesz and the Law and Justice party before their rise to power and, for the most part, absent from their pivotal election campaigns. In 2015, a pair of Polish scholars wrote, Law and Justice "softened its image. It placed signs of authoritarian leanings as well as controversial personalities . . . out of public view. Running on the slogan 'Good Change,'" the party "called for compassionate conservatism, and sought to offer undecided voters an alternative to the 'boring'" incumbent party.[24]

It was only *after* gaining power that these rather conventional-looking conservative parties embarked upon the project of "illiberal democracy." As they did so, they increasingly turned to scapegoating would-be immigrants and the European Union, bringing the bases of their support into somewhat closer alignment with those of right-wing populist parties elsewhere in Europe. However, even then, it seems likely that their popular support depended less on the appeal of radical nationalism than on the fact that they presided over substantial increases in prosperity and subjective well-being. As a result, both countries saw substantial increases in public trust in political elites and— ironically—in public satisfaction with the workings of democracy. While ordinary citizens in these cases were guilty of prioritizing the quality of their daily lives over democratic institutions and procedures, they were little more than passive bystanders to the erosion of democracy.

Public Opinion and Democratic Politics

Almost a century ago, the sage political analyst Walter Lippmann pointed to "immense confusions in the current theory of democracy which frustrate and pervert its action." Chief among these he noted "the fictitious power" of public

---

24. Fomina and Kucharczyk (2016: 60–61).

opinion in thinking about democratic governance.[25] In the decades since Lippmann wrote, the world has acquired vastly more experience with democracy, and social scientists have greatly refined our understanding of public opinion and political behavior. Yet, the immense confusions persist, a testament to the mythic power of the "folk theory" of democracy. The startling discrepancy between the perception of democratic crisis and the reality of public opinion in contemporary Europe is a dramatic case in point. I hope that exploring that discrepancy may help us learn "to think of public opinion as it is, and not as the fictitious power we have assumed it to be."

For democratic theorists, the pressing task is to identify and analyze the forces shaping the behavior of powerful political actors in democratic systems. If aggregate public opinion is seldom decisive, when and why are the intense preferences of slivers of the public more consequential? What factors govern the translation of right-wing populist sentiment, prevalent in most contemporary societies, into direct or indirect policy influence? Why do some elected leaders exploit opportunities to entrench themselves in power, as Orbán did in Hungary, while others forebear? These are fundamental political questions, but not central concerns of contemporary political science. A more forthrightly "elitist" theory of democratic crisis would help to bring them into clearer focus.

As Lippmann recognized, democratic theory is not merely an academic pursuit; misunderstanding the nature of democracy can "frustrate and pervert its action." In the United States, the rise of Donald Trump was facilitated by the putative "democratization" of the process by which major parties select their presidential candidates. In the United Kingdom, David Cameron promised Euro-skeptic voters a "referendum lock to which only they should hold the key," then blundered into inviting them to use it.[26] Across Europe, political analysts and mainstream party leaders have frequently misread modest flareups in support for right-wing populist parties as major shifts in public sentiment, magnifying the political influence of extremists.

For citizens and political leaders alike, better understanding the lessons of experience provided by two turbulent decades of European politics may help to surmount crises of democracy, both imagined and real.

---

25. Lippmann (1925: 200).

26. Deborah Summers, "David Cameron Admits Lisbon Treaty Referendum Campaign Is Over," *Guardian*, 4 November 2009.

2

The Euro-Crisis

THE GLOBAL FINANCIAL crisis that began in 2008 was the gravest economic calamity since the Great Depression of the 1930s. It began in the US, where a garden-variety recession triggered a collapse of the booming market in sub-prime mortgage derivatives. The resulting Wall Street meltdown disrupted financial markets around the world, revealed lurking vulnerabilities in the balance sheets of financial institutions and governments, and brought investment and economic growth to a grinding halt. Economic output in the 28 countries of the European Union would not return to its 2008 level until 2015, and unemployment remained above its 2008 level for a decade. In the worst-hit parts of Europe, things were even worse for even longer.[1]

One of my aims in this book is to assess the impact of the economic crisis on contemporary European politics and democracy. In this chapter, I focus on two specific arguments widely accepted among observers of European politics: first, that the institutional and political weaknesses of the European Union exacerbated the economic impact of the crisis; and second, that the result has been a significant erosion of public support for European integration.

As we shall see, the institutional limitations of the European Union—and political wrangling over whether and how to circumvent those limitations—did impede the ability of European leaders to manage the repercussions of the

---

1. Treas (2010: 3); Bermeo and Bartels (2014: 1). On the Great Recession and the policy response, see Bermeo and Pontusson (2012), Blinder (2013), Irwin (2013), Geithner (2014), Eichengreen (2015), and Tooze (2018), among many others. Data on economic output and unemployment are detailed in Figures 2.1 and 2.2 below. In Italy and Spain, the unemployment rate in 2018 was about four points higher than it had been in 2008; in Greece, it was 11.5 points higher.

Euro-crisis. Nonetheless, the economic pain was surprisingly localized and temporary; and, perhaps as a result, the public "backlash against the EU" was surprisingly brief and mild. Citizens' trust in the European Union declined during the Euro-crisis; but even in the worst of times, they expressed more trust in the EU than in their own national governments. Once the economy began to grow again, trust in both the EU and in national governments rebounded. More importantly, overall public support for further European integration was just as strong after the crisis as it had been before it began.

Writing in the midst of the crisis, political scientist Fritz Scharpf worried that "even though the international financial crisis had its origins beyond Europe, the Monetary Union has greatly increased the vulnerability of some member states to its repercussions. Its effects have undermined the economic and fiscal viability of some EMU [European Monetary Union] member states, and have frustrated political demands and expectations to an extent that may yet transform the economic crisis into a crisis of democratic legitimacy." While Scharpf's analysis of the economic "vulnerability" stemming from the relative weakness of European institutions proved cogent, his fear of "a crisis of democratic legitimacy" was largely unrealized. The durability of public support for European integration is one crucial instance of the resilience of European democracy in the face of the Euro-crisis.[2]

The Global Financial Crisis

Officially, the Great Recession began in December 2007; but it became a serious crisis the following March, when nervous investors soured on Bear Stearns, a US investment bank heavily invested in subprime mortgage securities and heavily dependent on short-term borrowing. Federal Reserve chairman Ben Bernanke, "convinced that the impact of Bear's bankruptcy on world financial markets would be devastating," stretched the Fed's legal authority by taking on $30 billion in questionable Bear Stearns assets, facilitating the company's sale to a sounder rival investment bank, J. P. Morgan. He also offered emergency loans to other vulnerable investment banks, staving off for the time being the prospect of a general financial panic.[3]

Despite the Fed's aggressive efforts to bolster the big banks, their balance sheets remained precarious. Through the summer, Fed officials pondered how

2. Scharpf (2013: 108–109).
3. Irwin (2013: 133–134).

to respond to the next looming crisis, a run on the venerable but highly lever-aged investment bank Lehman Brothers. Their conclusion was ominous: "There are no good options." Given Lehman's size, its toxic assets, and its complex ties to other precarious financial institutions, even a massive infusion of Fed funds would be insufficient to prevent an eventual collapse. When the run finally came, in early September, Fed officials pressured other major Wall Street players to come up with "joint funding mechanisms that [would] avert Lehman's insolvency"; but no buyers could be found, and the Fed reluctantly concluded that Lehman Brothers could not be saved. When Bernanke phoned his counterpart at the European Central Bank, Jean-Claude Trichet, to inform him of the impending bankruptcy, the Frenchman replied, "I think that the result of this will be very grave indeed."[4]

Lehman's bankruptcy prompted a 500-point drop in the Dow Jones stock market index, one of the largest single-day sell-offs in history. Investors were suddenly panicked by any exposure to the bursting subprime bubble. Within days, the giant insurance company AIG was on the brink of collapse as its once-lucrative sideline in guaranteeing subprime mortgage assets turned toxic. Bernanke and Treasury Secretary Hank Paulson went to Congress seeking support for a bailout of AIG. They also pressed Congress for a broader bailout measure, the $700 billion Troubled Asset Relief Program—then strong-armed every major bank into accepting assistance from the program whether they wanted it or not, minimizing any market stigma that might otherwise be attached to government aid for the weakest among them.[5]

According to historian Adam Tooze, "The ferocity of the financial crisis in 2008 was met with a mobilization of state action without precedent in the history of capitalism." *Time* magazine named Bernanke its "Person of the Year," observing that the Fed under his leadership had "conjured up trillions of new dollars and blasted them into the economy; . . . lent to mutual funds, hedge funds, foreign banks, investment banks, manufacturers, insurers and other borrowers who had never dreamed of receiving Fed cash; jump-started stalled credit markets in everything from car loans to corporate paper; . . . and generally transformed the staid arena of central banking into a stage for desperate improvisation."[6]

4. Irwin (2013: 139–143).

5. Irwin (2013: 144–157).

6. Tooze (2018: 166). Michael Grunwald, "Ben Bernanke," *Time*, 16 December 2009; quoted by Irwin (2013: 151).

Because the modern world's financial institutions are intricately inter-twined, financial panic and paralysis know no borders. Thus, the Fed's rescue efforts included lending hundreds of billions of dollars to foreign central banks and hundreds of billions more to individual foreign banks with US subsidiar-ies, including the Royal Bank of Scotland, Switzerland's UBS, Deutsche Bank, British Barclays, and Belgium's Dexia. The amounts and identities of the re-cipients were "so potentially explosive," both economically and politically, that they remained a closely held secret for more than two years.[7]

One of the most vulnerable financial sectors was in Ireland, which had ex-perienced a massive construction and housing price bubble built on precari-ous mortgage lending. In the early stages of the crisis, the government of Ire-land shocked Europe by announcing that it would fully guarantee the liabilities of six major Irish banks. No one really knew the extent of the banks' liabilities or whether the government could afford to cover them. It turned out not to matter, since the strength of the guarantee drew a wave of money into the Irish banks, further weakening those in Britain and elsewhere in Europe.[8]

At a hastily organized summit meeting in Paris, European leaders tried to cobble together a coordinated response to the crisis, but they were stymied by a lack of formal institutions for collective action and by the reluctance of Ger-many, Europe's most powerful economic player, to accept responsibility for other countries' problems. "To put it mildly," the German finance minister declared, "Germany is highly cautious about such grand designs for Europe." In private, Chancellor Angela Merkel was blunter, reportedly remarking to her French counterpart, "Chacun sa merde" (to each his own shit).[9]

Trichet, the head of the European Central Bank, tried diplomatically to make the best of a bad situation, telling reporters, "There is no lack of coordination—there is a European spirit. We have different governments, and they have different means of intervention."[10] In reality, as historian Tooze would write a decade later,

> There was no agreement on a common European response. . . . The EU would act as an agency of oversight and try to minimize the extent to which the European common market would be torn apart. But it was not a crisis

---

7. Irwin (2013: 154).
8. Irwin (2013: 158).
9. Irwin (2013: 159).
10. Irwin (2013: 159–160).

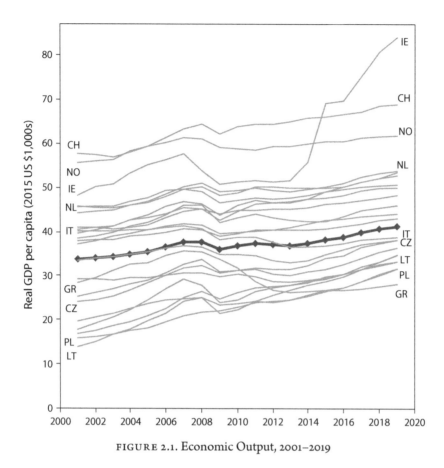

FIGURE 2.1. Economic Output, 2001–2019

fighter in its own right. . . . In retrospect it can seem as though it was the decisions taken in the first weeks of October 2008 that decided the future course
of events. The United States moved concertedly toward recapitalizing its
banks. In Europe, proposals for a common approach were vetoed in Berlin.
From there the crisis unfolded as a series of national struggles that after 2010
became once again entwined in the form of the eurozone crisis. In the end
Europe could not escape a common solution, but it would take years of
economic uncertainty and distress before it arrived at that point.[11]

The ramifications of the financial crisis for the "real economy" were slower
to evolve in Europe than in the US, but not by much, and not everywhere. As
the GDP growth trajectories shown in Figure 2.1 indicate, there was substantial

11. Tooze (2018: 193, 202).

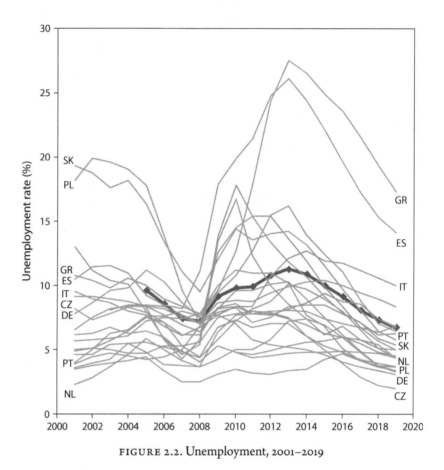

FIGURE 2.2. Unemployment, 2001–2019

national variation in the magnitude of the shock. In Ireland, real GDP per capita fell by 6.5% in 2008 and a further 6% in 2009. In Germany, real GDP per capita grew by 1.2% in 2008 before shrinking by 5.4% in 2009. Across the European Union, real GDP per capita grew by just 0.3% in 2008 and fell by a disastrous 4.6% in 2009. (By comparison, real GDP per capita in the US fell by 1.1% in 2008 and 3.4% in 2009.[12])

Unemployment rose only modestly at first, from 7.2% in 2008 to 9.1% in 2009 for the EU as a whole. But here the national variation was even greater, as the trendlines in Figure 2.2 make clear. The unemployment rate in Ireland rose from 6.8% to 12.6% in a single year, in Estonia from 5.4% to 13.5%, in Lithuania from

12. Country-level data from OECD, https://stats.oecd.org, are summarized in appendix Table A2.

5.8% to 13.8%, and in Spain from 11.2% to 17.9%. Moreover, unemployment continued to rise even after economic output began to rebound, peaking at 11.3% in 2013 and not falling back to its pre-crisis level until 2018.

The Sovereign Debt Crisis

In the US, the aggressive efforts of the Federal Reserve and the new Obama administration began to produce an economic turnaround in the summer and fall of 2009. But in Europe, things would get worse before they got better. Nervous lenders drove up interest rates just as economic conditions were driving tax revenues down and social spending up. As a result, most of Europe saw significant increases in government debt in 2009—20% of GDP in Ireland, 15% in France and Spain, 12% or more in Slovenia, Italy, Portugal, the United Kingdom, and Austria. Even Germany saw government debt increase by 7% of GDP. These increases are charted in Figure 2.3, which tracks levels of government debt in each of the 23 European countries over the whole period from 2001 to 2019.[13]

The sovereign debt crisis arose most acutely in Greece, where the global economic downturn depressed exports and tourism, reducing tax revenues and increasing demand for social services. A new government elected in late 2009 warned European authorities that the Greek budget deficit would be much higher than previously reported. In the eventual tally produced by the Organisation for Economic Co-operation and Development (OECD), public sector debt as a share of GDP ballooned by 18 percentage points in 2009. That was not wildly out of line with other hard-hit countries. However, unlike in the rest of Europe—with the notable exception of Italy—Greece's accumulated government debt had exceeded annual GDP for more than a decade. "What Greece needed to do was to restructure, to agree with its creditors to reduce their claims. To do anything else, to add new loans to an already insupportable debt burden, would postpone the problem but at the price of increasing its scale."[14]

Of Greece's €300 billion in debt, roughly one-third was held by European banks and another one-third by insurance and pension funds. Thus, restructuring would impose significant losses on major financial institutions that

---

13. OECD National Accounts at a Glance: Gross debt of general government, % of GDP, https://stats.oecd.org.

14. Tooze (2018: 323–324).

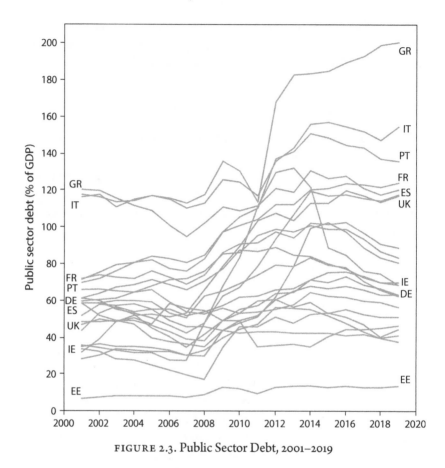

FIGURE 2.3. Public Sector Debt, 2001–2019

were already weakened by the global crisis. Moreover, any deal with Greece would have implications for even larger mountains of public debt in Italy and elsewhere. As Tooze put it, "The connecting thread between the crisis of subprime and the crisis of the eurozone was the fragility of Europe's bank balance sheets."[15]

European leaders scrambled to find a way out of the crisis that would minimize the risk of financial collapse for both precarious national governments and precarious financial institutions. German intransigence and the terms of the Maastricht treaty ruled out a direct bailout by the EU. Thus, in the spring of 2010, as Greece's financial crisis worsened and threatened to spread to other parts of the European periphery, European leaders cobbled together a complex

15. Tooze (2018: 317).

plan in which the IMF and individual countries would offer new loans allow-ing Greece to pay off its existing debts. Unfortunately, loan terms stringent enough to avoid constituting a bailout were too stringent to be sustainable. That problem was left to the Greeks, to be addressed with the magical elixirs of fiscal austerity and structural adjustment. "Instead of restructuring Greek's [*sic*] unsustainable debts, what would be restructured were its entire public sector and its creaky economy. Heroic assumptions about cost cutting and efficiency gains were the ways in which the IMF squared the Greek program with its conscience. Perhaps if it were shaken thoroughly enough, 'sclerotic' and 'clientelistic' Greece could be jolted onto a higher growth path that would make its debts sustainable after all." Some observers dubbed the strategy "ex-tend and pretend."[16]

"It is true," the prominent Greek economist (and later, briefly, finance min-ister) Yanis Varoufakis conceded,

> that in 2010 Greece's public and private sectors were incompetent, corrupt, bloated and indebted. That is why the euro crisis began there. . . . And yet none of this explains the depth of Greece's post-2010 crisis. . . . The gist of the bailout deal offered to Greece was simple: as you are now insolvent, we shall grant you the largest loan in history on condition that you shrink your national income by an amount never seen since the grapes of wrath. It would take a smart eight-year-old to see that such a "bailout" could not end well.[17]

However unworkable it might be in the long run, for the moment, at least, the deal could be billed as a "rescue" of Greece. For European leaders, that had three related benefits. First, it would buy some time for other countries on the EU periphery to get their fiscal houses in order without creating undue incen-tives for them to seek their own bailouts. Second, the focus on "incompetent, corrupt, bloated and indebted" Greece distracted attention from the fact that the main beneficiaries of the arrangement were the massive but still-vulnerable European financial institutions that had avoided taking losses on their bad loans. And third, the arrangement respected, however notionally, the German insistence that Europe would not usurp the national sovereignty of its member states by developing centralized institutions for financial risk-sharing.[18]

16. Tooze (2018: 323–337, 345).

17. Varoufakis (2017: 48–49; 2016: 156).

18. Tooze (2018: 344).

Over the course of the next year, the Greek "rescue" provided a template for similar deals in Ireland and Portugal, likewise organized by the Troika—the European Commission, the European Central Bank, and the IMF—to provide new loans in exchange for stringent austerity measures. Spain avoided a bailout but adopted tax hikes and budget cuts under EU pressure, an indication to some that the country "was already under de facto supervision from Brussels." The politics of each of these deals were complicated by the signals they might send to other actors. When Varoufakis asked one EU official why the commission was pushing Portugal to increase taxes in the face of a collapsing economy, he was "surprised to receive an honest answer. . . . 'The point is to demonstrate to Rome what it has coming its way if they do not comply with our demands for greater austerity there.'" "Greece, Portugal, Ireland, [and] Spain were beaten to a pulp," Varoufakis concluded, "in order to keep Italy and France in awe and the ECB in business."[19]

While austerity was being imposed upon the European periphery, the global downturn was being exacerbated by voluntary austerity elsewhere. In Germany, the constitution was amended to institute a "debt brake." "Despite its gaping deficit in 2009," Tooze observed, "Germany had no difficulty selling debt. It was not [financial] markets but the cross-party consensus on fiscal consolidation that had emerged before the crisis that dictated a decisive and irrevocable turn toward austerity." When the leaders of the world's major economies met in Toronto in June 2010 to address the crisis, they "committed themselves to simultaneously halving their deficits over the next three years. It was the householder fallacy expanded to the global scale. It was a recipe for an agonizingly protracted and incomplete recovery."[20]

Mody, the former IMF official, noted that "a general acceptance of the virtues of fiscal tightening had become integral to the eurozone's culture." In 2012, when prominent IMF economists released a report estimating much larger economic costs from aggressive austerity measures than the agency had previously been assuming, "European authorities reacted furiously." The vice president of the European Commission complained that the report had "not been helpful" and would "erode the confidence that we have painstakingly built up over the past years in numerous late-night meetings."[21]

19. Julien Toyer and Andrés González, "Spain Unveils New Austerity under European Pressure," Reuters, 11 July 2012. Varoufakis (2016: 192–193).

20. Tooze (2018: 287, 354).

21. Mody (2018: 287–289).

However much European officials might wish for austerity to restore prosperity, "By the summer it was already clear that the fix devised to contain the Greek crisis in May 2010 was not sustainable." The austerity measures reduced public and private spending, raising unemployment and cutting tax revenues, which worsened the deficit. Borrowing costs began to rise once again. "And yet in the face of failure, the troika remained committed to holding Greece to the May 2010 program." The European Central Bank tried, with modest success, to ease the pressure by buying Greek bonds, but then reversed course by raising interest rates, "one of the most misguided decisions in the history of monetary policy." Speculators in the financial markets were increasingly betting not just against Greece, but against the Euro. In July 2011, French president Nicolas Sarkozy cut a new deal with Merkel that would once again restructure Greece's debt, with €109 billion in new loans and, this time, modest losses for the debt-holders. But even those modest losses were a threat to financial stability. By that fall, "Europe's banks were sliding back toward the cliff edge," while "the eurozone [was] stuck on the German roadblock and divided over its future direction."[22]

The "German roadblock" was, in large part, a matter of domestic politics. As one Europe-watcher reported,

> Merkel faced intense pressures not to offer any financial help. German pensioners complained they did not want to see their precious resources lavished on their profligate neighbors to the south. The nation's most popular newspaper, *Bild Zeitung*, with 8 million daily readers, joined the campaign against the Greek bailouts. In one cover story depicting a plethora of yachts sailing in the Aegean Sea, the tabloid reported that while Germany had just raised its retirement age to sixty-seven, Greeks could still retire at fifty-five.

Of course, ugly stereotypes cut both ways. "On the streets of Athens, pictures of Merkel wearing swastikas and Hitler-style moustaches were plastered on walls throughout the capital."[23]

With conditions in Greece continuing to deteriorate, a provisional coalition government was formed including the two largest parties, the center-left PASOK (Panhellenic Socialist Movement) and center-right New Democracy. It fell to the new prime minister, a politically independent economist with ties

22. Tooze (2018: 357, 378, 401, 414).
23. Drozdiak (2017: 18).

to the European Central Bank, to negotiate the final terms of the latest bailout, which involved even stricter austerity measures and even larger losses for Greece's creditors—"the largest and most severe in history, larger in inflation-adjusted terms than the Russian revolutionary default or Germany's default of the 1930s. . . . Allowing for the much later repayment of the new long-term bonds, the net present value of claims on Greece was cut by 65 percent."[24]

An election the following May gave Greek voters an opportunity to express their unhappiness with the deal. Both coalition partners saw disastrous declines in support. With no party receiving even 20% of the vote, negotiations to form a new government broke down, necessitating another election the following month. This time, New Democracy won sufficient support to organize a new government with PASOK as a coalition partner; but the biggest vote-gainer was SYRIZA, a left-wing party that declined to join in a "unity government" pledged to honor the bailout agreement.

Across Europe, as Figure 2.3 shows, government debt was still escalating. In 2012, economic output stalled once again, and debt as a share of GDP rose by 15 percentage points in Spain, 18 percentage points in Ireland and Italy, 27 percentage points in Portugal, and even more in Greece. France, the UK, and Belgium were added to the list of countries in which debt exceeded annual GDP, with others not far behind. "The pressure the more fragile members of the eurozone were under depended not on some inescapable clash of peoples and markets, or global capitalism and democracy. It was dictated, first and foremost, by the willingness, or not, of the ECB to buy bonds." Without determined intervention, "Europe might face a doom loop of public and private insolvency and illiquidity. As in Greece, bad sovereign debts would pull down the banks. Or as in Ireland, failed banks would pull down the state's credit. Only the ECB could break this loop."[25]

In July 2012, Mario Draghi, Trichet's successor as head of the ECB, took a major symbolic step toward breaking the loop. In a speech to a global investment conference in London, he declared that observers outside the Euro area "underestimate the amount of political capital that is being invested in the euro," adding pointedly, "Within our mandate, the ECB is ready to do whatever it takes to preserve the euro." This bold commitment took even his ECB colleagues by surprise. "Nobody knew this was going to happen," one told Reuters. "Nobody." Draghi had "nothing precise in mind," another said.

24. Tooze (2018: 425–426).
25. Tooze (2018: 397, 415).

"It was a rash remark." Yet the effect was to rally public support for the euro from EU and national leaders, including Merkel, and to convince investors that the central bank would indeed do "whatever it takes" to stem the tide of bad debt. Draghi's pledge came to be seen as "the turning point of the Eurozone crisis. In the aftermath, markets immediately calmed. Yields for the most vulnerable borrowers came down. There was no more talk of a Eurozone breakup."[26]

While the eurozone might be safe, Europeans were not out of the woods. As Varoufakis put it, "Once in the eurozone member-states had entered a 'Hotel California' they could never leave." Without control of their own currencies, they could not inflate their way out of debt. Short of outright default, they could only accept relief on the Troika's terms, risking "death by a thousand austerity cuts." Across Europe, as Figure 2.2 records, unemployment continued to rise through 2012 and 2013. Real GDP per capita fell slightly in the Euro area, and substantially in the hardest-hit countries: Greece, Italy, Portugal, Spain, and Slovenia. According to historian Tooze, "Bad economics and faulty empirical assumptions had led the IMF to advocate a policy that destroyed the economic prospects for a generation of young people in Southern Europe."[27]

In Greece, the continuing deterioration in economic and social conditions "at the behest of the troika" fueled "a broad-based mood of protest." SYRIZA, the leftist party that had refused to endorse the previous bailout, was the primary beneficiary. A January 2015 election gave SYRIZA a near majority in the Hellenic Parliament, paving the way for a coalition government that would "force open the painful and unresolved question of Greek solvency." While "Germany would not budge" on debt restructuring, pressure was ratcheted up by the result of a July referendum in which Greeks voted by a 58-to-36% margin against accepting the Troika's latest debt proposal, and by the release of an IMF report baldly stating that "Greece's debt can now only be made sustainable through debt relief measures that go far beyond what Europe has been willing to consider so far." With much bitterness on all sides, a compromise was struck on yet another new bailout package and, in effect, ratified by the Greek electorate renewing SYRIZA's mandate in a snap election two months later. As Tooze summarized the deal,

---

26. Tooze (2018: 438–440).
27. Varoufakis (2016: 139–140, 221); Tooze (2018: 430).

Greece would receive new loans from Europe totaling 86 billion euros. In exchange, Athens accepted severe intrusions on its sovereignty. . . . Greece was still in the Eurozone. Europe had regained its capacity for a rather brutal form of collective action. The ECB had demonstrated the pacifying power of central bank intervention. Greece was held on the path of "reform" demanded by the troika. But as the IMF's démarche had made clear, this was a matter of politics as much as financial crisis management.[28]

Economic Disaffection

One useful way to gauge the impact of Europe's economic crisis is to track ordinary citizens' assessments of economic conditions. From 2002 through 2019, the European Social Survey asked successive waves of respondents, "On the whole, how satisfied are you with the present state of the economy in [country]?" Figure 2.4 summarizes their answers to this question, recorded on a zero-to-ten scale, over time and across countries.[29]

The direct impact of the Wall Street meltdown and the resulting economic downturn is evident in the sharp decline in satisfaction with the economy between the third (2006–2007) and fourth (2008–2009) ESS rounds. Across Europe, satisfaction with the economy fell by almost a full point on the ten-point scale, from 4.7 to 3.8. However, there is a great deal of variation across countries in the magnitude of this economic shock. In Ireland, where a run-up in real estate prices fed a substantial increase in average economic satisfaction between 2003 and 2005, the bursting of the bubble produced an even sharper downturn between 2007 and 2009, from 6.4 to just 2.7 on the zero-to-ten scale. Satisfaction with the economy fell by more than two points in Great Britain and by more than a point in Spain, Hungary, Belgium, and Sweden. At the

28. Tooze (2018: 516–517, 528, 532). International Monetary Fund, "Greece: An Update of IMF Staff's Preliminary Public Debt Sustainability Analysis," IMF Country Report No. 15/186, 14 July 2015, https://www.imf.org/external/pubs/ft/scr/2015/cr15186.pdf.

29. The heavy line in Figure 2.4 shows the average value of economic satisfaction for the entire sample in each ESS round, with respondents weighted to represent each country in proportion to its population. Since not all countries are included in each ESS round, the analysis from which these average values are derived includes country fixed effects (in order to avoid mistaking changes in the ESS sample for changes in levels of economic satisfaction). The lighter lines in the figure represent average values for each of the 15 countries included in all nine ESS rounds.

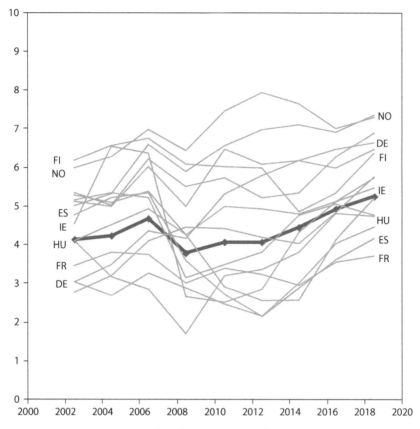

FIGURE 2.4. Public Satisfaction with the Economy, 2002–2019

opposite extreme, satisfaction with the economy fell by just 0.2 points in Germany and increased by 0.3 points in Poland.

What is just as striking in Figure 2.4, however, is that economic well-being almost immediately began to rebound. The data on GDP per capita presented in Figure 2.1 show that, for the European Union as a whole, economic growth resumed in 2010 and continued thereafter except for a slight dip in 2012. Similarly, satisfaction with the economy increased slightly between the fourth (2008–2009) and fifth (2010–2011) ESS rounds, then more significantly after 2013. By 2018–2019, average satisfaction with the economy was more than half a point higher than it had been at its peak 12 years earlier. This recovery was heavily influenced by Germany, where average economic satisfaction in 2018–2019 was 2.5 points higher on the zero-to-ten scale than it had been in 2006 (6.8 versus 4.2). However, the increase in economic satisfaction in Czechia

TABLE 2.1. Changing Public Attitudes in the Wake of the Euro-Crisis, by Country

	Satisfaction with national economy	Support for European integration	Conservative worldview
Austria	+.29 (.60)	−.15 (.29)	+.33 (.03)
Belgium	−.03 (.25)	+.39 (.19)	−.06 (.05)
Czechia	+1.73 (.39)	−1.12 (.07)	−.10 (.04)
Denmark	−1.04 (.19)	−.47 (.09)	+.03 (.04)
Estonia	−.02 (.41)	−.54 (.09)	−.09 (.04)
Finland	−.97 (.41)	+.37 (.17)	−.16 (.04)
France	−.26 (.22)	+.22 (.16)	−.02 (.03)
Germany	+2.81 (.36)	+.84 (.25)	−.15 (.02)
Great Britain	−.38 (.10)	−.15 (.23)	−.09 (.06)
Hungary	+1.08 (.42)	−.82 (.28)	−.03 (.04)
Ireland	−.86 (.61)	−.43 (.31)	−.10 (.04)
Italy	−.31 (.21)	—	—
Netherlands	+.65 (.50)	−.07 (.14)	−.14 (.07)
Norway	+.90 (.30)	−.14 (.08)	−.07 (.03)
Poland	+1.52 (.55)	−.91 (.16)	−.06 (.05)
Portugal	+.84 (.40)	+.67 (.30)	−.27 (.05)
Slovakia	+.74 (.61)	−1.35 (.13)	−.13 (.04)
Slovenia	−.56 (.70)	−.08 (.15)	+.07 (.03)
Spain	−1.56 (.36)	+.26 (.14)	−.12 (.05)
Sweden	+.83 (.30)	+.21 (.14)	−.18 (.03)
Switzerland	+1.49 (.44)	−.71 (.08)	+.07 (.04)
Population-weighted average	+.56 (.26)	+.05 (.12)	−.08 (.02)

Note: Change from 2002–2007 (ESS rounds 1–3) to 2014–2019 (ESS rounds 7–9) by country (with standard errors clustered by country-round in parentheses). Country-rounds are weighted by population.

over this period was similar in magnitude, while Hungary (1.8 points), Poland (1.7 points), and Portugal (1.3 points) also recorded substantial increases.

The data presented in the first column of Table 2.1 provide a broader comparison of economic attitudes before and after the economic crisis. For each country, it shows the change in average economic satisfaction on the ESS's zero-to-ten scale from 2002–2007 to 2014–2019. By this measure, 11 countries were better off after the crisis than they had been before it began, with ten of these gains registering at least half a point. Here, too, the biggest gainer was

Germany, which had been mired in recession even before the onset of the crisis, and which experienced a sharp rebound from the global downturn in 2010–2011. On the other hand, five countries experienced declines in economic satisfaction of half a point or more, with the greatest erosion in Spain. Greece does not appear in Table 2.1 because no ESS surveys were conducted there after 2011, but it almost certainly experienced an even more severe decline in subjective economic well-being.[30] Despite these instances of severe economic distress, the continent-wide pattern is one of surprising resilience. The average European's assessment of her nation's economy was more than half a point more favorable in the six years after the Euro-crisis than it had been in the six years before the Wall Street meltdown.

Table 2.2 provides a more detailed analysis of how European citizens' subjective economic assessments evolved over the course of the economic crisis. Separate statistical analyses for survey respondents in each income quintile relate subjective satisfaction with the national economy to shifting economic conditions—GDP per capita, changes in GDP, and unemployment—as well as to a variety of plausibly relevant personal characteristics, including household income,[31] education, age,[32] sex, religiosity,[33] union membership,

---

30. Economic satisfaction in Greece had already declined from a bleak 3.5 in 2003 and 2005 to 2.4 in 2009 and just 1.4 in 2011. Since GDP per capita was still lower in real terms in 2019 than it had been in 2011, and more than 17% of the workforce remained unemployed, there is every reason to think that economic satisfaction declined even further after 2011. Lithuania is also omitted from Table 2.1, because no ESS surveys were conducted there *before* 2011.

31. I use responses to a question on household income to characterize each respondent's relative position in the income distribution for her country and ESS round. However, this question was not asked in every country-round, and even when it was asked, a substantial fraction of respondents declined to answer. Overall, 22% of income data are missing, with over 40% missing in Portugal, Slovakia, Hungary, Italy, and Estonia. I imputed these missing data using the other personal characteristics listed in Table 2.2, country, and ESS round. Given the roughness of the imputation, the imputed data are clustered near the middle of the income distribution, accounting for the larger sample sizes in the middle-income quintiles in Table 2.2. However, simply excluding the cases with imputed income data would not materially alter the results of my statistical analyses.

32. I include both age in years and the natural logarithm of age in order to allow for potential nonlinearities in the relationship between age and economic perceptions. While an age-squared term is conventional, it seems more plausible here and elsewhere to suppose that similar age differences generally matter more to younger people. The logarithmic specification implies that the impact of an additional year is about twice as great among 30-year-olds as among 60-year-olds.

33. My measure of religiosity is based on a question asking, "Regardless of whether you belong to a particular religion, how religious would you say you are?" I have transposed the responses (on a zero-to-ten scale from "not at all religious" to "very religious") to range from zero to one.

TABLE 2.2. Economic Conditions and Economic Perceptions, by Income Quintile

	Bottom quintile	Second quintile	Third quintile	Fourth quintile	Top quintile
ln(GDP per capita)	.40	1.51	.93	.86	2.28
	(.80)	(.91)	(.71)	(.82)	(1.16)
Δ(GDP per capita) (%)	.098	.105	.117	.136	.173
	(.022)	(.027)	(.025)	(.026)	(.033)
Unemployment (%)	−.184	−.172	−.182	−.180	−.185
	(.020)	(.021)	(.020)	(.020)	(.022)
Income (percentile/100)	1.07	−.20	−.27	.20	1.57
	(.40)	(.44)	(.49)	(.45)	(.41)
Education (years)	.036	.028	.044	.031	.047
	(.007)	(.006)	(.007)	(.005)	(.006)
Age (years)	.082	.068	.057	.042	.026
	(.005)	(.004)	(.004)	(.004)	(.005)
ln(Age)	−3.66	−3.05	−2.53	−1.82	−1.17
	(.19)	(.18)	(.14)	(.19)	(.22)
Female	−.24	−.28	−.20	−.23	−.28
	(.04)	(.04)	(.04)	(.04)	(.05)
Religious	.86	.75	.73	.63	.41
	(.06)	(.07)	(.06)	(.07)	(.07)
Union member	.12	−.05	.02	−.11	−.05
	(.06)	(.05)	(.04)	(.03)	(.04)
Foreign-born	.79	.69	.56	.47	.31
	(.05)	(.07)	(.06)	(.07)	(.06)
Standard error of regression	2.18	2.15	2.10	2.00	1.99
Adjusted R²	.22	.23	.23	.28	.29
N	56,134	69,726	102,420	61,832	49,237

Note: Ordinary least-squares regression parameter estimates (with standard errors clustered by country-round in parentheses). Fixed effects for countries are included in the analyses but not shown. Country-rounds are weighted by population.

and nativity. The analyses also allow for stable differences in economic satisfaction across countries unrelated to objective economic conditions.[34]

Perhaps the most striking fact here is that levels of economic output had little discernible impact on subjective satisfaction with the economy, except perhaps among people in the top quintile of their country's income distribution. On the other hand, year-to-year changes in GDP did matter significantly. The difference between a good economic year (2% real growth) and a bad year (no real growth) would be expected to boost subjective satisfaction with the economy by about 0.2 points on the zero-to-ten scale among people in the bottom income quintile, and by almost twice that much among people in the top income quintile. Unemployment had a much more substantial impact on economic satisfaction, with each additional 1% of the labor force unemployed reducing satisfaction with the economy by almost 0.2 points. (Observed unemployment rates in the country-years included in this analysis ranged from less than 3% in Norway in 2008 to over 26% in Spain in 2013.) Unlike the impact of GDP growth, the impact of unemployment on satisfaction with the economy was essentially constant across income groups.

People's own household incomes also mattered, but only for those in the top and bottom income quintiles. These results probably suggest, once again, that levels of income had little impact on economic satisfaction, except in cases where people could make unambiguous comparisons between their own income and others'. Within the top income quintile, people with higher incomes were clearly better off than those below them; within the bottom quintile, people with lower incomes were clearly worse off than those above them; but in the intermediate quintiles people could easily compare upward or downward, making their ranking in the distribution, despite its unambiguous implication for real income levels, subjectively irrelevant.

Even after allowing for aggregate economic conditions and positions in the income distribution, subjective satisfaction with the economy varied with several personal characteristics. Men were consistently more satisfied than women with similar incomes, and people with more education were more satisfied than those with less education. Young people were substantially more satisfied than middle-aged people in similar economic circumstances,

---

34. Across the income spectrum, people in Switzerland, Finland, Norway, and Denmark were consistently somewhat more satisfied with the economy than would have been expected on the basis of economic conditions and personal characteristics. People in France, Slovenia, Portugal, and Hungary were generally less satisfied than would have been expected.

perhaps because they anticipated future income gains. This difference was especially pronounced among people who were less well off; the expected difference in economic satisfaction between a 20-year-old and a 45-year-old ranged from 0.3 points in the highest income quintile to 0.9 points in the lowest income quintile.[35] People who described themselves as more religious and those born outside their countries of residence were also substantially more satisfied with the economy than others in similar economic circumstances, and these differences, too, were significantly larger in the middle and lower income quintiles than in the top quintile. These differences underscore the fact that subjective economic well-being is not only an economic matter, but also a complex psychological and sociological phenomenon.[36]

The Euro-Crisis and Public Support for European Integration

The European Union has been under construction for more than six decades, since the Treaty of Rome established the first European Economic Community in the aftermath of World War II. The geographical and functional expansion of the European community has generally been portrayed as a top-down project of political elites. "Up to the early 2000s," historian Tooze wrote, "the

35. The statistical results for the bottom income quintile imply a nonlinear relationship between age and economic perceptions, with 20-year-olds 0.9 points more satisfied than otherwise similar 45-year-olds and 70-year-olds about 0.4 points more satisfied than otherwise similar 45-year-olds. The estimated age gradient for the top income quintile is similar in shape but much less steep, with 20-year-olds 0.3 points more satisfied than otherwise similar 45-year-olds and 70-year-olds about 0.1 points more satisfied than otherwise similar 45-year-olds.

36. The analyses reported in Table 2.2 are based on data from across Europe. However, there is some reason to think that the relationships they document might vary due to differences among countries in political institutions and socioeconomic conditions. For example, Anderson and Hecht (2014: 52–57) suggested that Europe's extensive welfare states "buffer" the relationship between objective economic conditions and public perceptions of the economy. Analyzing data from monthly consumer surveys conducted on behalf of the European Commission, they found much weaker effects of changes in unemployment and GDP growth on consumer confidence in countries with strong welfare states than in those with lower levels of social spending. However, the ESS data reveal no clear evidence of lesser sensitivity to economic conditions in countries with higher levels of social spending, either among lower-income people or overall. Indeed, if anything, economic satisfaction seems to have been *more* sensitive to fluctuations in unemployment rates in countries with higher levels of social spending.

EU operated against a backdrop of what political scientists called a 'permissive consensus.' Europe's population accepted the gradual push for ever closer union without enthusiasm but also without protest."[37]

That "permissive consensus" is supposed to have collapsed in the face of the EU's hapless response to the Euro-crisis. According to Tooze, by 2014 "a large segment of Europe's population had simply had enough. Across Europe, opinion polls showed a sharp decline in support for the EU even in states that had historically been overwhelmingly favorable."[38]

In fact, according to the authoritative Eurobarometer surveys, trust in the EU declined by about 20 percentage points over the course of the Euro-crisis, but was already rebounding by 2014, and in 2019 it reached its highest level since 2009. Moreover, survey respondents consistently expressed more trust in the EU than in their own national governments. And even at the worst point in the Euro-crisis, respondents in the Euro area supported "a European economic and monetary union with one single currency" by a margin of more than 30 percentage points; by 2019, that margin was 58 percentage points. Perhaps, as political scientists Sara Hobolt and Patrick Leblond surmised, people feared that a breakdown of the eurozone would "make the economic situation worse and even more uncertain." Whatever the logic, support for monetary union "remained high and relatively stable inside the eurozone during the crisis."[39]

The European Social Survey data likewise belie the notion of "a sharp decline in support" for the EU. Beginning with the second wave in 2004, most European Social Survey rounds have included an item tapping support for further European integration: "Now thinking about the European Union, some say European unification should go further. Others say it has already gone too far." The survey respondents were invited to place themselves on a

37. Tooze (2018: 112).

38. Tooze (2018: 513). The Eurobarometer report cited as evidence of "a sharp decline in support for the EU" actually showed some evidence that public opinion was already rebounding, with the gap between optimistic and pessimistic views "about the future of the EU" having widened from 2% in late 2011 to 19% in late 2014. TNS Opinion & Social, "Standard Eurobarometer 82: Public Opinion in the European Union, First Results," https://ec.europa.eu /commfrontoffice/publicopinion/archives/eb/eb82/eb82_first_en.pdf.

39. "Trust in EU at Its Highest in Five Years, New Poll Shows," Euronews, 6 August 2019, https://www.euronews.com/2019/08/06/trust-in-eu-at-its-highest-in-five-years-new-poll -shows. Hobolt and Leblond (2014: 143).

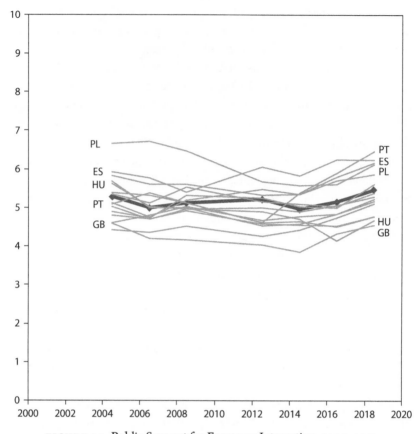

FIGURE 2.5. Public Support for European Integration, 2004–2019

zero-to-ten scale with the zero-point labeled "Unification has already gone too far" and 10 labeled "Unification should go further." Figure 2.5 shows the trend in public support for further integration for Europe as a whole and for each of the 15 countries included in the seven ESS waves including this item.

There is remarkably little evidence here of any substantial change in public attitudes toward the European project. For Europe as a whole, enthusiasm for European integration dipped from 5.3 on the zero-to-ten scale in the immediate wake of the 2004 EU expansion to 5.0 in the last survey before the Great Recession, then increased slightly over the course of the Euro-crisis before dipping again in 2014–2015. By 2018–2019, average support had risen again, reaching 5.6—the highest level since the advent of the ESS. While Europeans may have been dissatisfied with the EU's handling of the economic crisis, on balance they seemed to consider that a reason to continue the process of unification, not to reverse it.[40]

The second column of Table 2.1 shows changes in support for European integration in each of 20 countries from 2004–2007 to 2014–2019. The largest increase in support, more than 0.8 points, was in Germany—an endorsement, perhaps, of the EU's cautious approach to addressing the Euro-crisis. The largest declines in support, ranging from 1.3 to 0.8 points, were in Eastern European countries that joined the EU in 2004, and thus were in the first flush of enthusiasm at the time of the pre-crisis surveys—Slovakia, Czechia, Poland, and Hungary. In the latter two countries, the declines in support for further integration probably also reflected anti-EU agitation by nationalist governments that "have defied Brussels by cracking down on judges and the news media, refusing to take in migrants and lashing out at the European Union as elitist and antidemocratic."[41]

The resilience of public support for European integration is underlined by responses to a more direct question included in the 2018–2019 European Social Survey. Respondents in 17 EU countries were asked, "Imagine there were a referendum in [country] tomorrow about membership of the European Union. Would you vote for [country] to remain a member of the European Union or to leave the European Union?" The proportion of respondents who favored remaining in the EU ranged from a low of 66% in Czechia to a high of 89% in Ireland, while the proportion who favored leaving ranged from just 5% to 22%. The population-weighted average support for remaining in the EU was 80.2%, with only 11.8% in favor of leaving.[42]

A separate question in Great Britain referenced that country's 2016 EU referendum, then asked, "If there were to be a new referendum tomorrow, would you vote for the UK to remain a member of the European Union or leave the European Union?" A majority of respondents, 57%, said they would vote to remain in the EU, while just 35% said they would vote to leave. Even in the

---

40. Another item in the European Social Survey asked how much trust respondents placed in the European parliament. The average level of trust declined by about half a point on the zero-to-ten scale between 2008–2009 and 2014–2015, but it had rebounded to its pre-crisis level by 2018–2019.

41. Palko Karasz, "Leaders of Hungary and Poland Chafe at E.U., but How Do Their People Feel?," *New York Times*, 6 September 2017. Gergely Szakacs, "Hungary Could Resume Anti-EU Campaigns, Says PM Orban," Reuters, 24 March 2019.

42. The remaining respondents said they would submit a blank or spoiled ballot or wouldn't vote.

country where anti-EU sentiment took its most explosive form, many of those who had succumbed to frustration seem to have had second thoughts.[43]

To understand the politics of European integration, it is helpful to understand what kinds of people are more or less supportive of the European project. The statistical results reported in Table 2.3 summarize the relationship between support for further European integration and a variety of individual characteristics. The results presented in the first two columns of the table cover the entire period from 2004 through 2019, while those in the remaining three columns focus separately on the pre-crisis, crisis, and post-crisis periods.

In every case, the statistical analyses reveal a considerable gap in support between more affluent and better-educated people on the one hand and those with less income and education on the other. Other things being equal, someone in the top quintile of household income would be expected to be about a quarter of a point higher on the zero-to-ten scale than someone in the bottom quintile. Similarly, a person with 15 or 16 years of schooling would be expected to be about a quarter of a point higher than one with 12 years of schooling.

The analyses presented in the third, fourth, and fifth columns of Table 2.3 provide some evidence that the impact of education on support for the EU may have increased in recent years. However, that change is largely counterbalanced by changes in the estimated impact of age and religiosity, both of which are correlated with income and education. In purely descriptive terms, the gap in support for further European integration between people with less income and education and those with more has remained virtually constant over the whole period from 2004 through 2019.

Nor is there any evidence of generational erosion in public support for the European project. According to one prominent journalist, "Growing disaffection with Europe has become particularly acute among young people, who in the past embraced a borderless Europe." However, the statistical results reported in Table 2.3 document a consistent tendency for young people to be more enthusiastic about European integration than their elders, even after allowing for differences in income, education, and other factors.[44]

43. The UK survey firm YouGov has asked a somewhat different question in dozens of polls since the Brexit vote: whether "Britain was right or wrong to vote to leave the European Union." Since late 2017, the balance of opinion has consistently favored "wrong," albeit by smaller margins than for the ESS question.

44. Drozdiak (2017: xvii).

TABLE 2.3. Bases of Public Support for European Integration

	(1)	(2)	2004–2007	2008–2013	2014–2019
Income (percentile/100)	.52	.32	.32	.28	.31
	(.06)	(.05)	(.10)	(.12)	(.06)
Education (years)	.087	.066	.045	.070	.076
	(.006)	(.004)	(.006)	(.006)	(.007)
Age (years)	.041	.029	.011	.021	.041
	(.005)	(.004)	(.006)	(.006)	(.006)
ln(Age)	−2.08	−1.40	−.73	−1.00	−1.93
	(.19)	(.16)	(.29)	(.23)	(.23)
Female	−.06	.01	−.07	−.02	.08
	(.03)	(.03)	(.04)	(.05)	(.04)
Religious	.33	.36	.39	.39	.25
	(.05)	(.05)	(.08)	(.08)	(.08)
Union member	.07	.07	.08	−.07	.09
	(.03)	(.03)	(.07)	(.03)	(.04)
Foreign-born	.63	.54	.68	.46	.51
	(.07)	(.07)	(.07)	(.10)	(.13)
Conservative worldview	—	−.248	−.264	−.206	−.252
		(.012)	(.021)	(.023)	(.015)
Economic satisfaction	—	.191	.194	.205	.215
		(.015)	(.015)	(.018)	(.027)
Standard error of regression	2.57	2.52	2.49	2.51	2.52
Adjusted R^2	.08	.11	.12	.11	.12
N	254,530	254,530	71,313	75,588	107,629

Note: Ordinary least-squares regression parameter estimates (with standard errors clustered by country-round in parentheses). Fixed effects for countries are included in the analyses but not shown. Country-rounds are weighted by population.

What is more, young people were more supportive after the Euro-crisis than before. In 2018–2019, the average level of support for European integration among people under the age of 30 was 6.0, up from 5.6 in 2004–2007 (and well above the corresponding average among people over the age of 50, 5.3). Among young people in Germany, Portugal, Austria, Finland, Spain, and Belgium, support for further European unification increased by a half-point or more between 2004–2007 and 2018–2019; the corresponding increases in France, Sweden, and even Great Britain were smaller but still significant. Declines in support for European integration among young people, as in the broader public, were concentrated in the Eastern European countries that joined the EU in 2004. However, even in these places the balance of opinion among young people in 2018–2019 was at least slightly favorable toward further European integration. Indeed, the only country in which that was not the case was Switzerland, which has remained steadfastly outside the EU. (Young people in Norway were also less enthusiastic about further integration than those already inside the EU.)

The differences in attitudes toward the European Union documented in Table 2.3 presumably reflect some combination of perceived economic interests and what political scientist Matthew Gabel referred to as "affective allegiances." The "utilitarian" basis of attitudes toward the EU is reflected somewhat more directly in the relationship between satisfaction with the state of the national economy and support for further European integration. The statistical results suggest that a typical respondent satisfied with the economy (with a rating of 6 on the zero-to-ten scale) could be expected to be more than half a point more enthusiastic about further European integration than an otherwise similar respondent who was dissatisfied with the economy (with a rating of 3). Comparing the statistical results in the first and second columns of the table suggests that economic satisfaction mediated about 40% of the impact of income and about one-third of the impact of age. On the other hand, economic satisfaction mediated only about 20% of the impact of education, less than 15% of the impact of being foreign-born, and none of the impact of religiosity, suggesting that these effects reflected "affective allegiances" more than perceived economic interests.[45]

It is also worth noting that the relationship between economic disaffection and antipathy to European integration at the individual level does nothing to account for changes in attitudes toward European integration at the national level in the wake of the economic crisis. Germany saw the biggest gains in both economic satisfaction and support for further European unification between the pre-crisis period (2002–2007) and the post-crisis period (2014–2019).[46]

45. Gabel (1998).

46. Because the item on European unification was not included in the first round of the European Social Survey, the shifts in opinion for that item are tabulated based on data from 2004 to 2007 and 2014 to 2019.

Overall, however, the appetite for further integration held up as well or better in countries where economic satisfaction declined. Indeed, the most substantial declines in support for European integration occurred in countries with larger-than-average gains in economic satisfaction—Slovakia, Czechia, Poland, and Hungary. Clearly, these shifts in attitudes were a result of cultural and political frictions, not in any direct sense a reflection of economic disaffection.

Worldviews and Support for European Integration

One more potentially important factor in Europeans' views about the EU is attachment to convention and tradition, which in this context might be thought to imply attachment to traditional national authorities and institutions and an aversion to a still-evolving supranational government. Political scientist Erik Tillman, for example, has argued that "authoritarians, who have a predisposition towards order and conformity, are likely to oppose the EU as it threatens the established social and political order of the sovereign state and the dominant national culture."[47]

This is just one of a variety of respects in which public opinion in contemporary Europe is thought to be shaped (in some assessments, warped) by "authoritarian" dispositions. The study of "the authoritarian personality" flourished in the decades after World War II as scholars scrambled to understand the rise of fascism and the vulnerability of democratic societies to political extremism. The foundational work in this field, a book entitled *The Authoritarian Personality*, became mired in theoretical and methodological controversies. However, interest in authoritarianism was revived and recast by political psychologists Stanley Feldman and Karen Stenner, who advocated using survey measures of child-rearing values to capture "fundamental orientations toward authority/uniformity versus autonomy/difference." Marc Hetherington and Jonathan Weiler subsequently employed a similar concept and measures to explore "the recent rise of authoritarianism in defining political conflict" in the US, though they acknowledged the fraught connotations of the term and eventually abandoned it in favor of a more neutral focus on "fixed" and "fluid" worldviews.[48]

47. Tillman (2013: 566).

48. Adorno et al. (1950); Roiser and Willig (2002); Feldman and Stenner (1997); Stenner (2005: 24, emphasis in original); Hetherington and Weiler (2009: 63); Hetherington and Weiler (2018). Readers searching for the term "authoritarian" in Hetherington and Weiler's (2018) index are directed to "*See* worldview, fixed." Even more recently, Hetherington has used the term

Here, I follow Hetherington and Weiler in eschewing the language of "authoritarianism," referring instead to *conservative* and *liberal worldviews*. My measure of worldviews is based on responses to ten items in the European Social Survey. These items, listed in Table 2.4, resemble Feldman and Stenner's child-rearing items in making scant explicit reference to politics, focusing instead on the importance people place on particular social values and behaviors. I classify people who describe themselves as concerned about security, following rules, proper behavior, and tradition as having *conservative worldviews*, and those who value creativity, diversity, independence, and adventure as having *liberal worldviews*.[49] However, in adopting these labels I must emphasize that worldviews need not correspond to political ideologies. Indeed, the correlation between worldviews as measured here and self-assessed left-right ideology is quite modest, .15.

Obviously, most people value both security and tradition and adventure and creativity to varying degrees. Thus, the overall distribution of scores on my index of worldviews is bell-shaped, with 68% of scores falling between 4 and 6 on the zero-to-ten scale.[50] Of the remaining respondents, 18.0% expressed conservative worldviews (with scores of 6 or more), while 13.8% expressed liberal worldviews (with scores of 4 or less). Even further in the tails of the distribution, 3.6% of respondents had scores of 7 or more, while the same percentage had scores of 3 or less.

These differences in worldviews are sometimes assumed to reflect fundamental differences in personality. According to Hetherington and Weiler, for example, "People develop different worldviews because of impulses and orientations that emanate from deep inside them."[51] However, many observable

---

"conservative worldview" to refer to a somewhat broader construct closely related to Hetherington and Weiler's "fixed" worldview, and I adopt that terminology here.

49. One advantage of this terminology is that it implies theoretical symmetry between the opposing poles of security, following rules, proper behavior, and tradition on the one hand and creativity, diversity, independence, and adventure on the other. Hetherington and Weiler (2009: 43) criticized the scholarly literature's "lack of attention to understanding what motivates non-authoritarians," noting that "much of the explanatory power of authoritarianism in American politics over the past fifteen years or so derives from changes among those with moderate or low levels of authoritarianism, and not among authoritarians."

50. Three percent of ESS respondents did not answer any of the ten worldview items. (The missing data are concentrated in the first two ESS rounds, and in Ireland, Finland, Italy, and Sweden.) Another 4% declined to answer at least one item. My tabulations include only the 96.2% of respondents who answered at least eight of the ten items.

51. Hetherington and Weiler (2018: xix).

TABLE 2.4. Indicators of Conservative and Liberal Worldviews

Now I will briefly describe some people. Please listen to each description and tell me how much each person is or is not like you (very much like me; like me; somewhat like me; a little like me; not like me; not like me at all).

Conservative

It is important to her to live in secure surroundings. She avoids anything that might endanger her safety.	7.26 (.06)
She believes that people should do what they're told. She thinks people should follow rules at all times, even when no-one is watching.	5.48 (.09)
It is important to her that the government ensures her safety against all threats. She wants the state to be strong so it can defend its citizens.	7.33 (.05)
It is important to her always to behave properly. She wants to avoid doing anything people would say is wrong.	6.68 (.05)
Tradition is important to her. She tries to follow the customs handed down by her religion or her family.	6.39 (.08)

Liberal

Thinking up new ideas and being creative is important to her. She likes to do things in her own original way.	6.87 (.03)
She likes surprises and is always looking for new things to do. She thinks it is important to do lots of different things in life.	6.09 (.03)
It is important to her to listen to people who are different from her. Even when she disagrees with them, she still wants to understand them.	7.37 (.04)
It is important to her to make her own decisions about what she does. She likes to be free and not depend on others.	7.62 (.05)
She looks for adventures and likes to take risks. She wants to have an exciting life.	4.03 (.06)

Note: Average agreement on a zero-to-ten scale (with standard errors clustered by country-round in parentheses). Country-rounds are weighted by population.

differences in worldviews seem hard to account for on that basis. The differences across the countries of Europe documented in Figure 2.6 provide some examples. The black bars in the figure represent the percentage of the population in each country whose responses reflected a conservative worldview, while the gray bars show the percentage whose responses reflected a liberal

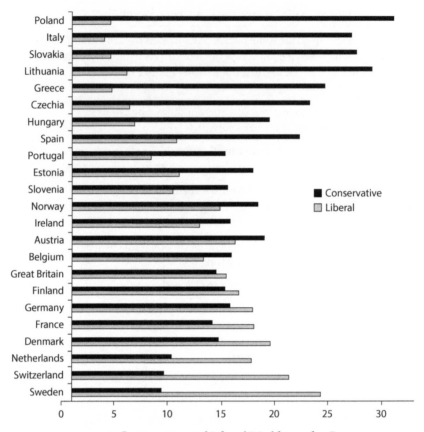

FIGURE 2.6. Conservative and Liberal Worldviews by Country

worldview.[52] Are Norwegians (18% conservative) really so different "deep inside" from Swedes (9% conservative), or Italians (27% conservative) from people in France (14% conservative)? Differences like these suggest that the translation of "impulses and orientations" into expressed preferences for security and tradition or adventure and creativity is strongly shaped by cultural and other factors.

The statistical analyses reported in Table 2.5 provide a broader picture of individual characteristics related to differences in worldviews—in the first

52. These distinctions, based on the threshold values of 4 and 6 on the zero-to-ten scale, are obviously somewhat arbitrary, but sufficient to illustrate the substantial variation in the distribution of worldviews across countries.

TABLE 2.5. Social Bases of Conservative Worldviews

	2002–2019	Northern Europe	Southern Europe	Eastern Europe
Income (percentile/100)	−.09	−.08	−.04	−.18
	(.01)	(.02)	(.03)	(.03)
Education (years)	−.055	−.068	−.048	−.045
	(.002)	(.003)	(.002)	(.003)
Age (years)	−.013	−.017	−.009	−.014
	(.002)	(.003)	(.004)	(.004)
ln(**Age**)	1.18	1.35	.99	1.21
	(.09)	(.14)	(.15)	(.13)
Female	.08	.07	.05	.19
	(.01)	(.01)	(.01)	(.01)
Religious	.63	.53	.77	.60
	(.03)	(.03)	(.04)	(.05)
Union member	.02	.05	−.06	.06
	(.01)	(.01)	(.02)	(.02)
Foreign-born	.12	.17	.06	−.02
	(.02)	(.03)	(.02)	(.03)
Pre-1930 cohort	.44	.52	.36	.40
	(.06)	(.09)	(.09)	(.07)
1930s cohort	.30	.34	.26	.23
	(.04)	(.05)	(.07)	(.06)
1940s cohort	.11	.13	.08	.14
	(.03)	(.04)	(.05)	(.04)
1950s cohort	.02	.00	.01	.04
	(.01)	(.02)	(.02)	(.02)
1970s cohort	.10	.13	.09	.02
	(.01)	(.02)	(.02)	(.03)
1980s cohort	.06	.09	.06	−.04
	(.02)	(.03)	(.04)	(.05)
Post-1989 cohort	.08	.12	.08	−.05
	(.04)	(.05)	(.08)	(.08)
Standard error of regression	.99	1.03	.97	.87
Adjusted R^2	.25	.20	.27	.28
N	342,313	152,310	95,619	94,384

Note: Ordinary least-squares regression parameter estimates (with standard errors clustered by country-round in parentheses). Fixed effects for countries are included in the analyses but not shown. Country-rounds are weighted by population.

column for all of Europe, and in the second, third, and fourth columns for subsets of countries roughly grouped by geography and culture.[53] In each of these analyses, conservative worldviews are most common among older and highly religious people, while liberal worldviews are more prevalent among the better educated and, to a lesser extent, among men and more affluent people. However, there are some marked differences across the subsets of countries in the strength of these associations, another indication of a complex interplay between worldviews and culture.

In substantive terms, the largest differences in worldviews are associated with age. Overall, and in each of the three subsets of countries, 45-year-olds were about 0.6 points closer to the conservative end of the zero-to-ten world-view scale than otherwise similar 20-year-olds, on average, while 70-year-olds were an additional 0.2 points more conservative than otherwise similar 45-year-olds. These life-cycle differences are magnified by differences across birth cohorts, with people born before 1930 about half a point more conserva-tive than those born in the 1960s (the modal cohort).[54] However, there is a noticeable regional difference in the worldviews of younger cohorts; in North-ern and Southern Europe, the post-1960s cohorts have been slightly more conservative in their worldviews than those born in the first decades after World War II, whereas in Eastern Europe there is no evidence of this conserva-tive cultural shift among younger cohorts.

In some cases, it is unclear whether the correlates of worldviews docu-mented in Table 2.5 reflect the impact of social characteristics on worldviews or the impact of worldviews on social characteristics. For example, there is a fairly strong correlation between formal education and liberal worldviews, especially in Northern Europe, where people with 15 years of schooling were about one-third of a point more liberal, on average, than otherwise similar people with ten years of schooling. One plausible interpretation of this differ-

53. I distinguish the former communist countries of Eastern Europe (Czechia, Estonia, Hun-gary, Lithuania, Poland, Slovenia, and Slovakia) from (mostly Catholic) Southern Europe (Aus-tria, France, Greece, Italy, Portugal, Spain, and Switzerland) and (mostly Protestant) Northern Europe and Scandinavia (Belgium, Denmark, Finland, Germany, Great Britain, Ireland, Neth-erlands, Norway, and Sweden). On the relevance of a similar typology for social and political change in contemporary Europe, see Bartels (2013b).

54. These estimates are based on the assumption that observed differences in worldviews are attributable to life-cycle and cohort effects rather than to fluctuations in worldviews across ESS rounds. Under that assumption, the 18-year span of the ESS interviews allows for a reason-ably reliable differentiation of life-cycle and cohort differences in worldviews.

ence is that education promotes more liberal worldviews; but an equally plausible alternative interpretation is that people who value novelty and creativity are more likely to pursue education. A similar ambiguity arises with respect to the even stronger correlation between religiosity and conservative worldviews. Religious commitment may promote attachment to tradition and proper behavior, especially in the Catholic religious culture prevalent in most of Southern Europe and parts of Eastern Europe; but people with more conservative worldviews may also be more likely to develop religious attachments in the first place. In each of these cases, more detailed analysis would be necessary to gauge how much of the observed relationship is attributable to the impact of life experiences on worldviews and how much is due to the impact of worldviews on life experiences.

My aim here is not to provide a detailed analysis of the social causes and consequences of variation in worldviews, but to explore the role of worldviews in shaping a variety of political attitudes, beginning with attitudes toward the European Union. The impact of worldviews on support for European integration is reflected in the statistical analysis reported in the second column of Table 2.3. That analysis implies that people who valued security and tradition were indeed substantially less enthusiastic about the project of European integration than those who emphasized new ideas and diversity, even after allowing for stable differences in national attitudes toward the EU, differences in individual social characteristics, and satisfaction with the national economy. The expected difference in support for further European integration between someone with a liberal worldview of 3 and an otherwise similar person with a conservative worldview of 7 amounts to a full point on the zero-to-ten scale.

While conservative worldviews have clearly diminished public enthusiasm for the European project, it is worth noting that there is nothing new about that fact. The tabulations presented in the third column of Table 2.1 indicate that conservative worldviews were, if anything, slightly more prevalent in Europe before the economic crisis than they have been since, while the statistical analyses reported in the third, fourth, and fifth columns of Table 2.3 indicate that the impact of worldviews on support for European integration was essentially similar before and after the Euro-crisis, though perhaps slightly weakened during the crisis.

Nor is it the case that national differences in worldviews account for national variation in support for European integration. Indeed, most of the countries that stand out in Figure 2.6 as having high proportions of people with conservative worldviews—including Poland, Slovakia, Lithuania,

Greece, Spain, Portugal, and Slovenia—have among the *highest* average levels of support for further European integration.[55] Clearly this is an instance in which differences in individual worldviews are swamped by other national considerations.

Summary

For many Europeans, the Euro-crisis was a significant economic challenge; for some, it was a protracted economic disaster. Yet, the worst possible scenarios— continent-wide depression, sovereign default, the collapse of the Euro—did not come to pass. Perhaps as a result, the authors of a 2016 assessment of the impact of the crisis found it

> striking that the political consequences of these developments have so far been comparatively small. Although there have been some protests, none of the debtor nations, with the possible exception of Greece, has experienced the kinds of political upheavals we have seen in previous debt and balance-of-payment crises. And although many governments have fallen and although Eurosceptic parties have recently gained in the polls, the basic institutional set-up, including EMU, remains essentially unchanged.[56]

To some observers, the project of European integration was fatally flawed from the start. Economist Ashoka Mody, for example, concluded his monumental history of the "Euro Tragedy" by arguing, "Logically, the Euro could do no economic or political good," and that "'more Europe' will not solve Europe's most pressing economic and social problems." To others, however, the path forward is indeed "more Europe." Adam Tooze concluded his own monumental history of "a decade of financial crises" by arguing that "the Eurozone needed to make bold steps toward further integration." However, Tooze's prescription for the European Union's "functional viability" came with a giant political caveat: "in light of the mounting popular backlash [against the EU] and the ongoing economic uncertainty, where was the political momentum to come from?"[57]

---

55. Average support for further European integration in these seven countries (net of fixed effects for ESS rounds) ranged from 5.4 in Slovakia to 6.1 in Poland. The only more liberal country with a similarly high level of public support for European integration (5.7) was Denmark.

56. Copelovitch, Frieden, and Walter (2016: 823–824).

57. Mody (2018: 458, 437); Tooze (2018: 515).

The analyses presented in this chapter suggest that the "popular backlash" against the EU is greatly exaggerated. Support for the EU was dented by the Euro-crisis, along with support for national governments and other institutions. But the damage was surprisingly modest and short-lived. Overall, public sentiment after the crisis was mildly favorable toward further European integration, just as it had been before the crisis began. Moreover, the characteristics of EU enthusiasts—younger, more affluent, better educated—imply that they are likely to be even more politically influential in the years to come than their numbers would suggest. If "political momentum" is a matter of public opinion, there is little evidence here of any significant obstacle to further, gradual European integration.

The European Union is an unlovable institution under the best of circumstances, a supranational conglomerate operating "by élite consensus and an irritating sort of mild bureaucratic snuffling," as one observer put it. To those on the receiving end of EU mandates, as Yanis Varoufakis was in his brief stint as Greek finance minister, it can be "a clueless, inefficient bureaucracy, complete with its own mystical beliefs, working tirelessly for politicians with an infinite capacity to recite unenforceable rules." The Euro-crisis highlighted the profound difficulties of managing a confederacy of sovereign states with diverse interests and substantial political and policymaking independence. Nonetheless, the EU proved sufficiently up to the task to muddle through the crisis with its popular legitimacy intact and the European project very much alive and well.[58]

58. James Wood, "Can You Forgive Her? How Margaret Thatcher Ruled," *New Yorker*, 2 December 2019. Varoufakis (2016: 142).

3

The Welfare State

LIKE DEMOCRACY, the modern welfare state seems to be in a protracted state of crisis. Writing in 1996, political sociologist Gøsta Esping-Andersen referred to "the beleaguered welfare states" of Western European and other affluent democracies, noting that there "seem to be as many diagnoses of the welfare state crisis as there are experts." In 1998, the managing director of the International Monetary Fund announced a "worldwide crisis in the welfare state," arguing that social programs "have come to represent an enormous drain on the resources and the efficiency of many of the so-called welfare states" and that "reforms will be necessary" in light of future trends—especially demographic change and globalization. Writing in 2004, policy analyst Frances Castles observed that for "more than three decades—since the time that the First Oil Shock spelled the end of an era of taken-for-granted, continuous economic growth—influential commentators have been arguing that the welfare state project is in dire trouble."[1]

In Castles's estimation, "the initial crisis warnings of the 1970s and 1980s were falsified by events," as social spending in affluent democracies continued to increase in real terms. Esping-Andersen likewise concluded, "In most countries what we see is not radical change, but rather a 'frozen' welfare state landscape." He added an explanation for this fact that suggested major rollbacks would remain unlikely in the future: "Resistance to change is to be expected: long-established policies become institutionalized, and cultivate vested inter-

---

1. Esping-Andersen (1996: ix, 1); Michel Camdessus, "Worldwide Crisis in the Welfare State: What Next in the Context of Globalization?," International Monetary Fund, 15 October 1998, https://www.imf.org/en/News/Articles/2015/09/28/04/53/sp101598; Castles (2004: 1).

ests in their perpetuation; major interest groups define their interests in terms of how the welfare state works."[2]

Nonetheless, the Euro-crisis spurred another wave of alarm about the welfare state. As we saw in Chapter 2, in the face of recession and soaring budget deficits, several countries adopted draconian austerity policies, in some cases under intense pressure from the European Commission, the European Central Bank, and the IMF, the so-called Troika. Indeed, according to historian Adam Tooze, "the European welfare state was hollowed out at the behest of the troika." He added, "The sense that Europe's welfare state was being subjected to a relentless program of rollback driven by the demands of bankers and bond markets provoked outrage."[3]

This chapter focuses on the state of the European welfare state in the wake of the economic crisis. Detailed data on social spending reveal a significant slowdown in the growth of Europe's welfare state after 2008, but rather little "hollowing out." In some places—most notably, Greece and Spain—social spending did clearly fail to keep pace with social needs, producing measurable declines in the well-being of the poor. For Europe as a whole, however, gradual increases in real social spending produced significant increases in the perceived quality of health services and education, while economic growth (as measured by GDP per capita) fueled a significant increase in overall life satisfaction.

I also explore the impact of the economic crisis on public attitudes toward the welfare state. Public support for redistribution and overall left-right ideology changed very little during and after the crisis. More detailed measures of perceived government responsibilities in specific domains, and preferences for spending increases or decreases for specific social programs, likewise remained virtually constant. There is no indication here of any diminution in public support for the welfare state, or in its prospects for continued gradual expansion.

The Resilience of the European Welfare State

In his attempt to distinguish "crisis myths and crisis realities" in welfare states in the last two decades of the 20th century, Castles examined data on social spending from the OECD Social Expenditure Database, an authoritative

2. Castles (2004: 1); Esping-Andersen (1996: 24).
3. Tooze (2018: 370, 374).

cross-national record of public spending on pensions, health care, housing, disability, childcare, unemployment benefits, job training, and other social programs, including both cash payments and in-kind benefits. He concluded that

> while there are real signs of a slowdown in expenditure growth compared with a previous era of welfare state expansion, there are equally no signs of a consistent trend to welfare retrenchment or diminishing welfare standards. . . . Over nearly two decades, in which welfare state crisis has been the leitmotif of informed social commentary, and welfare state reform an ostensibly major concern, many Western governments, welfare state structures, and priorities, at least in so far as these may be revealed by spending patterns, have remained much as they were in the early 1980s. . . . Crisis threats made with increasing stridency since the mid-1970s have remained uniformly unfulfilled.[4]

Castles' characterization of "a slowdown in expenditure growth" continues to fit the contemporary European welfare state. Figure 3.1 traces levels of social spending in 23 European countries from 2001 to 2017.[5] Average spending in these countries varied widely, from less than $4,000 per capita (in 2015 US dollars) in Lithuania and Estonia to more than $13,000 per capita in Denmark and Norway. Nonetheless, in every country but one, the welfare state expanded in real terms over this period. The sole exception was the Netherlands, where a reorganization and partial privatization of the national health care system reduced public spending on health care by half in 2006, taking a large bite out of what would otherwise have been a gradual increase in real social spending.[6]

The average level of spending across all 23 countries (weighted by population) grew from $8,040 per capita in 2001 to $10,310 per capita in 2017—a real increase of 1.6% per year. Most countries saw cumulative real increases of 25% to 45%. In Lithuania and Estonia, real per capita social spending more than

4. Castles (2004: 15, 168).

5. Data are from the OECD Social Expenditure Database (SOCX), https://stats.oecd.org.

6. Van de Ven and Schut (2008); Schut and van de Ven (2011); Maarse and Paulus (2011). The decline in health spending resulted in a 15% decline in total social spending per capita in 2006, even as spending in other areas remained essentially constant. Aside from that one-year decline, real social spending per capita in the Netherlands increased by 1% per year between 2001 and 2017.

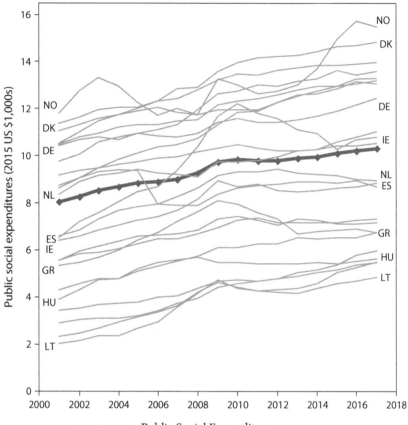

FIGURE 3.1. Public Social Expenditures, 2001–2017

doubled. Even Greece and Italy, which experienced cumulative declines of about 5% in real GDP per capita over this period, saw real increases in social spending of 26% and 15%, respectively.

Clearly, the notion that "the European welfare state was hollowed out" in the wake of the economic crisis is exaggerated. But the crisis did produce a further slowdown in expenditure growth. For Europe as a whole, the rate of real growth in social spending declined from 2.0% per year in 2001–2008 to 1.2% per year in 2009–2017. Moreover, the fact that spending continued to increase in real terms does not necessarily imply that it increased at a rate commensurate with people's needs.

The bulk of social spending in modern welfare states is targeted at three distinct groups of vulnerable citizens: the old, the young, and the unemployed. While the proportions of old and young people in most societies tend to change relatively slowly, the unemployment rate can change substantially from year to year. As we saw in Chapter 2, the average unemployment rate across Europe swelled from 7.0% in 2008 to 10.8% in 2013. Over the same period, the unemployment rate increased by 8.6 percentage points in Portugal, 14.9 percentage points in Spain, and 19.7 percentage points in Greece. Modest increases in spending could hardly be sufficient to address the rapid escalation in social distress implied by those numbers.

To gauge the response of European welfare states to the economic crisis, it will be helpful to establish a baseline of "usual" patterns of social spending in the pre-crisis period. Table 3.1 shows the results of statistical analyses relating levels of social spending in each country in 2001–2007 to economic and demographic conditions.[7] These analyses indicate that wealthier countries (as measured by GDP per capita in the preceding year) spent more on social programs; indeed, there is some statistically uncertain evidence that social spending was a "luxury good," with wealthier countries spending higher *proportions* of their GDP on social programs than poorer countries did. On the other hand, *changes* in GDP were negatively related to social spending, presumably because good economic times reduced—and downturns increased—the demand for social assistance. Finally, as expected, spending was greater in countries and years with higher levels of unemployment, higher proportions of people over the age of 64, and higher proportions of people under the age of 15.[8]

The analyses reported in Table 3.1 take no account of durable differences in social spending across countries resulting from distinctive cultural and historical legacies. The social democracies of Northern Europe generally spent more

---

7. Scholars more commonly analyze social spending as a share of GDP, rather than real spending levels. However, in a context of economic recession and recovery, that approach muddles shifts in the size of the welfare state and fluctuations in economic conditions. Since there is little reason to suppose that changes in social spending and GDP have similar causes or consequences, it seems preferable here to focus on real spending per capita, with real GDP per capita as one factor potentially driving shifts in spending.

8. A comparison of the parameter estimates in Table 3.1 seems to suggest that European welfare states spent less per capita on unemployed people than on children or older people. However, the direct comparison is misleading because the unemployment rate is expressed as a percentage of the labor force, not of the entire population. Fluctuations in unemployment accounted for greater changes in social spending; the within-country standard deviation of year-to-year fluctuations in the unemployment rate was 3.2%, whereas the corresponding standard deviations of changes in the shares of young and old people were 0.7% and 1.3%, respectively. The relative stability of young and old population shares is reflected in the larger standard errors associated with the estimated effects of those factors on social spending.

TABLE 3.1. Pre-Crisis Social Spending, 2001–2007

	(1)	(2)	(3)	(4)
ln(GDP per capita)t–1	1.130	1.304	1.175	1.133
	(.089)	(.125)	(.152)	(.141)
Δ(GDP per capita) (%)	—	−.0182	—	−.0115
		(.0086)		(.0088)
Unemployment rate (%)	—	.0233	.0249	.0230
		(.0108)	(.0104)	(.0102)
Population over age 64 (%)	—	—	.0526	.0497
			(.0237)	(.0237)
Population under age 15 (%)	—	—	.0377	.0351
			(.0310)	(.0317)
Intercept	−2.840	−4.825	−5.012	−4.433
	(.905)	(1.385)	(1.452)	(1.377)
Standard error of regression	.161	.130	.121	.120
Adjusted R²	.81	.87	.89	.89
N	161	148	148	148

Note: Dependent variable is ln(social spending per capita). Ordinary least-squares regression parameter estimates (with standard errors clustered by country in parentheses). Country-rounds are weighted by population.

than these analyses suggest, while liberal democracies and Mediterranean countries generally spent less.[9] Nonetheless, the five factors considered in the fourth column of Table 3.1 account for almost 90% of the observed variation in social spending levels across countries and years in the pre-crisis period. Thus, the statistical analysis provides a reasonable baseline for assessing how social spending *would have* changed in response to the economic crisis if welfare regimes themselves had remained unchanged.

For Europe as a whole, social spending in the aftermath of the economic crisis fell modestly below the expectations implied by this pre-crisis baseline. In absolute terms, the average level of social spending from 2009 through 2017

9. Even in the pre-crisis period, social spending per capita in the United Kingdom was about $1,000 lower, on average, than would have been expected on the basis of the common European pattern, while the shortfall in Ireland was almost $2,000 per capita. Conversely, social spending in Austria, France, Sweden, and Denmark was from $1,500 to as much as $2,400 higher, on average, than would have been expected.

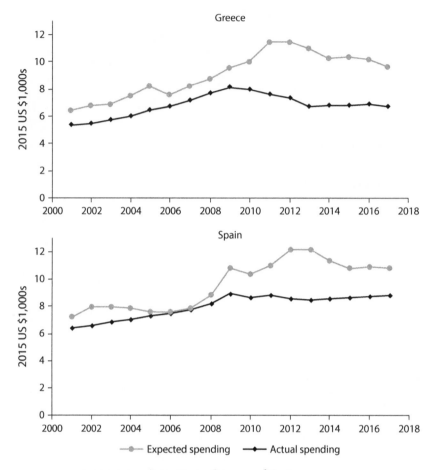

FIGURE 3.2. Austerity in Greece and Spain, 2001–2017

(weighting country-years by population) was $9,970 (2015 US dollars per capita), 16% higher than it had been in the pre-crisis period. Relative to pre-crisis spending patterns, after accounting for rising GDP and other post-crisis economic and demographic conditions, real spending per capita was less than 4% below the average "expected" level of $10,350. By either of those standards, the European welfare state was surprisingly resilient in the aftermath of the global financial crisis.

The story is less sanguine when we turn to some of the specific countries hardest hit by the Euro-crisis. For example, Figure 3.2 compares actual social spending with "expected" spending (based on the statistical analysis presented in Table 3.1) in Greece and Spain. Before the crisis hit, both countries were already spending slightly less on social programs, by general European standards, than their economic and demographic circumstances warranted; but the gaps between expected and actual spending widened substantially after 2008. In Spain, the shortfalls in 2012 and 2013 amounted to 30% of expected spending; in Greece, they reached almost 40%. These were genuine welfare state crises.

The figure underscores the fact that these shortfalls stemmed more from escalating need than from real cuts in spending. Even in Greece, which did experience substantial cuts, the welfare state at its low point in 2013 was larger than it had been as recently as 2005. But it was not nearly enough to cushion the hardship caused by the economic collapse; real per capita GDP was 20% lower in 2013 than it had been in 2005, while the unemployment rate had nearly tripled. These disastrous conditions were widely—and quite sensibly—seen as products, in substantial part, of austerity measures "driven by the demands of bankers and bond markets." And, yes, they "provoked outrage." But in most of Europe, social spending in the post-crisis period remained surprisingly consistent with the pre-crisis pattern.

Social Spending and Social Well-being

What is at stake in political battles over social spending? Sociologist Lane Kenworthy, surveying the political economies of a variety of affluent democracies, argued that "social democratic capitalism"—which he defined as "political democracy plus capitalism plus education plus a big welfare state plus high employment"—contributes significantly to a variety of social goods, including the well-being of the least well off, healthy life expectancy, innovation, social inclusion and security of women, intergenerational mobility, and life satisfaction. "Our historical experience and those of other rich democratic countries," Kenworthy concluded of the US,

> suggest that more expansive and generous social programs and employment-conducive public services would help in the United States, and they would do so without sacrificing other good outcomes, such as economic growth or individual freedom. These programs function as a floor, a safety net, and a springboard: they ensure a decent living standard for the least well-off, provide income security, and enhance opportunity. Properly formulated, they can also serve as an escalator, ensuring rising living standards over time.[10]

10. Kenworthy (2019: 19, 25–65, 160).

Political scientist Benjamin Radcliff provided a more detailed analysis of the impact of the welfare state on life satisfaction in affluent democracies. He concluded that

> "big government" is more conducive to human well-being, controlling for other factors. Indeed, the single most powerful individual- or national-level determinant of the degree to which people positively evaluate the quality of their lives is the extent to which they live in a generous and universalistic welfare state. . . . In the debate between Left and Right over the scope or size of the state, it is eminently clear that "big government" is more conducive to human well-being. As we have seen, the surest way to maximize the degree to which people positively evaluate the quality of their lives is to create generous, universalistic, and truly decommodifying welfare states.

While "the less prosperous have more to gain in an immediate way from a generous welfare state," Radcliff added, "the secondary effects on society in general (such as the reduction in crime, anomie, and other social pathologies that economic adversity fosters) benefit everyone," including the affluent.[11]

If the point of social spending is to bolster citizens' welfare and well-being, subjective assessments of welfare and well-being should provide a key indication of whether the welfare state is flourishing or in crisis. The European Social Survey has consistently included three items that may shed light on the success or failure of social spending in this respect. Two of these items focus on the quality of specific government services, asking people to rate "the state of health services in [country] nowadays" and "the state of education in [country] nowadays." Of course, people's assessments of these services may be impressionistic and, in some cases, flatly mistaken. For example, their assessments of "the state of education nowadays" may reflect their own children's idiosyncratic experiences, or second-hand reports or folk-wisdom regarding educational success or failure.[12] Nonetheless, it seems hard to deny that significant erosion in average ratings of these services would be a troubling indication of something amiss in a country's welfare state.

The first two columns of Table 3.2 show how responses to these ESS items, recorded on a zero-to-ten scale, changed in the wake of the economic crisis in

---

11. Radcliff (2013: 7, 177, 132).

12. Lerman (2019) argued that US governments' "reputation crisis" is based, in significant part, on stereotyped perceptions of government waste and incompetence that are often impervious to objective information.

TABLE 3.2. Changes in Subjective Social Welfare in the Wake of the Euro-Crisis

	Health services	Education	Life satisfaction
Austria	+.34 (.17)	−.05 (.36)	+.10 (.15)
Belgium	+.21 (.12)	+.08 (.05)	+.09 (.04)
Czechia	+.99 (.18)	+.15 (.21)	+.34 (.11)
Denmark	+.21 (.09)	+.27 (.06)	−.14 (.06)
Estonia	+.95 (.08)	+.99 (.19)	+.63 (.24)
Finland	+.30 (.16)	−.09 (.03)	−.00 (.03)
France	+.39 (.17)	−.07 (.07)	+.20 (.06)
Germany	+1.35 (.13)	+.74 (.15)	+.71 (.06)
Great Britain	+.65 (.15)	+.22 (.10)	+.18 (.05)
Hungary	+.27 (.19)	+.05 (.25)	+.58 (.15)
Ireland	+.14 (.06)	−.19 (.15)	−.35 (.08)
Italy	+.77 (.18)	+.22 (.17)	−.09 (.07)
Netherlands	+.56 (.16)	+.54 (.09)	+.19 (.06)
Norway	+1.41 (.15)	+.87 (.14)	+.16 (.04)
Poland	+.24 (.30)	+.61 (.17)	+.81 (.22)
Portugal	+1.42 (.20)	+.92 (.25)	+.57 (.22)
Slovakia	−.76 (.63)	−.29 (.17)	+.46 (.18)
Slovenia	−.19 (.13)	+.10 (.21)	+.20 (.21)
Spain	−.31 (.36)	−.45 (.28)	+.03 (.16)
Sweden	+.34 (.20)	−.08 (.20)	+.06 (.04)
Switzerland	+.83 (.12)	+.81 (.05)	+.05 (.04)
Population-weighted average	+.59 (.10)	+.25 (.08)	+.32 (.06)

Note: Change from 2002–2007 (ESS rounds 1–3) to 2014–2019 (ESS rounds 7–9) by country (with standard errors clustered by country-round in parentheses). Country-rounds are weighted by population.

each of 21 European countries.[13] On the whole, these data are more indicative of a flourishing welfare state than of a "hollowing out" or crisis. Citizens in 18 of the 21 countries were more satisfied with their nation's health services after the Euro-crisis (in 2014–2019) than they had been before (in 2002–2007). In nine of those countries, the improvement exceeded half a point on

13. Ratings of health services and education are recorded on scales with 0 labeled "extremely bad" and 10 labeled "extremely good." (The responses for satisfaction with life and with the incumbent government range from 0 for "extremely dissatisfied" to 10 for "extremely satisfied.") Greece does not appear in the table because there are no ESS data after 2011; Lithuania does not appear because there are no ESS data before 2011.

the zero-to-ten scale, and the population-weighted average change was +0.6 points. The trend in satisfaction with education is less dramatic, but still upward, with improvements exceeding half a point in seven countries, and a population-weighted average improvement of a quarter of a point. Portugal, Norway, Germany, Estonia, Switzerland, and the Netherlands all registered substantial improvements in both health services and education, while only Slovakia and Spain registered even small declines in both. Overall, judging by these measures, public satisfaction with the services provided by the European welfare state has increased markedly in recent years.

What factors account for these increases in satisfaction with the welfare state? Table 3.3 reports the results of statistical analyses relating these perceptions to a variety of national conditions and individual characteristics. Ratings of health services and education were substantially higher, on average, among young people, the foreign born, and people who described themselves as very religious, and to a lesser extent among the affluent, men, and people with conservative worldviews.[14] Even after allowing for these differences, stable differences across countries, and fluctuations associated with current economic conditions (real GDP and unemployment), social expenditures seem to have had a substantial positive impact on ratings of health services. Social spending was also positively related to assessments of the state of education, albeit less strongly.[15]

These statistical results imply that the population-weighted average increase in European social expenditures from 2001 to 2017 boosted the average rating of health services by about 0.7 points on the zero-to-ten scale, and the average rating of education by about 0.2 points. Comparing those estimates with the overall increases in ratings of health services and education in Table 3.2 (0.59 and 0.25 points, respectively), the statistical analyses imply that most or all of the net increase in ratings of social services over this period was attributable to the gradual expansion of European welfare states.

---

14. Other things being equal, the average rating of health services was .83 points lower among 45-year-olds than among comparable 20-year-olds, but .39 points *higher* among 70-year-olds than among comparable 45-year-olds. Education ratings were about 0.6 points lower among 45-year-olds than among 20-year-olds, but didn't vary much among older people.

15. The latter association presumably reflects a positive correlation between education spending and other social spending, since the OECD measure of social expenditures takes no direct account of education spending. To allow time for survey respondents to perceive and react to changes in economic conditions and social spending, my analyses employ data from the previous year as the relevant values for people interviewed in the first half of each calendar year.

TABLE 3.3. Bases of Subjective Social Welfare, 2002–2017

	Health services	Education	Life satisfaction	Life satisfaction (bottom income tercile)
ln(social expenditures per capita)	2.68	.84	.44	.22
	(.70)	(.41)	(.23)	(.32)
ln(GDP per capita)	−1.68	.17	1.43	1.98
	(1.14)	(.63)	(.38)	(.49)
Unemployment (%)	−.058	−.047	−.025	−.029
	(.022)	(.013)	(.007)	(.010)
Income (percentile/100)	.25	.17	1.72	3.25
	(.05)	(.04)	(.06)	(.20)
Education (years)	.013	−.026	.029	.034
	(.004)	(.004)	(.003)	(.005)
Age (years)	.074	.025	.067	.100
	(.003)	(.003)	(.004)	(.006)
ln(Age)	−3.31	−1.49	−2.98	−4.45
	(.12)	(.12)	(.16)	(.26)
Female	−.36	−.12	.03	.00
	(.03)	(.02)	(.01)	(.03)
Religious	.61	.65	.76	1.06
	(.04)	(.05)	(.05)	(.06)
Union member	−.09	−.02	.05	.08
	(.02)	(.02)	(.02)	(.04)
Foreign-born	.74	.61	−.09	−.01
	(.06)	(.05)	(.03)	(.06)
Conservative worldview	.068	.131	−.053	−.090
	(.010)	(.010)	(.007)	(.015)
Standard error of regression	2.25	2.13	2.07	2.33
Adjusted R^2	.17	.12	.12	.13
N	304,854	293,982	307,269	89,316

Note: Ordinary least-squares regression parameter estimates (with standard errors clustered by country-round in parentheses). Fixed effects for countries are included in the analyses but not shown. Country-rounds are weighted by population.

A third item in the European Social Survey provides a broader and more direct measure of subjective well-being. Survey respondents were asked how satisfied they were "with your life as a whole nowadays." If, as Radcliff has argued, "'big government' is more conducive to human well-being," then overall life satisfaction should capture, at least in part, the impact of the welfare state. Here, too, the data—presented in the third column of Table 3.2—are surprisingly encouraging. Eighteen of 21 countries registered at least small improvements in average reported life satisfaction between 2002–2007 and 2014–2019, with the average improvement amounting to one-third of a point on the zero-to-ten scale.

These increases in subjective well-being are especially notable because national changes in average life satisfaction were generally quite modest in magnitude. Figure 3.3 shows the average level of life satisfaction in each ESS round for Europe as a whole and for the 15 countries that participated in every round. The countries with the highest overall levels of life satisfaction—Switzerland, Finland, Norway, and Sweden—all fluctuated in a very narrow range, between 7.7 and 8.2 on the zero-to-ten scale, over the entire period. More generally, there is rather little evidence in the figure of declines in subjective well-being even in the midst of the Euro-crisis. A notable exception is Ireland, where average life satisfaction fell from 7.7 in 2005, at the height of the country's pre-crisis economic boom, to 6.6 in 2011, then gradually rebounded, reaching 7.2 in 2019. In Poland, average life satisfaction gradually rose from 5.8 in 2002 to 7.1 in 2012, while Hungary experienced a smaller but still substantial decade-long increase, from 5.2 in 2009 to 6.2 in 2019.

Is the gradual overall increase in life satisfaction in Figure 3.3 plausibly attributable to the gradual overall increase in social spending in Figure 3.1? The statistical analysis reported in the third column of Table 3.3, which relates variation in life satisfaction to social spending, economic conditions, and individual characteristics, suggests that increased social spending probably contributed, at least modestly, to increased life satisfaction. However, the estimated effect is a good deal smaller than for assessments of education and, especially, health services. It implies that the overall expansion of welfare states during the period covered by the ESS data increased Europeans' average life satisfaction by a bit more than 0.1 points on the zero-to-ten scale, accounting for about one-third of the overall increase. The difference in expected life satisfaction between typical high-spending European countries (Finland, France, or Sweden) and typical low-spending country (Portugal, Czechia, or Greece) is somewhat larger—about 0.3 points in 2017—providing more substantial but

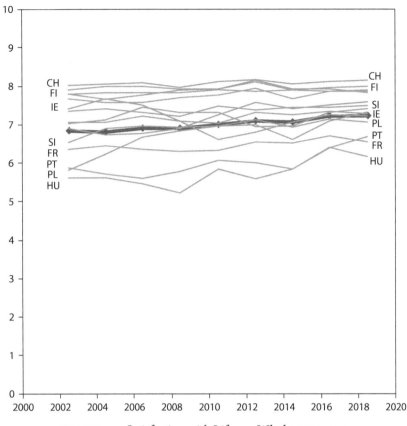

FIGURE 3.3. Satisfaction with Life as a Whole, 2002–2019

still modest support for the claim that "'big government' is more conducive to human well-being, controlling for other factors."

Perhaps focusing on the life satisfaction of entire populations misses a stronger impact of social spending on the well-being of the people who are most dependent on the welfare state. The analysis reported in the fourth column of Table 3.3 parallels the one reported in the third column, but focuses solely on people whose family incomes were in the bottom third of their national income distribution. Here, the estimated effects of GDP and income on subjective well-being are stronger than in the overall population, but the estimated effect of social spending is even weaker. At least in contemporary Europe as a whole, variation in the size of the welfare state had rather little apparent impact on the subjective well-being of its primary beneficiaries.

In his influential study of welfare states, Esping-Anderson argued that "expenditures present a circumspect and possibly misleading picture of welfare-state differences. If what we care about is the strength of social rights, equality, universalism, and the institutional division between market and politics, social-spending levels may camouflage more than they reveal." However, measures of variation in institutional features of welfare states provide even less evidence of a relationship between welfare state generosity and life satisfaction.[16]

The larger factor in accounting for differences in life satisfaction—both for poor people and for nonpoor people—was increasing national affluence, as measured by GDP per capita. The population-weighted increase in GDP per capita from 2001 to 2017 probably boosted average life satisfaction by more than a quarter of a point, accounting for most of the overall increase in life satisfaction documented in Table 3.2. The estimated impact on the subjective well-being of lower-income people was even larger. The plausibility of these effects is bolstered by the very substantial cross-sectional difference in life satisfaction between more and less affluent people in the same country and year, even after statistically adjusting for the effects of age, education, religiosity, and other factors—and especially among lower-income people. Money may not buy happiness on a day-to-day basis, but it *does* seem to buy significant increases in satisfaction with life as a whole, especially for those who are economically worst off.[17]

---

16. Esping-Anderson (1990: 106). The Comparative Welfare Entitlements Project led by Lyle Scruggs has produced comparable data on the structure of welfare entitlements in a variety of affluent democracies; see Comparative Welfare Entitlements Dataset, http://cwed2.org/. Adding the most recent (2010) measure of overall welfare state generosity as an explanatory variable in analyses of life satisfaction paralleling those in Table 3.3 produces small but statistically precise *negative* relationships, both overall and for lower-income people. Rueda (2012) used data from the Luxembourg Income Study to assess the impact of welfare state structures on the relationship between unemployment and poverty. His analysis suggested that the trend toward "more demanding" welfare policies in the 1990s and early 2000s magnified the impact of unemployment on poverty. However, repeating the analyses reported in the last column of Table 3.3 separately for countries with low, intermediate, and high levels of "benefit generosity" suggests that unemployment and social spending both had much larger effects on life satisfaction among lower-income respondents in countries with intermediate levels of "benefit generosity" (Austria, Finland, Germany, Ireland, Norway, Sweden, and Switzerland) than in those with less generous (France, Great Britain, Greece, Italy, and Spain) or more generous (Belgium, Denmark, and the Netherlands) unemployment benefits.

17. Kahneman and Deaton (2010).

The Steel Strings of Austerity

If social spending is not strongly related to subjective well-being, what are we to make of the common perception that the victims of the Troika's heavy-handed conditional bailouts suffered what Greek economist Yannis Varoufakis characterized as "death by a thousand austerity cuts"? Perhaps the consequences of cuts in social spending are simply exaggerated, and the real cost of austerity programs is macroeconomic rather than fiscal. That would be consistent with the evidence in Table 3.3 suggesting that GDP and unemployment, not social spending, drove variation in subjective well-being, especially for the poor. Alternatively, gauging the true impact of social spending may require us to focus more specifically on places where "the European welfare state was hollowed out at the behest of the troika."[18]

The most obvious place to look for the impact of austerity on social well-being is in Greece, where years of draconian budget-cutting in the face of economic depression and sky-high unemployment produced the massive shortfalls in social spending documented in Figure 3.2. According to Varoufakis, "The steel strings of austerity that accompanied the massive loan agreement demolished Greece's social economy."[19]

Unfortunately, the full impact of austerity on Greece's social economy is not captured in the ESS data because surveys were not conducted there after 2011. However, the early stages of the crisis are reflected in measures of subjective well-being from 2009 and 2011. In the first of these readings, overall life satisfaction in Greece had already fallen by half a point on the zero-to-ten scale from its 2005 level. By 2011, it had fallen by another 0.3 points, producing an average reading of 5.7, 1.3 points below the European average. People in the bottom third of the income distribution were even worse off, with average life satisfaction of just 5.2.

While these data from Greece are suggestive, Spain provides a more comprehensive record of the impact of austerity on subjective well-being. As we saw in Chapter 2, Spain avoided a full-scale bailout, but adopted substantial budget cuts and tax hikes under pressure from the Troika.[20] As a result, as

---

18. Varoufakis (2016: 139–140); Tooze (2018: 370).

19. Varoufakis (2016: 209).

20. Julien Toyer and Andrés González, "Spain Unveils New Austerity under European Pressure," Reuters, 11 July 2012. Giles Tremlett, "Spain: The Pain of Austerity Persists," Guardian, 1 January 2013. Gonzalo Cavero, "The True Cost of Austerity and Inequality: Spain Case Study,"

Figure 3.2 shows, Spain's social spending remained virtually flat from 2009 to 2013, even as GDP fell by almost 10% and unemployment soared to 26.1%. In 2012 and 2013, the gap between actual social spending and expected spending based on the pre-crisis European pattern reached 30%. The Spanish economy began to recover in 2014, reducing the shortfall somewhat, but GDP did not return to its pre-crisis peak (in real, per capita terms) until 2017, and unemployment did not fall below 15% until 2019.

Spaniards' satisfaction with the state of their economy tracks these developments, falling from 5.3 in 2006 to just 2.2 in 2013, then gradually rebounding to 4.2 by 2019. Average satisfaction with life as a whole shows a similar but much less pronounced trend, falling from 7.5 in 2006 to 6.9 in 2013, then gradually rebounding to 7.4 by 2019. Figure 3.4 shows these trends separately for affluent people (in the top quarter of the Spanish income distribution, represented by double lines) and poor people (in the bottom one-third of the income distribution, represented by single lines). Not surprisingly, affluent people were almost always somewhat more satisfied with the state of the economy than poor people were; but the two groups' assessments shifted in close parallel over the whole period, declining precipitously from 2006 to 2013, then rebounding strongly and steadily from 2013 to 2019.

Spaniards' satisfaction with life as a whole followed a rather different pattern. The differences in average levels of life satisfaction between affluent and poor people were considerably larger than for assessments of the economy. What is even more striking is that affluent Spaniards' subjective well-being was almost entirely stable throughout the economic crisis, never dipping by more than two-tenths of a point on the zero-to-ten scale. Despite the magnitude of the economic calamity, they seem to have been effectively insulated from personal harm.

The trend in life satisfaction looks quite different for people in the bottom one-third of the Spanish income distribution. Their life satisfaction was largely impervious to the beginning of the economic downturn in 2008; but it declined by half a point on the zero-to-ten scale between 2011 and 2013, as

---

Oxfam, September 2013, https://oxfamilibrary.openrepository.com/bitstream/handle/10546/301384/cs-true-cost-austerity-inequality-spain-120913-en.pdf. Amnesty International, "Spain: Cruel Austerity Measures Leave Patients Suffering," 24 April 2018, https://www.amnesty.org/en/latest/news/2018/04/spain-cruel-austerity-measures-leave-patients-suffering/. Lopez-Valcarcel and Barber (2017).

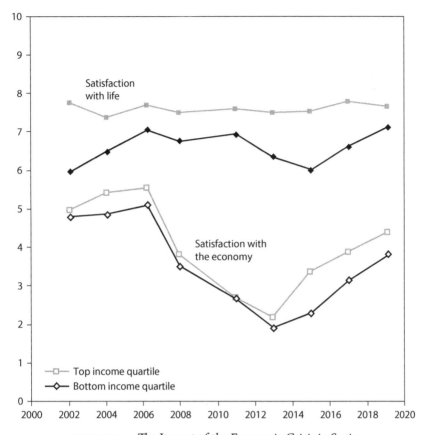

FIGURE 3.4. The Impact of the Economic Crisis in Spain

unemployment continued to rise and social spending fell. The gap in life satisfaction between people in the top and bottom income quartiles swelled from
0.6 points in 2011 to a full point in 2013 and 2015 before gradually narrowing
again in 2017 and 2019. Compared to more affluent counterparts, poor Spaniards seem to have been far less insulated from the cumulative fallout of the
economic crisis.

Lest the slump in low-income well-being in Spain be considered a fluke, it
is worth noting that a similar, but even sharper pattern appears in Ireland,
which experienced a rather different economic crisis and a rather different
flavor of austerity. The Wall Street meltdown of 2008 triggered a massive
collapse of Ireland's overleveraged financial sector. After years of sustained,
robust growth, real per capita GDP fell by a disastrous 6.5% in 2008 and a

further 6% in 2009. The crisis was exacerbated by the government's early decision (in September 2008) to guarantee a vast pool of domestic bank debt. Bailing out and restructuring the banks cost €64 billion—roughly 40% of Ireland's annual GDP.[21]

An "emergency budget" announced in late 2008 included new income taxes and government spending cuts. But with the economy continuing to contract and unemployment escalating, the government agreed in November 2010 to a €68 million bailout from the EU and IMF. The aid was conditioned on further structural reforms, including income tax increases, spending cuts, changes in eligibility for pensions, and the adoption of a new "Fiscal Responsibility Law."

The size and influence of Ireland's business and financial sectors probably made the government officials who designed and implemented these austerity plans "particularly sensitive to and compliant with the interests of international financial capital," and "the priority accorded to maintaining Ireland's low tax regime . . . transfer[red] the burden of fiscal adjustment onto the public sector, through cuts in pay and services, including downward pressure on social welfare payments where demand is increasing due to rising unemployment." The result was a sharply regressive distribution of economic pain. "In 2010," Oxfam reported, "those in the lowest income band saw their disposable income fall by more than 26 per cent, while those in the highest income band saw their disposable income rise by more than eight per cent."[22]

According to the most comprehensive analysis of the Irish case,

> The major policies agreed with the Troika had been initiated by the Irish Government before the country was forced into accepting a bailout. . . . The government's decision to opt for austerity reflected a long-established procyclical bias in fiscal policy and in politics. The sustainability of austerity was reinforced by support from the main political parties for the decision to implement austerity and for most of the measures involved.[23]

---

21. Roche, O'Connell, and Prothero (2017: 11).

22. Dukelow and Kennett (2018); Dukelow and Considine (2014). Niamh Hardiman and Aidan Regan, "The Politics of Austerity in Ireland," January 2013, https://researchrepository.ucd .ie/handle/10197/4222. Jody Clarke, "The True Cost of Austerity and Inequality: Ireland Case Study," Oxfam, September 2013, https://www-cdn.oxfam.org/s3fs-public/file_attachments/cs -true-cost-austerity-inequality-ireland-120913-en_0.pdf.

23. Roche, O'Connell, and Prothero (2017: 2).

While elite support for austerity policies crossed party lines, electoral retribution for the economic downturn focused on the incumbent Fianna Fáil party. In the next general election, a few months after the new bailout agreement was announced, Fianna Fáil suffered a shattering defeat, losing more than half of its first-preference vote share. The party that had governed Ireland for most of the preceding 80 years was supplanted by its longtime rival Fine Gael, which formed a coalition government with the social democratic Labour Party.

The new government continued to implement the bailout plan, to wide applause from European leaders who viewed Ireland as "Europe's poster child" for the benefits of austerity. Real GDP, which had begun to rebound in 2010 after two disastrous years, leveled off in 2011 and hardly grew through 2012 and 2013. The unemployment rate remained over 15%. Nonetheless, in 2012 Fine Gael prime minister Enda Kenny was named "European of the Year" in Germany and appeared on the cover of *Time* magazine as the hero of "The Celtic Comeback." IMF Director Christine Lagarde and German Chancellor Angela Merkel congratulated the Irish on their successful weathering of the crisis.[24]

In fact, as a team of Irish social scientists argued, Ireland was less a "poster child" than a "beautiful freak" in the context of Europe as a whole. "Ireland recovered not because of but despite eurozone-imposed strictures and policies. . . . Ireland's special advantage arose from its nearly three-decades-old corporate-tax regime, which combined a low corporate tax rate with assorted additional side deals to attract foreign investors." The social cost of this "success" was considerable. Unemployment rose from 100,000 in 2007 to 295,000 in 2012. Even more remarkably, "560,000 people left Ireland between 2008 and 2015. Almost half were Irish nationals." Those who stayed experienced Europe's largest decline in average life satisfaction in the wake of the Euro-crisis.[25]

Perhaps the oddest twist in this story is that Ireland's austerity campaign persisted well after the economic crisis abated. According to the OECD, Ireland's real GDP per capita grew by an astounding 35% (the equivalent of almost $18,000) between 2012 and 2015. Yet, public social spending per capita fell by more than 15% (almost $2,000 in 2015 dollars) between 2010 and 2015, with most of that decline coming after 2012.

24. Roche, O'Connell, and Prothero (2017: 1–2). Hardiman and Regan, "Politics of Austerity in Ireland."

25. Roche, O'Connell, and Prothero (2017: 1–2).

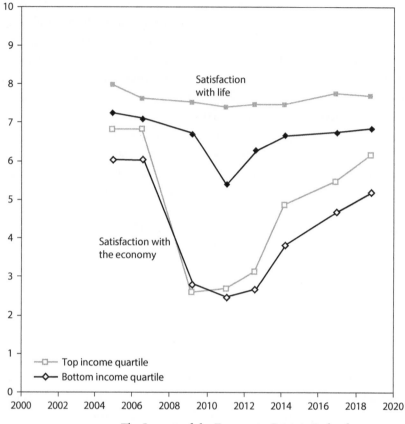

FIGURE 3.5. The Impact of the Economic Crisis in Ireland

Ireland's remarkable GDP growth was partly a reflection of complex book-keeping by multinational corporations exploiting Ireland's low tax rates.[26] Nonetheless, the robust upturn appears clearly in public perceptions of the economy. The bottom two trendlines in Figure 3.5 record average levels of satisfaction with the economy among the top and bottom income quartiles of the Irish population (the gray and black lines, respectively). Both trendlines clearly reflect the dramatic economic turnaround between 2012–2013 and 2014–2015, with further improvement in 2017 and 2019. As in Spain, the re-bound in economic optimism was somewhat faster and stronger among high-income people, reestablishing the consistent gap in economic perceptions

26. Mody (2018: 431).

(about two-thirds of a point on the zero-to-ten scale) that had disappeared in the immediate wake of the financial crisis.[27]

The trendlines for satisfaction with Irish "life as a whole" show a distinctly different pattern. Here, too, affluent people were consistently more satisfied than poor people were. But, unlike their economic assessments, their satisfaction with life was only gradually dented by the economic crisis, falling by three-quarters of a point on the zero-to-ten scale between 2005 and 2012–2013, then regaining most of that ground. In contrast, the average level of life satisfaction among lower-income people fell by twice as much, and even after eight years of recovery it remained half a point below its 2005 level, and more than half a point below the corresponding level for affluent people.

The statistical analyses reported in Table 3.4 shed additional light on the bases of life satisfaction in Spain and Ireland. In each case, separate analyses focus on people in the bottom third of the income distribution and those in the top two-thirds.[28] The explanatory factors include aggregate indicators of social spending, GDP, and unemployment, as well as a variety of personal characteristics. The results suggest that income, education, age, and religiosity were all strongly related to life satisfaction in both countries, especially for lower-income people.

With just seven or eight rounds of surveys in each country, it is very difficult to disentangle the distinct effects of social spending, GDP, and unemployment on subjective well-being.[29] Thus, while unemployment seems to have been robustly associated with declines in life satisfaction in both countries, especially for lower-income people, the corresponding estimated effects of GDP are implausibly negative. Nonetheless, these analyses seem to provide the best evidence the European Social Survey data can offer regarding the impact of austerity on life satisfaction.

For Spain, the statistical results suggest that fluctuations in social spending contributed substantially to shifts in life satisfaction, especially for lower-income

27. On the sensitivity of high incomes to financial downturns and recoveries, see Guvenen, Ozkan, and Song (2014).

28. The analyses for Ireland begin in 2005 because the first round of Irish ESS interviews did not ascertain family income. The analyses for both countries end in 2017 because, at the time of this writing, the OECD Social Expenditure Database does not yet include spending data for more recent years.

29. The correlation between logged GDP per capita and unemployment is −.60 in Spain and −.39 in Ireland. The correlation between logged social spending per capita and unemployment is +.74 in Spain and +.89 in Ireland.

TABLE 3.4. Life Satisfaction in Spain and Ireland

	Spain (2002–2017)		Ireland (2005–2017)	
	Bottom income tercile	Middle and top income terciles	Bottom income tercile	Middle and top income terciles
ln(social expenditures per capita)	5.88	2.94	1.67	−.41
	(1.41)	(.71)	(1.08)	(.59)
ln(GDP per capita)	−9.64	−2.76	−1.23	−.21
	(3.31)	(1.64)	(.52)	(.28)
Unemployment (%)	−.115	−.055	−.170	−.058
	(.028)	(.014)	(.034)	(.019)
Income (percentile/100)	3.31	.87	1.94	1.10
	(.39)	(.11)	(.39)	(.12)
Education (years)	.023	.004	.052	.010
	(.010)	(.005)	(.014)	(.008)
Age (years)	.068	.026	.097	.081
	(.009)	(.005)	(.009)	(.006)
ln(Age)	−3.16	−1.33	−3.73	−3.04
	(.40)	(.20)	(.40)	(.25)
Female	−.23	.01	.10	.07
	(.07)	(.04)	(.08)	(.04)
Religious	1.15	.68	1.52	.98
	(.15)	(.07)	(.17)	(.09)
Union member	.45	.12	.19	.01
	(.20)	(.06)	(.15)	(.05)
Foreign-born	−.42	−.15	.12	.00
	(.13)	(.07)	(.11)	(.06)
Conservative worldview	−.129	−.019	−.015	−.081
	(.037)	(.020)	(.041)	(.023)
Standard error of regression	2.21	1.78	2.25	1.84
Adjusted R²	.06	.03	.12	.07
N	4,382	11,546	5,414	10,813

Note: Ordinary least-squares regression parameter estimates (with standard errors in parentheses). Country-rounds are weighted by population.

people. Taken at face value, they imply that the increasing gap between expected and actual social spending documented in Figure 3.2—from just 1% in
2007 to about 35% in 2012 and 2013—may have reduced average life satisfaction
among lower-income Spaniards by two full points on the zero-to-ten scale,
while the corresponding estimated effect for middle- and high-income people
was about half that large.

In Ireland, social spending seems to have had no effect on life satisfaction
among people with middle and high incomes, and even among those with lower
incomes, the estimated impact of social spending was much more modest than
in Spain. The statistical analysis reported in Table 3.4 implies that the ballooning
gap between expected and actual social spending in Ireland—from 4% in 2010
to 21% in 2012 and 2013—may have reduced average life satisfaction among
lower-income people by about 0.3 points on the zero-to-ten scale. Most of the
gradual decline in their life satisfaction is more likely attributable to the direct
effect of increasing unemployment. From 2005 to 2011, the Irish unemployment
rate rose from 4.3% to 15.4%. The estimated impact of unemployment in Table 3.4
implies that that increase reduced average life satisfaction among lower-income
people by almost two points, fully accounting for the overall decline documented in Figure 3.5, while the estimated impact on middle- and high-income
people was about two-thirds of a point on the zero-to-ten scale.

If the impact of social spending on subjective well-being is difficult to trace
in Spain and Ireland, it is even more fugitive elsewhere in Europe—even in
countries wrapped in "the steel strings of austerity." For example, historian
Tooze described the United Kingdom as Europe's "most remarkable instance
of austerity contagion." Yet, it is surprisingly hard to see much evidence of the
impact of austerity in the survey responses of ordinary Britons. The UK suffered a severe but relatively brief economic downturn in 2008–2009. Public
debt swelled from around 50% of GDP before the crisis to almost 90% in 2010.
Unlike the distressed countries on the periphery of the eurozone, the UK had
its own currency, and thus a good deal of latitude to pursue monetary as well
as fiscal remedies for its problems. Nonetheless, a congenial alliance between
a new Conservative government and a conservative Bank of England produced a policy of austerity that was, even more than in Ireland, a matter of
ideological choice rather than necessity.[30]

From 1997 to 2007, the Labour government of Prime Minister Tony Blair
had instituted a variety of major policy changes intended to alleviate poverty

30. Tooze (2018: 348–349).

and bolster social well-being, including a national minimum wage, an education maintenance allowance, increased maternity and paternity leave for working families, and a new employment support allowance. Real public social spending per capita increased by almost 50%, with health expenditures and housing and family programs growing even faster.[31] Social spending continued to increase under Gordon Brown, the longtime chancellor of the exchequer who succeeded Blair as prime minister in 2007. But with the onset of the Great Recession, much of the increased spending was in direct response to the economic downturn; spending on unemployment benefits increased by 75% in just three years.

In 2010, a bad election year for incumbents globally, Brown's Labour government was replaced in power by a Conservative coalition government led by David Cameron. The Tories used the economic crisis as the rationale for a sharp reversal in social policy. The growth rate in spending on health care slowed considerably, old-age pensions stagnated, and the rest of the social budget shrank by 2.0% per year in real terms during Cameron's first five years as prime minister. As a share of GDP, total public social spending fell from 22.4% in 2010 to 21.6% in 2015 and 20.6% in 2018.

According to a 2018 *New York Times* report, "The protracted campaign of budget cutting, started in 2010 by a government led by the Conservative Party, has delivered a monumental shift in British life. A wave of austerity has yielded a country that has grown accustomed to living with less, even as many measures of social well-being—crime rates, opioid addiction, infant mortality, childhood poverty and homelessness—point to a deteriorating quality of life." The following year, a United Nations official reported that the budget cuts had produced "tragic social consequences" for Britain: "It might seem to some observers that the Department of Work and Pensions has been tasked with designing a digital and sanitized version of the 19th-century workhouse, made infamous by Charles Dickens."[32]

31. Mike Brewer, Alissa Goodman, Robert Joyce, Alastair Muriel, David Phillips, and Luke Sibieta, "Have the Poor Got Poorer under Labour?," London: Institute for Fiscal Studies, 13 October 2009, https://ifs.org.uk/publications/4637. Spending figures are from the OECD's Social Expenditure Database.

32. Peter S. Goodman, "In Britain, Austerity Is Changing Everything," *New York Times*, 28 May 2018. Ceylan Yeginsu, "U.K. Austerity Has Inflicted 'Great Misery,' U.N. Official Says," *New York Times*, 22 May 2019.

This sounds grim, indeed. Yet, the tabulations presented in Table 3.2 indicate that ordinary Britons were more satisfied with their lives in 2014–2018, after years of Tory austerity, than they had been in 2002–2006, toward the end of Tony Blair's decade in power. Even people in the bottom third of the income distribution expressed the same level of subjective well-being as they had before the crisis, and significantly higher levels of satisfaction with health services and education—hardly a Dickensian picture.[33]

One possible explanation for this striking disparity between alarmed perceptions and the more sanguine response of the people on the receiving end of Tory austerity is that the significant cuts in social spending after 2012 followed years of rapid increases; in 2017, the most recent year covered by the OECD data, the UK's social spending was still 8% higher in real terms than it had been when Tony Blair left office a decade earlier. Another, related possibility is that perceptions of crisis are partly a matter of perspective—especially when austerity is a matter of ideological choice rather than economic necessity. As Castles wrote of the shift from "the 'golden age' of the welfare state" to the period of constrained growth in the 1980s and 1990s, "Those fighting to extend its frontiers have had to fight harder in recent decades than they did in the years of plenty. Clearly, too, some battles have been lost, making it extremely tempting for those involved to seek compelling explanations of why the forces of 'social progress' are now apparently on the back foot."[34]

Public Support for the Welfare State

Writing in the 1990s, political scientist Paul Pierson assessed the impact of conservatives' attempts to scale back the welfare state under Ronald Reagan in the US and Margaret Thatcher in the UK. "Despite the aggressive efforts of retrenchment advocates," he concluded, "the welfare state remains largely intact." His explanation for this resilience emphasized "the high political costs associated with retrenchment initiatives. Despite scholarly speculation about declining popular support for the welfare state, there remains little evidence

---

33. The average level of life satisfaction among Britons in the bottom income tercile was 6.6 in 2002; it reached a low point of 6.5 in 2010 and fluctuated between 6.7 and 7.1 thereafter. The overall change from 2002–2006 to 2014–2018 was .02 (with a standard error of .08). The corresponding changes in satisfaction with health services and education were +.47 (with a standard error of .09) and +.21 (with a standard error of .08), respectively.

34. Castles (2004: 45).

of such a shift in opinion polls, and even less in actual political struggles over social spending. On the contrary, efforts to dismantle the welfare state have exacted a high political price."[35]

Pierson's emphasis on popular support for the welfare state as an important factor in accounting for the failure of aggressive retrenchment efforts is consistent with sociologists Clem Brooks and Jeff Manza's broader account in their book *Why Welfare States Persist*. Brooks and Manza pointed to a strong cross-national correlation between public opinion and social spending in affluent democracies as evidence that "mass policy preferences are a powerful factor behind welfare state output." While their statistical evidence is subject to alternative interpretations, it certainly suggests that a significant decline in public support for social spending could be a sign of political trouble for contemporary welfare states.[36]

The European Social Survey has consistently included two items shedding light on public attitudes toward the welfare state. One asked whether "the government should take measures to reduce differences in income levels." This question has been used by Brooks and Manza, among others, to measure public support for the welfare state. While income redistribution might reasonably be characterized as a byproduct of the welfare state rather than a primary goal, substantial public opposition to redistribution might well be a significant political hurdle to increasing social spending. As it turns out, however, there has been strong and steady support across Europe for reducing income differences. Figure 3.6 shows average levels of support for redistribution in Europe as a whole and in each of the 15 countries included in every ESS round. In Europe as a whole, enthusiasm for redistribution increased during the Euro-crisis, from 7.0 on the zero-to-ten scale in 2002–2007 to a high of 7.3 in 2012–2013. The average level in the post-crisis period was 7.2.

While there is significant variation across countries in support for redistribution, from Hungary and Portugal (and Greece and Lithuania, not shown in the figure) at the high end to the Netherlands and Czechia (and Denmark) at the low end, there are only two countries—France and Norway—in which support for redistribution fell by as much as a quarter of a point in the

---

35. Pierson (1994: 179–181).

36. Brooks and Manza (2007: 36, 141). On the limitations of Brooks and Manza's cross-sectional evidence, see Kenworthy (2009). On the limits of responsiveness to public demand for social spending, see Bartels (2017).

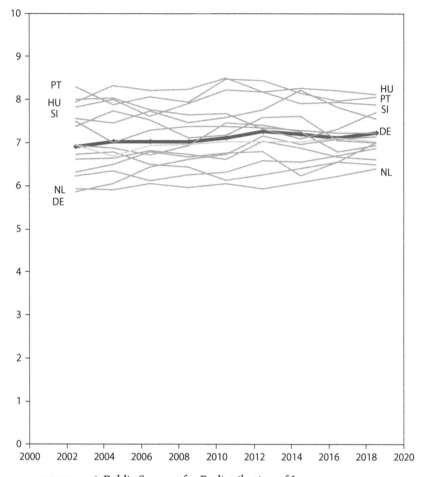

FIGURE 3.6. Public Support for Redistribution of Income, 2002–2019

wake of the economic crisis. Ironically, the one country in which support for redistribution dipped (very slightly) below the midpoint of the zero-to-ten scale at any point between 2002 and 2019 was Denmark, which has one of the lowest levels of economic inequality and one of the highest levels of social spending in the world. Presumably, Danish survey respondents were expressing a lack of enthusiasm for further reductions in income inequality beyond those already achieved. In any case, it is clear from the very high and steadily growing level of social spending in Denmark in Figure 3.1 that their relative hesitance to endorse "measures to reduce differences in income levels" has done rather little to constrain the scope of the Danish welfare state.

TABLE 3.5. Bases of Public Support for Income Redistribution

	(1)	(2)	2002–2007	2008–2013	2014–2019
Income (percentile/100)	−1.35	−1.27	−1.32	−1.26	−1.12
	(.05)	(.06)	(.09)	(.11)	(.08)
Education (years)	−.039	−.034	−.052	−.037	−.025
	(.005)	(.005)	(.008)	(.006)	(.006)
Age (years)	−.018	−.012	−.012	−.016	−.013
	(.002)	(.002)	(.004)	(.003)	(.003)
ln(Age)	.87	.61	.44	.73	.69
	(.10)	(.09)	(.19)	(.14)	(.12)
Female	.29	.26	.29	.24	.22
	(.02)	(.02)	(.04)	(.03)	(.03)
Religious	−.38	−.35	−.26	−.33	−.30
	(.05)	(.05)	(.09)	(.08)	(.08)
Union member	.34	.34	.33	.32	.36
	(.03)	(.03)	(.05)	(.04)	(.05)
Foreign-born	−.00	.04	.02	.09	−.01
	(.03)	(.03)	(.06)	(.05)	(.05)
Conservative worldview	—	.040	.070	.082	−.011
		(.013)	(.020)	(.018)	(.023)
Economic satisfaction	—	−.089	−.105	−.122	−.124
		(.016)	(.014)	(.015)	(.015)
Standard error of regression	2.46	2.45	2.44	2.45	2.42
Adjusted R²	.09	.10	.14	.10	.08
N	348,300	348,300	113,430	121,754	113,116

Note: Ordinary least-squares regression parameter estimates (with standard errors clustered by country-round in parentheses). Fixed effects for countries are included in the analyses but not shown. Country-rounds are weighted by population.

Table 3.5 summarizes the correlates of support for income redistribution at the individual level. Perhaps unsurprisingly, affluence is a powerful source of opposition to income redistribution, with the expected difference between people at the top and bottom of the income distribution amounting to more than a full point on the ten-point scale of support for redistribution. Formal education also tended to dampen support for income redistribution, though that opposition seems to have weakened in response to the economic crisis.

Finally, the impact of conservative worldviews on support for redistribution was modestly positive before the economic crisis (consistent with the notion that people who valued security and order might favor government provision of *economic* security). However, in more recent surveys, the link between worldviews and support for redistribution seems to have disappeared entirely.

ESS respondents have also consistently been invited to characterize their own political views using a left-right scale running from zero on the extreme left to ten on the extreme right.[37] Left-right ideology is not entirely about the welfare state; this summary measure also captures, to varying degrees in different times and places, attitudes toward a variety of social and cultural conflicts only tangentially related to the conflicts over social provision that loomed so large in European politics in the post-war era. Nonetheless, attitudes toward the welfare state continue to be a major ingredient of political ideology and partisan conflict in contemporary Europe, especially for people on the left side of the political spectrum.[38]

At the aggregate level, these left-right placements reflect consistent moderation. For Europe as a whole, the average position is almost perfectly moderate and almost precisely constant from 2002 to 2019, ranging from a low of 4.9 to a high of 5.0 on the zero-to-ten scale.[39] Indeed, in the 148 separate country

37. Despite the ubiquity of "left-right" imagery in public discourse on European politics, ideological self-identification is far from universal. Overall, 12% of ESS respondents declined to place themselves on the left-right scale. (The proportion ranged from 5% or less in Norway, Sweden, Finland, and the Netherlands to more than 20% in Greece, Slovenia, Italy, and Portugal and 30% in Lithuania.)

38. Knutsen (1995); Kriesi et al. (2012); Lachat (2018). In an analysis of data from the 2008–2010 European Values Study, which included a wider variety of items tapping specific political attitudes than the European Social Survey, a summary measure of economic views had almost five times as much impact on left-right placements as a summary measure of cultural views. Among the strongest indicators of economic views were items touching on the state's responsibility to ensure that everyone is provided for, equalizing incomes, and whether people receiving unemployment benefits should be required to take any job available.

39. Some of this apparent moderation may reflect a lack of ideological orientation in segments of the European public. In addition to the 12% of ESS respondents who declined to place themselves on the left-right scale, a further 31% placed themselves at the exact midpoint of the scale. Kinder and Kalmoe (2017: 157–159), using US data, found that ideological moderates were no more consistent or stable in their specific political preferences than people who declined to place themselves on the (7-point) ideological scale, though they were significantly more likely to display an understanding of ideological labels. They concluded that there is "little reason to regard moderation as an ideological category."

surveys, there is not a single average reading as far to the left as 4.0 or as far to the right as 6.0 on the zero-to-ten scale. Moreover, only a few countries display meaningful shifts in ideology within that limited range.[40]

Neither the Great Recession nor the Euro-crisis seems to have produced any hint of systematic ideological shifts in Europe, whether to the left or the right; nor is there much evidence of significant shifts in the demographic and social bases of ideology, which for the most part mirror the bases of attitudes toward redistribution reported in Table 3.5. Contrary to some accounts of the political implications of economic disaffection, people who were dissatisfied with the state of their national economies generally placed themselves a bit further to the ideological left than those who were satisfied, and that tendency probably increased after the economic crisis. The relationship between conservative worldviews and right-wing ideology also seems to have increased somewhat in recent surveys. That change may reflect a shift in the meaning of "left" and "right" to incorporate cultural concerns in addition to traditional controversies regarding the role of government. However, the relationship between conservative worldviews and right-wing ideology is negligible or even reversed in some of the most conservative countries in Europe, including Slovakia, Czechia, Estonia, and Hungary.

A different cross-national survey, the International Social Survey Programme (ISSP), provides more detailed evidence regarding public attitudes toward the welfare state. Responses to a series of questions included in the ISSP's Role of Government module in 2006 and again in 2016 offer a valuable window on shifts in public support for the welfare state in 11 countries included in both those surveys.[41] The ISSP questions asked people whether their government should be responsible for each of four key aspects of social welfare—providing health care for the sick, a decent standard of living for the old, decent housing for those who can't afford it, and a decent standard of living for the unemployed. Respondents were also asked whether they favored increases or decreases in spending on a variety of specific government pro-

40. Most notably, Hungary moved a full point to the right on the zero-to-ten scale between 2005 and 2010, before moderating somewhat following the election of Victor Orbán. Poland moved two-thirds of a point to the right between 2002 and 2006, but with no additional movement thereafter.

41. The 11 countries surveyed in both 2006 and 2016—Czechia, Denmark, Finland, France, Germany, Great Britain, Hungary, Norway, Spain, Sweden, and Switzerland—provide a fairly representative cross-section of Europe, aside from the overrepresentation of Nordic countries.

grams, including four focused on core elements of the modern welfare state—health, education, old-age pensions, and unemployment benefits.

Responses to these questions demonstrated widespread public support for the responsibilities and programs of the modern European welfare state. In the case of government spending on health care, the relatively few people who did *not* want their government to spend more were outnumbered by people who wanted it to spend *much* more. Substantial majorities of citizens also favored spending more on education and old-age pensions. The only welfare state program that produced a near-even split between people who favored more spending and those who favored *less* spending was unemployment benefits—and even in that area the modal survey respondent acknowledged that the government probably should be responsible for providing a decent standard of living for the unemployed.

Ultimately, of course, the benefits of the welfare state must be weighed against its costs. As part of a battery of questions about "some things the government might do for the economy," ISSP respondents were also asked whether they favored or opposed "cuts in government spending." Paradoxically, though perhaps unsurprisingly, the same survey respondents who expressed strong support for increases in spending on the major social programs constituting much of their governments' budgets also expressed strong support for cuts in government spending. Enthusiasm for budget-cutting was overwhelming in France and, to a lesser extent, Hungary, but also strong in Germany, Czechia, Norway, Switzerland, and Sweden; the only countries that expressed net opposition to spending cuts were Finland (in 2006) and Great Britain (in 2016). However, this public support for spending cuts was generally exceeded by support for *increases* in spending on specific social welfare programs.

Even more remarkable than the *level* of public support for the welfare state in these data is the *consistency* of that support between 2006 and 2016. Despite the economically and politically tumultuous decade separating the two surveys, the shifts in perceived government responsibility and spending preferences were miniscule. The largest shift in overall support for the welfare state was in Germany, where increasing prosperity fueled increasing demands for social spending. Sweden and Spain experienced smaller increases in public support. The only countries where support for the welfare state declined perceptibly were Finland and Denmark; but those declines were modest in magnitude, and both countries remained among the most supportive of the welfare state even in 2016. Of all the specific attitudes and preferences tapped in the ISSP surveys, the only one that showed a perceptible shift between 2006 and 2016 was enthusiasm for government budget-cutting, which declined by about one-fourth of a point on average.[42]

In short, the ISSP surveys strongly reinforce the less detailed but temporally and geographically richer evidence provided by the European Social Survey in suggesting that public support for the welfare state was essentially impervious to the Euro-crisis. If there was any real change in Europeans' attitudes toward the welfare state in the wake of the economic crisis, it was a modest *increase* in their willingness to pay for it. There is certainly no support in these data for the notion that Europeans have turned against the welfare state, either in principle or in practice.

Summary

The Euro-crisis generated renewed alarm regarding the viability of Europe's supposedly embattled welfare states. However, real per capita social spending continued to increase in most of Europe throughout the crisis, and most citizens were more satisfied with health services, education, and their overall lives in the years after the crisis than they had been before it began. By these measures, the contemporary European welfare state not only survived the Euro-crisis—it thrived.

The perception of a welfare state in crisis is partly a matter of focus. In Greece, Spain, and Ireland, aggressive austerity programs did constrain government responses to severe economic downturns, producing significant shortfalls in social spending and, probably though not certainly, a significant negative impact on the well-being of lower-income people. But in most countries, even lower-income people were more satisfied with social services, and with their overall lives, during the crisis than they had been before, and more satisfied after the crisis than they had been while it unfolded.[43]

---

42. Translating responses to the various ISSP survey items on government responsibilities, spending on specific welfare state programs, and support for spending cuts on to zero-to-ten scales, the largest overall shift in attitudes between 2006 and 2016 was a quarter-point decline in support for cutting government spending; only one of the eight items on government responsibilities and spending on specific programs showed an overall shift of even one-tenth of a point. Combining the items into a summary scale of support for the welfare state (with support for spending cuts weighted four times as heavily as the other items), the increase in support in Germany amounted to a bit more than half a point on the zero-to-ten scale, while the declines in Finland and Denmark amounted to about one-third of a point.

43. The average life satisfaction of Europeans in the bottom tercile of their national income distributions increased from 6.31 in 2002–2007 to 6.48 in 2008–2013 to 6.63 in 2014–2019. These

More broadly, insofar as public opinion is an important factor in accounting for why welfare states persist, that opinion seems as conducive as ever to continued, gradual expansion of European welfare states. Indeed, the only notable shift in public opinion in recent years has been a modest decline in enthusiasm for *cuts* in government spending. Electorates may sometimes appear to "vote for austerity," as in the United Kingdom in 2010; but that is primarily an illusion, a misreading of pragmatic electoral responses to hard times as ideological mandates. In fact, public support for redistribution in Great Britain was probably higher at the time of the 2010 election than it had been when Tony Blair left office in 2007, and it continued to increase through the next several years of Tory government.[44]

The constancy of public support for the welfare state before, during, and after the Euro-crisis may seem puzzling to those who expect political attitudes and policy preferences to shift sharply in response to economic conditions. However, there is ample precedent in the scholarly literature for finding "surprisingly weak" effects of economic crises on policy preferences.[45] Europeans' response to the Euro-crisis seems to be another case in point. While economic adversity led disgruntled citizens to turn against incumbent governments, it made no dent in their appetite for government action.

Alas, just as Europe seemed to be putting the Euro-crisis in the rearview mirror, another emerging crisis seemed to threaten the stability of the welfare state. Years of increased immigration, capped by a dramatic influx of asylum-seekers in 2015, led some observers to fear that a rising tide of anti-immigrant sentiment would fuel fierce opposition to the extension of Europe's generous social benefits to newcomers. As we shall see in Chapter 4, however, this "immigration crisis" was just as exaggerated as the "crisis" of the welfare state.

---

gains were comparable in magnitude to those among middle-income and affluent people, albeit starting from a lower base.

44. On ideology and retrospection in electoral responses to the economic crisis, see Bartels (2014). The average level of support for redistribution in the British ESS data increased from 6.1 in 2006 to 6.3 in 2008 and 2010, then continued to increase gradually but steadily to 6.9 in 2018.

45. Kenworthy and Owens (2011); Bartels (2013a); Schlozman and Verba (1979).

4

Immigration

IMMIGRATION HAS EMERGED as a momentous policy issue and a major political flashpoint in many of the world's affluent democracies. "The Immigration Crisis Is Tearing Europe Apart," according to Bruce Stokes in *Foreign Policy*. In the *Washington Post*, Max Ehrenfreund warned that "Europe's Immigration Crisis Is Just Beginning," noting that "demographers project more and more immigrants for decades to come" and adding that recent events "raise troubling questions about the ability of political institutions in the developed world to cope with their arrival." In *American Prospect*, Georg Diez argued that "migration will remain central to the politics of the continent, raising fundamental questions about European societies, challenging the legitimacy of the system, and increasing the political strength of the far right." In the wake of the 2015 refugee crisis, he wrote, "The sense of democratic inevitability that Europeans had taken for granted ever since the fall of the Berlin Wall in 1989 has been shattered."[1]

In its broad outlines, the "immigration crisis" is hardly a surprise. Sagging birthrates in the decades after World War II increased the "old-age dependency ratio"—the number of people over the age of 65 for every 100 between the ages of 15 and 64—in the 28 countries of the EU from 20.6 in 1990 to 30.7 in 2018. In Italy it increased from 21.7 in 1990 to 35.4 in 2018. These figures imply a substantial burden on economic resources.[2] In *The Future of the Welfare State* (2004),

---

1. Bruce Stokes, "The Immigration Crisis Is Tearing Europe Apart," *Foreign Policy*, 22 July 2016, http://foreignpolicy.com/2016/07/22/the-immigration-crisis-is-tearing-europe-apart/. Max Ehrenfreund, "Europe's Immigration Crisis Is Just Beginning," *Washington Post*, 1 July 2016. Georg Diez, "The Migration Crisis and the Future of Europe," *American Prospect*, 5 April 2019.

2. By comparison, the old-age dependency ratio in 2018 was 24.5 in the United States and 13.7 in the world as a whole.

policy analyst Francis Castles observed that migration offers a promising source of labor and tax revenue for employers and governments "concerned about the social expenditure demands of an ageing population." However, he warned that "substantial increases in migration could well lead to political tensions and provide a platform for anti-immigrant populist movements with a real potential to destabilize the political systems of Western democracies."[3]

In 2015 and 2016, the political tensions stemming from rising immigration from Eastern Europe, Turkey, and North Africa were exacerbated by a flood of asylum-seekers, most fleeing from war-torn Syria, Afghanistan, and Iraq. The refugee crisis produced significant disruptions in Europe, ranging from "mass brawls at overcrowded refugee centers" to attempts by thousands of migrants to reach the United Kingdom through the Channel Tunnel. EU authorities struggled to address the situation by attempting to coordinate the resettling of refugees, offering member states substantial subsidies for each refugee they accepted, and eventually cutting a deal with Turkey to curb the flow of refugees.[4]

As Castles foresaw, immigration has generated significant political tensions and openings for "anti-immigrant populist movements." Yet the overall public reaction to Europe's "immigration crisis" has been remarkably muted. Analyzing European Social Survey data from the first decade of the 21st century, political scientists Rafaela Dancygier and Michael Donnelly concluded that "most countries have not seen dramatic shifts in beliefs about the impact of immigration or in preferences for immigration policies."[5] A decade later, the European public's support for immigration has still seen no significant erosion. Indeed, insofar as attitudes toward immigrants have changed at all, they have generally

3. Castles (2004: 144).

4. Dan Harris and Jackie Jesko, "Anti-Immigrant Protests Grow as Thousands of Refugees Flood Europe," ABC News, 21 December 2015. Margot Haddad and Holly Yan, "2,000 Migrants Try to Storm Channel Tunnel in France to Reach UK," CNN, 30 July 2015. James Kanter, "E.U. Offers New Immigration Plan, Hoping to Sway Reluctant Countries," New York Times, 13 July 2016. Kyilah Terry, "The EU-Turkey Deal, Five Years On: A Frayed and Controversial but Enduring Blueprint," Migration Policy Institute, 8 April 2021, https://www.migrationpolicy.org /article/eu-turkey-deal-five-years-on.

5. Dancygier and Donnelly (2014: 178). They found that workers in sectors of the economy employing relatively large numbers of immigrants from outside the European Union expressed more negative views about the economic impact of immigration during periods of heightened economic pessimism. But those effects were not large enough to significantly dampen overall support for immigration, even during the Euro-crisis.

become more favorable, not less. And younger cohorts of Europeans are consistently, substantially more favorable toward immigrants and immigration than older cohorts, suggesting that continued generational replacement will produce further gradual increases in support for immigration for years to come.

That is not to say that the painfully slow economic recovery from the global financial crisis, the dramatic challenge of the refugee crisis, and vigorous agitation by anti-immigrant populist movements have had no effect. The political salience of immigration has increased, especially among opponents of immigration. Anti-immigrant parties have gained electoral support, and mainstream parties in some countries have adjusted their own rhetoric and policies in hopes of blunting those gains. However, upon somewhat closer inspection, all those developments seem to have less to do with the sheer influx of immigrants in specific countries than with the ways in which political elites have responded to that influx.

The Immigration Crisis

Figure 4.1 tracks immigration rates in the countries of Europe from 2001 to 2019.[6] Because new immigrants are most likely to be socially and politically salient, I focus here on the *inflow* of foreigners in each year (relative to the total population) rather than on the total *stock* of foreigners at any given time.

The figure reveals a great deal of heterogeneity in the immigration experiences of different European countries. Some, like Ireland, Spain, and Slovenia, experienced a massive boom-and-bust cycle, with very high levels of immigration followed by dramatic plunges in the wake of the global financial crisis. Switzerland experienced a similar boom and bust, though on a much smaller scale, and with relatively high levels of immigration both before and after the economic crisis. Sweden provides an example of relatively steady growth in immigration, from 5 per thousand population in 2001–2004 to more than 14 per thousand in 2016. Germany experienced an even sharper run-up, from roughly 7 per thousand population in 2003–2009 to almost 25 per thousand in 2015. Finally, Hungary (among other countries) experienced low rates of immigration throughout this period, reaching just 5 per thousand population in 2018.

---

6. The annual inflows of immigrants and asylum-seekers in each country are recorded in the OECD's International Migration Database: Inflows of foreign population by nationality and Inflows of asylum-seekers by nationality, http://stats.oecd.org.

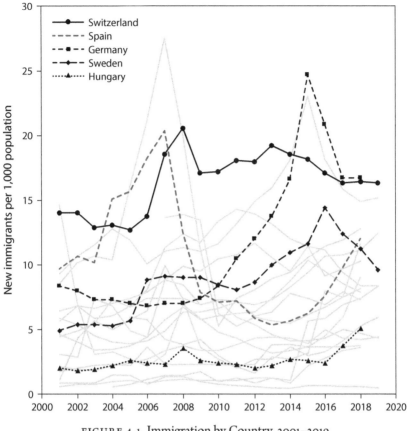

FIGURE 4.1. Immigration by Country, 2001–2019

It is worth bearing in mind that the OECD figures include all immigrants regardless of their circumstances or country of origin. The political and social ramifications of immigration are likely to hinge in significant part upon the ethnicity, culture, and economic circumstances of the new arrivals. Northern European pensioners buying retirement homes in sunny Mediterranean climes pose different challenges to their host countries than young guest workers from Eastern Europe or North Africa. Disparities in unemployment rates shed some light on the economic circumstances of different groups of immigrants: in 2006, before the onset of the Great Recession, the EU average unemployment rate was 6.5% for nationals, 10.2% for immigrants from elsewhere in the EU, and 18.5% for immigrants from outside the EU.[7]

7. Boswell and Geddes (2011: 23–25, 222).

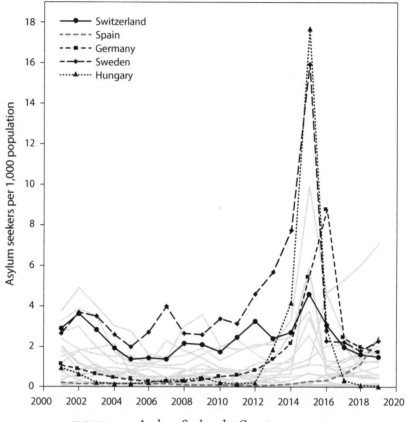

FIGURE 4.2. Asylum-Seekers by Country, 2001–2019

The subsequent influx of refugees, mostly from Syria, Afghanistan, and Iraq, presented even greater challenges. Figure 4.2 summarizes a separate OECD tabulation of the number of asylum-seekers in each European country from 2001 through 2019. Here there is much clearer evidence of a "crisis," with dramatic increases in asylum-seeking in most countries after 2012 and a huge, concerted peak in 2015. The population-weighted European average fluctuated between 0.5 and 1.0 per thousand population from 2001 to 2013, but it reached 2.7 per thousand in 2015 before receding somewhat.

While the timing of the ebb and flow of asylum-seeking was relatively consistent across countries, the magnitude of the asylum crisis varied greatly. In Sweden, which had relatively large numbers of asylum-seekers throughout this period, it peaked at 16 per thousand population—almost six times the European average. Switzerland, which likewise had relatively large numbers of asylum-seekers before and during the Euro-crisis, saw a much more modest increase to 4.6 per thousand in 2015. Hungary experienced the most sudden and massive increase in asylum-seekers anywhere in Europe, from just 0.2 per thousand in 2012 to almost 18 per thousand in 2015. In stark contrast, the crisis almost entirely bypassed Spain, Portugal, Poland, and Czechia, among other places, though some of these countries experienced modest increases (and Greece experienced a substantial increase) after 2016. Germany fell between these extremes, with the number of asylum-seekers increasing from 0.5 per thousand in 2010 to 8.8 per thousand in 2016.

The Impact of the Crisis on Public Attitudes

The European Social Survey has consistently included a battery of six items tapping public attitudes toward immigrants and immigration. The wording of these items appears in Table 4.1. Three of the items asked respondents how many people from specific ethnic groups and parts of the world should be allowed "to come and live here." The other three items invited respondents to say whether immigrants to their country are bad or good for the economy, culture, and the country as a whole.[8]

Table 4.1 shows the average level of support for immigrants and immigration in 2018–2019 as measured by each of these items. In every case, average support was moderately favorable, ranging from 5.0 to 6.4 on the zero-to-ten scales. However, differences in average support across the items reveal some important nuances in immigration opinion. For example, there was a good deal more support for allowing immigrants "of the same race or ethnic group" as the current national majority than for allowing "people of a different race or ethnic group" or "people from the poorer countries outside Europe." And there was more concern about the impact of immigrants on the receiving country's economy than on its cultural life. Nonetheless, the responses to the various items are highly correlated, so for the most part I focus here on overall support for immigration as measured by a simple average of responses to all six items.[9]

8. The response options for the first three items were "many," "some," "few," and "none"; responses for the latter three items were recorded on zero-to-ten scales. To facilitate comparison, I recoded each item to range from zero (for responses most opposed to immigration) to ten (for those most favorable to immigration).

9. Factor analyzing the six items produces one strong common factor with roughly equal factor loadings. My analyses employing the summary scale includes respondents (95.5%) who answered at least five of the six items.

TABLE 4.1. Dimensions of Immigration Opinion

	Average support (2018–2019)	Δ (2002–2007 to 2018–2019)
To what extent do you think [country] should allow people of the same race or ethnic group as most [country] people to come and live here?	6.51 (.16)	+.69 (.19)
How about people of a different race or ethnic group from most [country] people?	5.61 (.22)	+.59 (.24)
How about people from the poorer countries outside Europe?	5.47 (.20)	+.53 (.22)
Would you say it is generally bad or good for [country]'s economy that people come to live here from other countries?	5.51 (.11)	+.65 (.14)
Would you say that [country]'s cultural life is generally undermined or enriched by people coming to live here from other countries?	5.74 (.13)	+.19 (.13)
Is [country] made a worse or a better place to live by people coming to live here from other countries?	5.28 (.10)	+.57 (.11)
Support for immigration (index)	5.69 (.14)	+.53 (.16)

Note: Average levels and changes in support for immigration on zero-to-ten scale (with standard errors clustered by country-round in parentheses). Fixed effects for countries are included in the analyses but not shown. Country-rounds are weighted by population.

Figure 4.3 shows average levels of overall support for immigration from 2002 to 2019 in Europe as a whole and in each of the 15 countries represented in all nine ESS rounds. Sweden clearly stands out as having the most favorable attitudes toward immigration. The other most supportive countries are mostly wealthy northern European countries (Switzerland, Norway, Germany, and Denmark), while the least supportive countries are generally less affluent countries on the eastern and southern periphery of Europe—Greece, Hungary, Czechia, Portugal, and Estonia. However, Poland is a notable exception

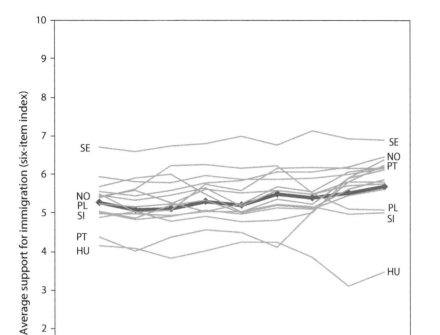

FIGURE 4.3. Public Support for Immigration, 2002–2019

to this pattern, with much more favorable attitudes toward immigration than in the rest of Eastern Europe.[10]

Remarkably, given the widespread perception of an "immigration crisis," the overall trend in public support for immigration was generally upward, with the average level of support across Europe gradually climbing from 5.1 on the zero-to-ten scale before the onset of the economic crisis to 5.7 in 2018–2019.

10. Some of the countries with the most and least supportive attitudes toward immigration (including Denmark, Czechia, Estonia, and Greece) do not appear in Figure 4.3 because they are not represented in every ESS round. However, all those countries are reflected in the overall upward trendline for Europe as a whole, which is derived from a regression analysis with indicator variables for survey rounds and fixed effects for countries to guard against distortions stemming from variation in the set of countries included in each survey round.

Great Britain, Germany, Norway, Belgium, Spain, France, the Netherlands, and Ireland all registered increases in support ranging from half a point to 1.2 points on the zero-to-ten scale between 2002–2007 and 2018–2019. In most cases, these increases in support for immigration were gradual, with few substantial fluctuations in opinion. The most notable shifts were in countries with relatively low overall levels of support in the pre-crisis period. Portugal saw a dramatic increase in support for immigration, from 4.2 in 2002–2007 to 6.2 in 2018–2019. On the other hand, support for immigration in Czechia and Hungary, similarly low before the economic crisis, declined even further thereafter—to 3.6 in Czechia and 3.1 (before rebounding to 3.5) in Hungary.

Of course, average levels of support may be misleading about what is happening at the extremes. But there is no evidence of a rise in extreme anti-immigrant sentiment, either. In 2002–2007, before the onset of the economic crisis, 14% of ESS respondents had index scores below 3.0 on the zero-to-ten scale of support for immigration. Over the next five survey rounds (and allowing for changes in the set of countries participating in each round), that percentage fluctuated between 13% and 15% before falling to 12% in 2018–2019. Even further in the tail of the distribution, the percentage of ESS respondents with index scores below 1.0 on the zero-to-ten scale fell slightly, from 2.9% in 2002–2007 to 2.7% in 2018–2019.

The overall increase in support for immigration evident in Figure 4.3 is not limited to just one or a few of the six separate items in the ESS. The rightmost column of Table 4.1 shows the change in average support for each item from before the Wall Street meltdown (2002–2007) to 2018–2019, after the refugee crisis. Every one of the six items shows at least a small increase in support for immigration, and for five of the six items the increase amounts to half a point or more on the zero-to-ten scale, reinforcing the conclusion that public attitudes toward immigration have become broadly and substantially more favorable in recent years.

But then, what of the "immigration crisis" that is supposedly "tearing Europe apart"? As it turns out, there is remarkably little evidence that the surges in immigration and asylum-seeking documented in Figures 4.1 and 4.2 have produced significant erosion in public attitudes toward immigrants. Statistical analyses across countries and years reveal no systematic relationship between inflows of immigrants or asylum-seekers and aggregate public support for immigration. Rather, immigration attitudes are mostly marked by stable national differences and very gradual change. These analyses, like the generally stable country-by-country trend lines in Figure 4.3, suggest that marked shifts of any

sort in public support for immigration have been surprisingly rare in contemporary Europe, and essentially unrelated to fluctuating immigration rates.
This impression of stability is bolstered by data from several panel studies
conducted in Europe and the US, which show that individuals' "immigration
attitudes are remarkably persistent and hard to change, even during economic
and political crises."[11]

This is not to suggest that there has been no public response to the immigration surge. "Rather than changing attitudes toward immigration," one team of
researchers suggested, "exogenous shocks such as a refugee crisis may simply
increase the salience and issue importance of immigration to individual voters." Others argued that "the effect of the 'crisis' was to activate latent concern
about immigration among those already predisposed to be concerned about
the issue." In the wake of the asylum crisis, some countries saw substantial
increases in the proportion of people citing immigration as an "important
issue"; and the aggregate salience of immigration was strongly correlated with
support for anti-immigration parties in public polls. One interpretation of this
correlation is that people agitated by immigration turned to anti-immigrant
parties; another is that the salience of immigration as an issue was stimulated,
in part, by the mobilizing efforts of prominent anti-immigrant parties.[12]

The salience of the "immigration crisis" was also bolstered by widespread press attention to instances of anti-immigrant backlash. In Brussels,
thousands of demonstrators mobilized by Flemish right-wing parties pro-
tested against a UN migration pact, clashing with police wielding tear gas
and water cannons. In Copenhagen, an anti-Muslim provocateur sparked a

---

11. On individual stability, see Kustov, Laaker, and Reller (2021: 1490). Country fixed effects
account for 58% of the variation in aggregate support for immigration in the 178 country-years
covered by the ESS data. Prior public support (measured at two-year intervals, to maximize the
leverage of the mostly biennial surveys) accounts for an additional 20% of the variation. By
comparison, fluctuations in immigration and asylum-seeking, measured with either a one-year
or two-year lag, seem to have vanishingly small estimated effects. An inflow of ten immigrants
per thousand population—in the top quartile of the European distribution—may have depressed public support for immigration by as much as one-tenth of a point on the zero-to-ten
scale, by comparison with no immigration at all; but even this estimate is statistically imprecise
and variable across specifications. The estimated response to asylum-seekers was even more
modest, with five asylum-seekers per thousand population—a flow observed in only 12 of 440
country-years covered by the OECD data—depressing support for immigration by just one-
twentieth of a point.

12. Kustov, Laaker, and Reller (2021: 1479); Dennison and Geddes (2019: 116, 114).

clash between immigrants and the police. However, the widespread perception of a political crisis seems to owe as much to the glare of the media
spotlight on these isolated events as to genuine public outrage. "Anti-Migrant
Protesters Rally in Several Major European Cities," one headline reported—
but a careful reader would have noted that in two of the three cities receiving
more than cursory mentions in the article, protesters numbered "about 200"
(with riot police outnumbering both protesters and counterprotesters) and
"fewer than 200."[13]

Real social frictions caused by immigration can be blown out of proportion in the journalistic quest for larger meaning. In 2019, a 3,000-word report
in the *New York Times* described fallout from the refugee crisis in Sweden,
asking portentously whether the Nordic model of social welfare can "survive
immigration." The article's evidence that it might not came from one small
town, Filipstad, in which immigrants—mostly recent refugees—made up
one-fifth of the population. Funds from the central government to subsidize
their integration into the community (about $2,500 per person) proved in-
adequate. The mayor, a member of the nationalist party Sweden Democrats,
wanted them to assimilate; she "would start by forcing them to learn Swedish" (though most had less than a high school education, and many were
illiterate). A bus driver who served on the municipal council, another Sweden Democrat, said, "The services that you pay taxes for have been reduced
drastically. . . . When there are so many people arriving who don't work, the
whole thing falls apart."[14]

But does it, really? The *Times* reporter concluded that Swedes' faith in the
social welfare system is "imperiled" by providing benefits to too many people
"who stand out as different from the majority." There is certainly good reason
to believe that ethnic diversity puts strains on generous welfare states. A detailed cross-national analysis of the politics of immigration in Europe suggested that "sustained intergroup conflict is more likely to emerge when the
state is in charge of distributing scarce economic goods" and emphasized "the

13. Frey (2020). Harris and Jesko, "Anti-Immigrant Protests Grow as Thousands of Refugees
Flood Europe." "Brussels Protest over UN Migration Pact Turns Violent," BBC News, 16 De-
cember 2018. Martin Selsoe Sorensen, "In Copenhagen, Reaction to an Anti-Muslim Event
Turns Violent," *New York Times*, 15 April 2019. VOA News, "Anti-Migrant Protesters Rally in
Several Major European Cities," *Voice of America*, 6 February 2016.

14. Peter S. Goodman, "The Nordic Model May Be the Best Cushion against Capitalism.
Can It Survive Immigration?," *New York Times*, 11 July 2019.

significance of immigration regimes in influencing resource shortages in the cities and towns where immigrants settle."[15]

Yet, one would hardly guess from the *New York Times* article that Swedes had among the most favorable attitudes in Europe toward immigrants, despite many years of significant immigration—including one of the biggest waves of asylum-seekers in Europe in 2015. In the wake of that influx, average support for immigration among ESS respondents fell only slightly, from 7.1 on the zero-to-ten scale in 2014 to 6.9 in 2016 and 2018. Support for immigration "from the poorer countries outside Europe" fell from 7.5 to 7.2. In both cases, support remained slightly higher in 2018 than it had been before the Great Recession— and a good deal higher than anywhere else in Europe. A separate 2017 Eurobarometer survey likewise found substantial support for immigration in Sweden. The average score on an index of positive attitudes regarding the impact of immigrants on society was considerably higher than in any of the 27 other countries surveyed. Overwhelming majorities of respondents agreed that immigrants "enrich Swedish cultural life" and "have an overall positive impact on the Swedish economy," while the proportion saying that "immigration from outside the EU is more of a problem" than "an opportunity" was the second lowest in Europe, about 20%.[16]

Survey data from the University of Gothenberg's SOM Institute shed additional light on Swedes' reactions to the refugee crisis. In annual surveys going back to 1990, one question asked whether "accepting fewer refugees" would be a good or bad proposal. In the immediate wake of the refugee crisis, the proportion of respondents supporting a reduction in the inflow of refugees jumped from 40% to 53%, and by 2019 it had risen to 58%. Still, that proportion was no higher than it had been in the early 1990s, when Sweden's foreign-born population was half its recent size. The proportion of respondents mentioning "integration" as one of the most important issues of the day spiked in 2015, and while it declined thereafter, it remained well above pre-crisis levels. However, responses to more specific questions shed light on the nature of those concerns. About as many respondents reported being very worried about "increased social

---

15. Dancygier (2010: 296, 293). For a broader analysis of the impact of racial and ethnic heterogeneity on redistribution, see Alesina and Glaeser (2004: chap. 6).

16. Lenka Drazanova, Thomas Liebig, Silvia Migali, Marco Scipioni, and Gilles Spielvogel, "What Are Europeans' Views on Migrant Integration?," OECD Working Paper No. 238, 21 February 2020, 24, 25, 54, https://ec.europa.eu/migrant-integration/library-document/oecd-working-paper-no-238-what-are-europeans-views-migrant-integration_en.

inequality" as about "worsened welfare," while even more reported being very worried about "increased racism/xenophobia."[17]

In the ESS data, public satisfaction with Swedish health services and education was higher in 2018 than before the economic crisis, while support for government redistribution of income remained unchanged. Asked more directly whether immigrants were a "burden on our welfare system," a clear majority of Swedes in the 2017 Eurobarometer survey disagreed. None of these trends are consistent with the notion of a welfare state "imperiled" by a public backlash against immigration. Apparently Filipstad's Sweden Democrats were less representative of national opinion than the municipal manager who said, "Immigration doesn't shake the Swedish welfare model in any way. . . . When we have succeeded with these people, this is a huge resource for Sweden."[18]

The Bases of Anti-Immigrant Sentiment

Overall, European public opinion seems to have been remarkably sanguine in the face of increased immigration. But while some people view immigrants as "a huge resource," others do see them as a serious threat to their national economy and culture. Why is that? The statistical analyses reported in Table 4.2 relate public support for immigration to a variety of individual characteristics, including demographic and social characteristics, economic circumstances, and worldviews.

These analyses suggest that the most important factors in accounting for variation in attitudes toward immigration, aside from stable national differences, were age and education. Other things being equal, 45-year-olds were about 0.6 points less favorable toward immigrants than 20-year-olds, while 70-year-olds were slightly less favorable than 45-year-olds. Older people also spent less time in school, on average, which reinforced this difference. People with 15 years of schooling (the 75th percentile of the European distribution) were more than half a point more favorable toward immigrants than otherwise similar people with 10 years of schooling (the 25th percentile). Further in the tails of the distribution, people with 18 years of schooling (the 90th percentile) were almost a full point more favorable than otherwise similar people with 8 years of schooling (the 10th percentile). It is impossible to tell from these data how much of these differences reflects the impact of time spent in schools

17. Martinsson and Andersson (2021: 46, 40, 22).

18. Goodman, "Nordic Model May Be the Best Cushion against Capitalism."

TABLE 4.2. Bases of Public Support for Immigration

	(1)	(2)	2002–2007	2008–2013	2014–2019
Income (percentile/100)	.60	.42	.35	.48	.45
	(.03)	(.03)	(.05)	(.07)	(.04)
Education (years)	.140	.116	.099	.118	.117
	(.006)	(.004)	(.008)	(.006)	(.006)
Age (years)	.024	.015	.001	.010	.026
	(.003)	(.002)	(.004)	(.003)	(.004)
ln(Age)	−1.45	−.80	−.31	−.61	−1.28
	(.13)	(.10)	(.18)	(.13)	(.16)
Female	−.05	.01	−.03	.00	.06
	(.02)	(.02)	(.03)	(.03)	(.03)
Religious	.22	.33	.44	.35	.21
	(.06)	(.05)	(.09)	(.09)	(.09)
Union member	.19	.20	.20	.16	.20
	(.02)	(.02)	(.03)	(.03)	(.03)
Foreign-born	.91	.86	.99	.82	.74
	(.06)	(.06)	(.05)	(.08)	(.12)
Conservative worldview	—	−.352	−.317	−.321	−.386
		(.012)	(.016)	(.022)	(.019)
Economic satisfaction	—	.162	.160	.162	.174
		(.010)	(.014)	(.013)	(.016)
Standard error of regression	1.95	1.89	1.83	1.87	1.90
Adjusted R^2	.17	.22	.20	.24	.25
N	337,352	337,352	109,331	117,695	110,326

Note: Ordinary least-squares regression parameter estimates (with standard errors clustered by country-round in parentheses). Fixed effects for countries are included in the analyses but not shown. Country-rounds are weighted by population.

and how much reflects other characteristics of the sorts of people who got more schooling. Whatever the reason, antipathy toward immigrants was concentrated among older and less educated people.[19]

19. Cavaille and Marshall (2019) exploited changes in compulsory schooling policies in various European countries to estimate substantial effects of additional secondary schooling on

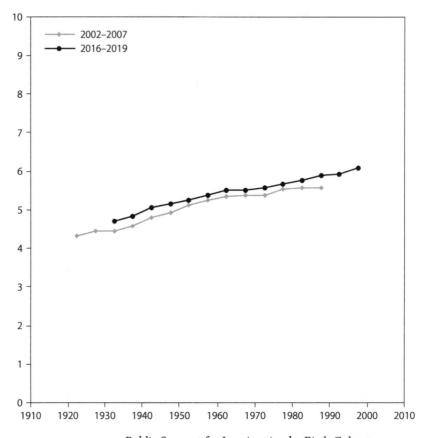

FIGURE 4.4. Public Support for Immigration by Birth Cohort

Figure 4.4 provides a different perspective on the age gradient in attitudes toward immigration, and on the gradual overall shift in those attitudes visible in Figure 4.3. The gray line in the figure shows the average level of support for immigration in the 2002–2007 surveys for successive half-decade birth cohorts, from people born in the early 1920s to those born in the late 1980s. The pattern is a steady, nearly linear increase in pro-immigrant sentiment among younger cohorts totaling nearly 1.3 points on the zero-to-ten scale. The black line in the figure shows the average level of support for immigration in the 2016–2019 surveys, beginning with people born in the early 1930s and ending with those born in the late 1990s. Here, too, there is a marked, nearly linear

immigration attitudes. However, their analysis did not assess the effect of tertiary education, where selection effects are likely to be larger.

increase in pro-immigrant sentiment, with the youngest cohorts almost 1.4 points more favorable toward immigrants than the oldest cohort.[20]

The gap between these two lines indicates that, within each cohort, attitudes toward immigration became slightly more positive in recent years, notwithstanding the overall increase in immigration and the 2015 asylum crisis. However, the main explanation for the overall increase in pro-immigration sentiment was generational replacement. On average, people born in the 1990s were a great deal more favorable toward immigration than those born in the 1920s. Moreover, given the consistency of the overall relationship between birth years and immigration attitudes in both periods, there is good reason to expect that this process of generational replacement will continue to produce increasing support for immigration in the years to come, as the oldest, least sympathetic cohorts in the current population are gradually replaced by younger people with more favorable attitudes toward immigrants and immigration.

The analysis reported in the second column of Table 4.2 includes two additional explanatory factors—conservative worldviews and satisfaction with economic conditions. These factors had substantial independent effects on immigration attitudes. People with typical conservative worldviews (5.8 on the zero-to-ten scale) were half a point less enthusiastic about immigration than those with typical liberal worldviews (4.4), other things being equal. Conversely, people at the 75th percentile of economic satisfaction (6.0) were half a point more enthusiastic than those at the 25th percentile (3.0), other things being equal. Together, these differences account for about half of the apparent effect of age, mostly because older people had distinctly more conservative worldviews, on average. They also account for about one-third of the apparent positive effect of income on immigration attitudes, mostly because people with higher incomes tended to be more satisfied with the state of the economy.

The third, fourth, and fifth columns of Table 4.2 present separate analyses of the bases of public support for immigration before, during, and after Europe's economic crisis. Whether due to the crisis itself or the rising tide of immigrants or shifts in the political climate, patterns of support for immigration seem to have shifted in two important respects. First, income became a

---

20. Each of the half-decade cohorts represented in Figure 4.4 includes at least 2,000 survey respondents. The average level of support for immigration in each cohort is derived from an analysis including fixed effects for countries.

somewhat stronger predictor of immigration attitudes during and after the economic crisis than they had been before, with opposition to immigration increasingly concentrated among people with low incomes. Second, support for immigration became increasingly strongly related to the basic attitudes toward change and tradition reflected in my measure of worldviews. In 2002–2007, the immigration attitudes associated with typical conservative and liberal worldviews differed by 0.7 points on the ten-point scale; by 2014–2019, that difference had increased to 0.9 points.

The impact of worldviews was especially strong for the questions about allowing immigrants from minority racial and ethnic groups and from "poorer countries outside Europe," and for the question about the impact of immigration on national cultural life. Presumably, these differences reflect the fact that people who value security, order, and tradition are especially likely to oppose immigration that might threaten ethnic, social, or cultural homogeneity.[21]

The strength of the relationship between worldviews and immigration attitudes also varied significantly from country to country. Perhaps surprisingly, most of the weakest relationships between worldviews and support for immigration appeared in places where conservative worldviews were most prevalent, including Greece, Slovakia, Poland, Lithuania, and Czechia. Conversely, conservative worldviews seem to have depressed support for immigration most strongly in places where those worldviews were relatively uncommon, such as Austria, Switzerland, and France. As a result, while worldviews are a strong predictor of which *individuals* support or oppose immigration, they contribute little to explaining which *countries* support or oppose immigration.

Political Leadership

Political contention over immigration is often portrayed as a clash between cosmopolitan political elites and nationalist masses. For example, political scientist Anthony Messina posed as a "vexing" puzzle "how to explain the perceived gap between public opinion (generally antagonistic and restrictionist) and public policy (generally supportive and expansionist) on questions related to immigration."[22] That framing seems to overstate the extent of public antipathy

---

21. The partially countervailing impact of union membership was also greatest for these same three items—suggesting, perhaps, that unions' efforts to promote solidarity blunted the impact of ethnic nationalism on immigration attitudes.

22. Messina (2007: 13).

to immigration; as we have seen, overall immigration sentiment in most of Europe has been and continues to be quite moderate. Nonetheless, Messina's puzzle raises the question of how public opinion, the beliefs and commitments of political elites, and public policy are related in the domain of immigration.

There is certainly good reason to think that political leaders have exercised considerable leeway in responding to Europe's "immigration crisis," and even played an important role in shaping public reactions to that crisis. Their impact is most evident for the political leaders personifying the liberal and conservative responses to the asylum crisis of 2015—German Chancellor Angela Merkel and Hungarian Prime Minister Victor Orbán.

As we saw in Chapter 2, Merkel's reluctance to support concerted action by the EU in response to Europe's sovereign debt crisis was a significant roadblock to economic recovery. However, her role in the asylum crisis was very different. As the crisis mounted, Merkel pressed her EU colleagues to construct a coordinated European response. She also took unilateral actions signaling that Germany would act regardless of whether the rest of Europe went along.

> Merkel was besieged with warnings from her EU colleagues, who were surprised and exasperated by her action. They warned that her unilateral decision would backfire and exacerbate the refugee crisis in ways that could inflict political and economic damage on all of Europe. At a tense summit meeting convened at EU headquarters in Brussels, Hungary's prime minister, Viktor Orban, sharply lectured her about what he viewed as a foolhardy policy that he would not follow under any circumstances.
>
> "I don't care what you may think, but I am going to protect my borders even if it becomes necessary to build fences all around my country," Orban said huffily. "I will not accept your moral imperialism. And believe me, Madame Chancellor, in the end you will be forced to do the same thing as I am doing on my borders." Merkel shoved her papers aside and stared icily across the vast conference table. . . .
>
> "I grew up staring at a wall in my face," Merkel told Orban, with emotion rising in her voice. "And I am determined not to see any more barriers being erected in Europe during the remainder of my lifetime." The other heads of government sat back in stunned silence as they absorbed her message and realized how Merkel's fierce determination to maintain open borders for the refugees had become for her a personal test of humanitarian morality.[23]

23. Drozdiak (2017: 3–4).

Merkel's "fierce determination to maintain open borders for the refugees" was widely viewed as a remarkable act of political courage. According to one prominent commentator, the chancellor weathered "a storm of opposition over her brave decision to welcome hundreds of thousands of refugees from Syria and elsewhere." Following a much-publicized eruption of violence by refugees in Cologne and other cities on New Year's Eve, her public approval rating fell to its lowest level since the depths of the Euro-crisis. Her support in the Bundestag seemed to be eroding as well, with forty members of her own party calling for a reversal of her open-door asylum policy. A May 2016 poll found that two-thirds of Germans opposed a fourth term for Merkel, while support for the anti-immigrant party Alternative for Germany had increased to 15%.[24]

Merkel persisted. In 2016, the flow of asylum-seekers, which was receding significantly elsewhere in Europe, continued its rapid increase. At the end of the year, Germany was rocked by terrorism when a Tunisian man who had been denied asylum drove a stolen truck into a Christmas market in Berlin, killing 12 people and injuring dozens more. The attack "bolstered critics of Ms. Merkel's open-door immigration policy of 2015 who said it added to the country's vulnerabilities."[25]

When Germans went to the polls nine months later, they dealt the chancellor a setback. Support for her Christian Democratic Union (and their Bavarian allies, the Christian Social Union) fell by more than 8 percentage points, from 41.5% to 32.9%, while Alternative for Germany vaulted from 4.7% to 12.6%, earning representation in the Bundestag for the first time. The result "was largely viewed as a rebuke of her open-door refugee policy." However, this was a far cry from the electoral debacle that had been predicted in some quarters. Merkel's main rival party, SPD, also lost substantial support, leaving a vacuum of power that only she could fill. After months of negotiation and a failed attempt to construct a governing coalition with two minor parties, the Free Democrats and Greens, she eventually persuaded the reluctant Social Demo-

24. E. J. Dionne Jr., "Germany's Political Crisis," *Washington Post*, 2 December 2015. Patrick Donahue, "Merkel's Popularity Drops to Four-Year Low after Cologne Attacks," Bloomberg News, 15 January 2016. Agence France-Presse, "Angela Merkel Faces Party Rebellion over Germany's Stance on Refugees," *Guardian*, 20 January 2016. Chase Winter, "Two-Thirds of Germans Oppose Fourth Term for Merkel: Poll," *Deutsche Welle*, 12 May 2016, http://www.dw.com/en /two-thirds-of-germans-oppose-fourth-term-for-merkel-poll/a-19250905.

25. Melissa Eddy, "A Year after the Berlin Market Attack, Germany Admits Mistakes," *New York Times*, 19 December 2017.

crats to join her in yet another grand coalition of Germany's two largest parties, ensuring her a fourth term as chancellor.[26]

It is impossible to know exactly how steep a political price Merkel paid for her courageous insistence on "her open-door refugee policy." Antipathy to immigration certainly played a major role in the alarming rise of Alternative for Germany.[27] However, evidence from public opinion polls suggests that most Germans' support for immigration was remarkably resilient throughout the refugee crisis. The ESS data provide no evidence of a decline in support for immigration in Germany in four successive surveys conducted between 2012 and 2019, even in the immediate wake of the Berlin terrorist attack.[28] The impression of resilience is confirmed by other opinion readings. For example, a large-scale survey conducted in the months before and after the 2017 election found that 63.8% of native Germans "viewed the immigration situation positively," a decline of just 1.6% from 2015. The survey's results cast doubt on the notion that opposition to immigration stemmed from direct experience of economic competition or social disruption; "reservations about immigration and integration" were concentrated in "areas where few migrants live, such as in the eastern German states."[29]

26. Steven Erlanger and Melissa Eddy, "Angela Merkel Makes History in German Vote, but So Does Far Right," *New York Times*, 24 September 2017. Melissa Eddy and Katrin Bennhold, "Angela Merkel Averts Crisis, Forming Government with S.P.D. Again," *New York Times*, 4 March 2018. A simple election forecast based on the relationship between GDP growth and incumbent vote shares in European elections during the Great Recession (Bartels 2014: 192) suggests that Merkel's CDU/CSU should have lost about 3.3 percentage points in 2017 even if immigration had no effect on the outcome. The standard error of the regression analysis from which that forecast is derived, 7.1 percentage points, underlines the fact that substantial shifts in vote shares based on other factors are not uncommon.

27. Mader and Schoen (2019); Arzheimer and Berning (2019).

28. The average level of support for immigration in Germany was 6.16 in 2012–2013, 6.18 in 2014–2015, 6.17 in 2016–2017, and 6.17 in 2018–2019. (The standard error associated with each of these estimates is .04.) While most of the 2016–2017 interviews were conducted before the Berlin terrorist attack, the 329 respondents interviewed in early 2017, after the attack, expressed nearly identical support for immigration. With or without adjustment for demographic differences between the two groups, the decline in support for immigration from 2016 to 2017 amounted to just .02 points (with a standard error of .12) on the ten-point scale. The results for immigration by "people of a different race or ethnic group" were identical, while support for immigration by "people from the poorer countries outside Europe" *increased* slightly (though the difference is too imprecisely estimated to be meaningful).

29. "Germans Upbeat about Immigration, Study Finds," *Deutsche Welle*, 17 September 2018, https://www.dw.com/en/germans-upbeat-about-immigration-study-finds/a-45519655. A

Germans' support for immigration also remained high by European standards. In the 2017 Eurobarometer survey, overall attitudes regarding the impact of immigrants were more positive than in most other European countries, despite a substantial majority agreeing that immigrants "worsen the crime problems in Germany." In the 2018–2019 ESS round, only Sweden, Norway, Ireland, Portugal, and Spain reported higher average levels of support for immigration than Germany, and most of these differences were negligible in magnitude. Similarly, in a spring 2018 survey from the Pew Research Center, 82% of Germans expressed support for "taking in refugees from countries where people are fleeing violence and war," while just 16% were opposed. Of ten countries surveyed, only Spain and the Netherlands had (slightly) higher levels of support, while Sweden's distribution of opinion resembled Germany's.[30]

If the resilience of Germans' support for immigration is a testament to Chancellor Merkel's determined political leadership, the antipathy of Hungarians seems due in significant part to President Orbán's equally determined opposition to what he called "an invasion of outsiders."[31] Of the 21 countries represented in the 2018–2019 ESS, Hungary had the lowest level of average support for immigration; only Czechia and Slovakia were close. Hungary was likewise an outlier in the 2018 Pew Survey, the only country surveyed in which most respondents opposed taking in refugees (54%, with only 32% in favor).

Hungarians' attitudes toward immigrants had always been relatively unfavorable by European standards. Yet, as recently as 2012, the average level of support for immigration in Hungarian ESS interviews was 4.2; by 2017, it had sunk to 3.1. The timing of the decline coincided not only with the refugee crisis, but also with a concerted anti-immigrant campaign by the Orbán regime. In

---

study of Canadians' reactions to the even deadlier 2015 Islamic State attack in Paris, which killed 130 civilians, found that attitudes and policy preferences were "resilient, even in the face of substantial, widely covered attacks." The authors expressed surprise that "the effects of a massive real-world terrorist attack are clearly ephemeral" (Breton and Eady 2022: 558–559).

30. Drazanova et al., "What Are Europeans' Views on Migrant Integration?," 25, 54. Phillip Connor, "A Majority of Europeans Favor Taking in Refugees, but Most Disapprove of EU's Handling of the Issue," Pew Research Center FactTank, 19 September 2018, https://www.pewresearch.org/fact-tank/2018/09/19/a-majority-of-europeans-favor-taking-in-refugees-but-most-disapprove-of-eus-handling-of-the-issue/. Survey respondents in France, the United Kingdom, Greece, Italy, and Poland all supported taking in refugees, though by smaller pluralities (ranging from 79%–20% down to 49%–36%).

31. Cantat and Rajaram (2019: 183).

May 2015, the government launched a "National Consultation Regarding Immigration and Terrorism." Eight million Hungarians received a 12-item questionnaire accompanied by a letter of introduction from the president. The letter offered a lurid reminder of the terrorist attack on the French satirical newspaper *Charlie Hebdo* earlier that year:

> In Paris they extinguished the lives of innocent people in merciless cold blood and with frightening brutality. That which took place appalled every one of us. At the same time, this humanly incomprehensible monstrosity also showed that Brussels and the European Union are not capable of handling the question of immigration in an adequate manner.

The questionnaire went on to frame immigration as a national crisis and to solicit support for a crackdown. For example, one question asked, "Did you know that subsistence immigrants cross the Hungarian border illegally and that the number of immigrants in Hungary has risen twentyfold over the recent period?" Another asked, "Would you support the Hungarian government if, contrary to the permissive policy of Brussels, it introduced stricter regulation of immigration?"[32]

Orbán's "national consultation" sparked international outrage. Human Rights Watch accused him of "stoking the flames of intolerance toward migrants and asylum seekers." The United Nations human rights office called the effort "extremely biased" and "absolutely shocking." The European Parliament officially denounced it as "highly misleading, biased and unbalanced," calling for "responsible governance aimed at securing democratic political solutions and respect for fundamental European values." Journalists portrayed it as part of "a pointed government anti-immigration campaign which critics say is aimed at shoring up faltering support for the ruling Fidesz party and divert[ing] attention from escalating poverty and corruption scandals."[33]

32. The Orange Files, "National Consultation on Immigration and Terrorism," 19 May 2015, https://theorangefiles.hu/2015/05/19/national-consultation-on-immigration-and-terrorism/.

33. Lydia Gall, "Dispatches: Hungary's Wrong Focus on Migration," Human Rights Watch, 29 April 2015, https://www.hrw.org/news/2015/04/29/dispatches-hungarys-wrong-focus-migration. Tom Miles, "U.N. Office Outraged by 'Biased' Hungarian Survey on Migration," Reuters, 22 May 2015. "European Parliament Resolution of 10 June 2015 on the Situation in Hungary," http://www.europarl.europa.eu/doceo/document/TA-8-2015-0227_EN.html. Daniel Nolan, "Hungary Government Condemned over Anti-Immigration Drive," *Guardian*, 2 July 2015.

Within Hungary, however, the government's campaign seems to have succeeded handsomely in stoking anti-immigrant sentiment. When the 2015 ESS interviews began in April, the average level of support for immigration on the ten-point scale was 4.1—only slightly below the 4.2 recorded two years earlier. But the average among people interviewed in May (the bulk of the respondents) was 3.9, and in June just 3.6. Consistent with the notion that this was a response to Orbán's agitation, the decline was concentrated among people who reported having voted for his Fidesz party or for the right-wing nationalist Jobbik party in the previous year's election. On the other hand, there is no evidence in the ESS data that the anti-immigration campaign was successful in "shoring up faltering support" for Fidesz. Indeed, the proportion of respondents who reported feeling closer to Fidesz than to any other party declined from 18% in May to 14% in June, while the proportion who reported feeling "very close" held steady at 4%.[34]

As the summer wore on, the flow of asylum-seekers mounted. The government built a 100-mile razor-wire fence along Hungary's border with Serbia in hopes of diverting refugees to Croatia or Romania—EU member states that would then be responsible for them while their claims were being processed. In September, the parliament passed a law allowing the government to declare a "state of migration emergency" under which refugees who entered Hungary could be detained while their asylum claims were considered. An emergency was duly declared the following April (despite the flow of asylum-seekers having dramatically decreased), and a few months later the "crisis" was used as a pretext to pass a package of "counterterrorism" laws granting additional powers to Orbán. In October 2016, a national referendum asked whether the European Union should "be able to mandate the obligatory resettlement of non-Hungarian citizens into Hungary even without the approval of the National Assembly?" Too few votes were cast to make the result binding; nonetheless, Orbán trumpeted the "no" vote as a victory for his government.[35]

---

34. After statistically controlling for demographic characteristics, worldviews, and satisfaction with the economy, the decline in support for immigration from May to June amounted to .48 points (with a standard error of .13). Including self-reported vote choices in the preceding election as an additional control variable increased the estimated decline to .56 points (with a standard error of .16).

35. Kim Lane Scheppele, "The Hungary Games: How Budapest Evades Its Migrants Obligation," Politico, 24 August 2015. Moreover, virtually every asylum claim could be denied, since a previous law prohibited asylum for refugees who had entered Hungary through a "safe country." As Scheppele pointed out, "Since Serbia and all EU states were declared safe under this law, the

Meanwhile, the number of asylum-seekers in Hungary fell from 177,000 in 2015 to just 671 in 2018. Yet, in a 2018 survey, "56 percent of Hungarians said that immigration was one of the two most pressing issues the EU faces." The Migration Policy Institute and the Brookings Institution reported that "Fidesz has been able to keep immigration on the top of the agenda via continuous campaigns based on hate-inciting rhetoric, conspiracy theories (e.g., about the existence of a so-called 'Soros-plan') and disinformation," resulting in "a string of anti-immigrant actions and policies," including a law criminalizing assistance to unauthorized immigrants. "Controlling borders and separating those 'who belong' from those who don't have become central aspects of the government's discourses and practices."[36]

The difference between Germans and Hungarians in views about immigration was of long standing, but it was significantly exacerbated by the asylum crisis, and by Merkel and Orbán's contrasting leadership in response to it. Figure 4.5 shows the trends in overall public support for immigration in these countries from 2002 to 2019. In Hungary, consistently unfavorable attitudes regarding immigration were becoming even more unfavorable by the spring of 2015. The refugee crisis and Orbán's vigorous anti-immigrant agitation accelerated that downward trend. By 2017, average support for immigration in Hungary had fallen substantially, from 3.9 to just 3.1 on the zero-to-ten scale, the lowest level recorded in any country in any round of the European Social Survey. By 2019, however, part of that effect seems to have worn off, as average support for immigration rebounded by four-tenths of a point. In Germany, on the other hand, attitudes toward immigration became significantly more positive over the course of Merkel's first several years as chancellor, then remained steady throughout the asylum crisis.

The wave of asylum-seekers in Hungary in 2015 was nearly matched in Sweden, where the overall share of the population that was foreign-born increased from 11.3% in 2001 to 19.5% in 2019, second only to Switzerland among major

---

only way a refugee traveling by land could enter Hungary without passing through a safe state is if the refugee entered through Ukraine. And that's not where these refugees are coming from." Kim Lane Scheppele, "Orban's Police State: Hungary's Crackdown on Refugees Is Shredding the Values of Democracy," Politico, 14 September 2015. Cantat and Rajaram (2019: 186).

36. Elżbieta M. Goździak, "Using Fear of the 'Other,' Orbán Reshapes Migration Policy in a Hungary Built on Cultural Diversity," Migration Policy Institute, 10 October 2019, https://www.migrationpolicy.org/article/orban-reshapes-migration-policy-hungary. Péter Krekó, Bulcsú Hunyadi, and Patrik Szicherle, "Anti-Muslim Populism in Hungary: From the Margins to the Mainstream," Brookings Institution, 24 July 2019. Cantat and Rajaram (2019: 188).

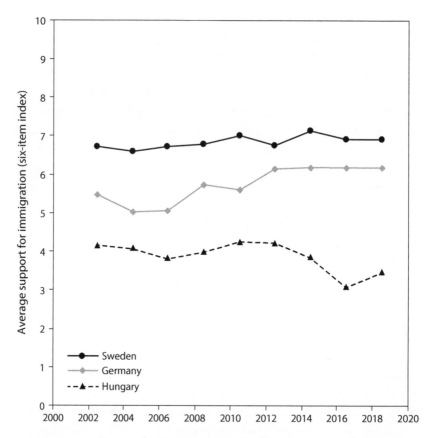

FIGURE 4.5. Support for Immigration in Sweden, Germany, and Hungary

European countries. However, the popular reaction to this influx of immigrants was very different in Sweden, as Figure 4.5 also shows. The already-high level of support for immigration declined only slightly, from 7.1 in late 2014 to 6.9 in 2016–2017 and 2018–2019—still the highest level in Europe by far. Clearly, immigration does not in itself constitute an "immigration crisis."

While the experience of Sweden demonstrates that even a massive influx of immigrants is not *sufficient* to produce a political crisis around the issue of immigration, the experience of Denmark demonstrates that a massive influx of immigrants is not *necessary* to produce a political crisis, either. The inflow of asylum-seekers in Denmark peaked at 3.7 per thousand, less than one-fourth what it was in Sweden, and in 2019, the total foreign-born population was 10%, about half what it was in Sweden. Yet, the center-left Social Democratic Party and other mainstream parties "have supported and pushed further tightening of an already restrictive immigration system, often adopting the same policies that far-right parties have recommended." New regulations were adopted to disperse immigrant "ghettos"; refugees receiving government assistance faced bolstered work requirements; and authorities revoked some immigrants' residence permits, insisting that it was safe for them to return to Syria.[37]

For the media, where there is policy smoke there must be public opinion fire. The *Economist* asked, "Why Have Danes Turned Against Immigration?" But the politics of immigration in Denmark cannot be explained by unusually hostile public opinion. Although no European Social Survey has been conducted in the country since 2015, the Eurobarometer survey data from 2017 portray rather favorable attitudes toward immigration in the wake of the asylum crisis. The proportion of respondents who viewed immigration more as a problem than an opportunity was about 25%, the fourth lowest among the 28 countries in the survey. While most Danes agreed that immigrants created a burden on the welfare system, their average attitude regarding the overall impact of immigrants on society was the ninth-most favorable in Europe.[38]

The issue of immigration did seem to be more *salient* in Denmark than elsewhere. In mid-2021 Eurobarometer data, 17% of Danish respondents considered immigration one of the two most important issues facing the country, well above the 10% EU average. But that is more plausibly an *effect* than a *cause* of controversial policy shifts; just six months earlier, the share mentioning immigration had been only 11%. A Danish immigration scholar argued that "party political dynamics and associated politicization pressures," rather than public opinion, were "decisive factors" in "pushing immigration and immigrant integration policy in a more restrictive direction." The most important source of "politicization pressures" was the sudden rise of the anti-immigrant Danish People's Party from 12.3% of the vote in 2011 to 21.1% in 2015, in the early stages of the asylum crisis. But if mainstream party leaders were panicked by

37. Regin Winther Poulsen, "How the Danish Left Adopted a Far-Right Immigration Policy," *Foreign Policy*, 12 July 2021, https://foreignpolicy.com/2021/07/12/denmark-refugees-frederiksen-danish-left-adopted-a-far-right-immigration-policy/. Ellen Barry and Martin Selsoe Sorensen, "In Denmark, Harsh New Laws for Immigrant 'Ghettos,'" *New York Times*, 1 July 2018. "Denmark Tells Some Migrants to Work for Benefits," BBC News, 8 September 2021. Elian Peltier and Jasmina Nielsen, "They 'Bombed My Dream': Denmark Strips Some Syrians of Residency Status," *New York Times*, 14 April 2021.

38. "Why Have Danes Turned Against Immigration?," *Economist*, 18 December 2021. Drazanova, et al., "What Are Europeans' Views on Migrant Integration?," 24, 25, 54.

the rise of the Danish People's Party, they seem not to have been equally responsive to its subsequent collapse, to just 8.7% of the vote in 2019. The politics of immigration in Denmark seem mostly to reflect a failure of nerve on the part of political elites.[39]

Summary

As immigration scholars James Dennison and Andrew Geddes put it, "The notion that Europeans are becoming more negative to immigration and that this is the cause of the increase in support for anti-immigration parties is not supported by major social science surveys." Perhaps it should not be surprising that the Euro-crisis seems to have had little impact on Europeans' immigration attitudes. Previous studies of public opinion toward immigrants have concluded that "considerations of national identity dominate those of economic advantage in evoking exclusionary reactions to immigrant minorities," and that "opinion about immigration is unrelated to the demographic and economic circumstances of countries." What is more surprising is that Europe's chronic "immigration crisis," and even the acute asylum crisis of 2015, have likewise had remarkably little impact on Europeans' attitudes regarding immigration. In most countries, public opinion has been moderate and stable, despite substantial fluctuations in immigration rates and, in some places, a massive influx of asylum-seekers.[40]

The few places where anti-immigrant sentiment increased in the wake of the Euro-crisis and the asylum crisis—Slovakia, Czechia, Italy, Hungary, Poland, and possibly Greece—are among the most conservative (and most religious) countries in Europe; yet conservative worldviews account for only a fraction of their distinctive anti-immigrant attitudes. The population of Italy is significantly older and less educated than elsewhere in Europe, but Slovakia and Czechia are younger than average and no less educated. Greece and Italy were wracked by the Euro-crisis, but the others have experienced relatively robust economic growth. Perhaps the closest thing to a common thread uniting these countries is the vigor of anti-immigrant rhetoric from prominent

---

39. Standard Eurobarometer 95, Spring 2021, https://europa.eu/eurobarometer/surveys/detail/2532, T16. Simonsen (2020: 609).

40. Dennison and Geddes (2019: 111); Sniderman, Hagendoorn, and Prior (2004: 35); Sides and Citrin (2007: 500).

nationalist political leaders in and out of government.[41] Prime Minister Orbán's anti-immigrant campaign in Hungary illustrates the potential for that sort of agitation to stoke anti-immigrant sentiment. However, the rebound in Hungarians' opinion of immigrants in 2019 may hint at the limits of a long-term diet of heavy-handed anti-immigrant propaganda.

For Europe as a whole, public sentiment toward immigrants and immigration has become significantly more favorable over the course of the 21st century, largely due to the gradual passing from the scene of older cohorts with less favorable views. The trend toward more welcoming attitudes extends even to the youngest cohorts in the most recent European Social Survey rounds, and even in countries where overall immigration sentiment has become more negative.[42] Thus, while the challenges of immigrant integration will no doubt continue to cause significant frictions, and to inspire some ugly politics, there is good reason to expect that public opposition to immigration will continue to ebb in the years to come.

41. Jan Culik, "Beyond Hungary: How the Czech Republic and Slovakia Are Responding to Refugees," *Conversation*, 7 September 2015. Davide Lerner, "Why Slovakia Won't Embrace Migration," Politico, 16 August 2016. David Frum, "The Toxic Politics of Migration in the Czech Republic," *Atlantic*, 23 October 2017. Patrick Wintour, "Migrants to Europe 'Need to Go Home,' Says Czech Prime Minister," *Guardian*, 25 October 2018.

42. In Poland, Slovakia, Italy, and Greece, younger cohorts are just as favorable toward immigrants, relative to older cohorts, as in the rest of Europe. In Czechia, the gradient is about one-third less steep, and in Hungary only about half as steep.

5

Democratic Frustrations

IN AN ATTENTION-GETTING 2016 essay in the *Journal of Democracy*, Roberto Stefan Foa and Yascha Mounk used data from the World Values Survey to argue that "democratic deconsolidation may already be underway" in some of the world's most venerable democracies.

> Citizens in a number of supposedly consolidated democracies in North America and Western Europe have not only grown more critical of their political leaders. Rather, they have also become more cynical about the value of democracy as a political system, less hopeful that anything they do might influence public policy, and more willing to express support for authoritarian alternatives. The crisis of democratic legitimacy extends across a much wider set of indicators than previously appreciated.[1]

Foa and Mounk's analyses of the World Values Survey data have come in for significant criticism.[2] But criticism of their analyses ignores a deeper question: why should we care what people say in surveys about democracy as a political system? The authors "suspect" that public opinion is "one of the most important factors in determining the likelihood of democratic breakdown," but they provide no evidence of such a connection. Indeed, one eminent scholar of comparative politics, Adam Przeworski, has argued that "there is not a shred of evidence" that survey responses "predict anything. . . . Whether democracy requires democrats, whether its continued existence depends on individual attitudes is a controversial issue. Even if it does, the causal relation

---

1. Foa and Mounk (2016: 15).
2. Erik Voeten, "Are People Really Turning Away from Democracy?," https://www.journalofdemocracy.org/wp-content/uploads/2018/12/Journal-of-Democracy-Web-Exchange-Voeten_0.pdf.

between answers to survey questions and the erosion of democracy must depend on the actions of organized political groups."[3]

One reason to be wary of survey data on democratic values is that, as Przeworski noted, "no one knows what people in different countries and at different times understand by 'democracy.'" People in China are just as likely as those in the US to say that it is "important . . . to live in a country that is governed democratically." Even more surprisingly, they are just as enthusiastic as Americans are about how democratically their own country is being governed. More specific questions about "essential characteristics of a democracy" produce disparate results even in generally similar liberal democracies. For example, in the 2010–2014 World Values Survey, 66% of Spaniards and 64% of Germans said it is "an essential characteristic of democracy" that "people receive state aid for unemployment," but only 43% of the respondents in the Netherlands and 27% in the US agreed. On the other hand, Germans were only slightly more likely (69%), and Spaniards were slightly *less* likely (61%), to say it is essential that "civil rights protect people's liberty against oppression" than to say that democracy requires unemployment insurance.[4]

Concerns about a "crisis of democratic legitimacy" are sometimes stoked by pointing to the success of right-wing populist parties in many parts of Europe. However, it is risky to conflate support for right-wing populism with bad attitudes about democracy as a political system. As political scientists Roger Eatwell and Matthew Goodwin have observed, supporters of populist parties

> are generally not anti-democrats who want to tear down our political institutions. . . . In several of these democracies national populist voters are actually *more* supportive of representative democracy than the general population. In Britain, Poland, Italy, the Netherlands, Hungary and Germany, eight or nearly nine in ten of these voters feel that representative

---

3. Foa and Mounk (2016: 15); Przeworski (2019: 101). An unusually careful and comprehensive recent study (Claassen 2020) provides some support for the hypothesized relationship between survey responses and expert ratings of democracy, though the interpolation of missing year-by-year survey data risks muddling the potentially reciprocal relationship between public opinion and democratic practice.

4. Przeworski (2019: 101); Achen and Bartels (2016: 4–6). Percentages from the 2010–2014 World Values Survey represent responses of 8 to 10 on a 10-point scale with endpoints labeled "not at all an essential characteristic of democracy" and "definitely is an essential characteristic of democracy." Data are available from the World Values Survey website, http://www .worldvaluessurvey.org/WVSOnline.jsp.

democracy is a good way of governing their countries. Differences between these voters, the general public, and those who oppose national populism are small or non-existent.[5]

In any case, it is far from clear how citizens' attitudes toward democracy are related to "the likelihood of democratic breakdown." Public satisfaction with "the way democracy works" was higher in Poland on the eve of the election that began its illiberal slide than it was in France, Spain, or Portugal—and higher than it had been in Poland a decade earlier. Even more paradoxically, as we shall see in Chapter 7, Poles' satisfaction with the working of their democracy *increased* substantially after their leaders cracked down on the judiciary and independent media. Hungary followed a similar pattern.

The significance of political distrust is not so obvious, either. As Jack Citrin observed when trust in the US government was plummeting half a century ago, "Allegiance to the political system . . . does not preclude criticism of specific policies, authorities or institutions." Moreover, "the burgeoning ranks of the politically cynical may include many who are verbalizing a casual and ritualistic negativism rather than an enduring sense of estrangement that influences their beliefs and actions." Recently, in "Political Trust and the 'Crisis of Democracy,'" political scientist Tom van der Meer surveyed a considerable body of scholarly work on determinants of political trust, including corruption, macroeconomic performance, political socialization, and political institutions. But when it came to the *consequences* of political trust, van der Meer concluded that "systematic empirical knowledge about these consequences is strikingly absent."[6]

I shall explore the impact of democratic disaffection and distrust on support for right-wing populist parties in Chapter 6, and their relevance for the erosion of democratic institutions in Hungary and Poland, specifically, in Chapter 7. In the meantime, however, this chapter takes concerns about a "crisis of democratic legitimacy" at face value, providing an assessment of trends in trust in government and satisfaction with democracy in contemporary Europe and shedding some light on the bases of those trends. As it turns out, here as elsewhere, the perception of "crisis" is greatly overblown. Overall levels of political trust and satisfaction with democracy have been quite stable in Europe over the course of the 21st century. Moreover, the increases in frustration

5. Eatwell and Goodwin (2018: 117–120).
6. Citrin (1974: 974–975); van der Meer (2017).

with democracy that *have* occurred seem mostly to reflect dissatisfaction with economic conditions rather than specifically political grievances.

Political Trust

Several items included in the European Social Survey since 2002 have tapped public trust in a variety of social and political institutions—the police, the legal system, the national parliament, the European Parliament, politicians, and political parties.[7] Figure 5.1 shows overall trends in trust in each of these institutions for Europe as a whole. The average ratings are all fairly stable, with few dramatic fluctuations from round to round and few sustained trends over almost two decades. There is a clear overall tendency for Europeans to express the greatest trust in the institutions most insulated from conventional politics (the police and the legal system), middling trust in national and European parliaments, and the lowest levels of trust in the most overtly political entities on the list, politicians and political parties. This pattern hardly suggests a strong public appetite for the give-and-take of democratic politics. In this respect, Europeans may not be so different from Americans. Perhaps, as John Hibbing and Elizabeth Theiss-Morse wrote in an insightful study of "stealth democracy" in the US, "People do not want responsiveness and accountability in government; they want responsiveness and accountability to be unnecessary."[8]

Nor is there much evidence here that "citizens have grown deeply mistrustful of their political institutions," as Foa and Mounk argued. At the worst point in the Euro-crisis, the average level of trust in national parliaments and politicians was about half a point lower than it had been a decade earlier; but as the crisis eased, that decline was almost entirely reversed. The most substantial remaining decline in trust, as of 2018–2019, was in the European Parliament.

7. "How much do you personally trust [institution]?" Survey respondents rated each entity on a zero-to-ten scale ranging from "no trust at all" to "complete trust." The trend lines reflect European average responses, with each country's responses weighted in proportion to the share of Europe's population they represent. In order to avoid confounding changes in trust with changes in the set of countries represented in each round of ESS, the analyses on which the figure is based include fixed effects for countries. The item on trust in political parties was not included in ESS round 1.

8. Hibbing and Theiss-Morse (2002: 4). In the same vein, but somewhat more narrowly, Mudde (2004: 557–558) suggested, "While the populists of the 'silent revolution' wanted more participation and less leadership, the populists of the 'silent counter-revolution' want more leadership and less participation."

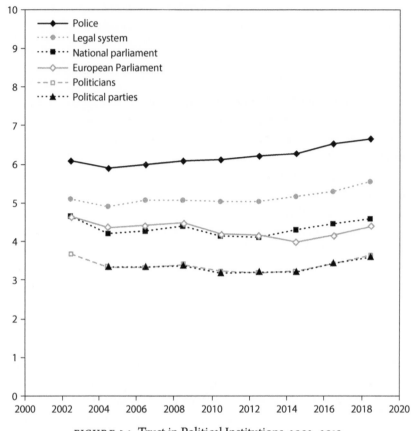

FIGURE 5.1. Trust in Political Institutions, 2002–2019

Even that decline amounted to just a quarter of a point on the zero-to-ten scale. Moreover, as we saw in Chapter 2, public support for further European integration was higher after the crisis than before, suggesting that the decline in trust in existing European institutions did not imply anything like a crisis of legitimacy for the EU, much less for democracy.

While average levels of trust in political institutions do not seem to have changed much in Europe as a whole, there is a good deal of variability in both levels and trends across countries. Figure 5.2 illustrates this variability using a composite measure of political trust combining the separate measures for national parliaments and politicians. The heavy line in the figure represents average political trust for all of Europe, while the lighter lines show the corresponding averages for each of the 15 countries represented in all nine ESS

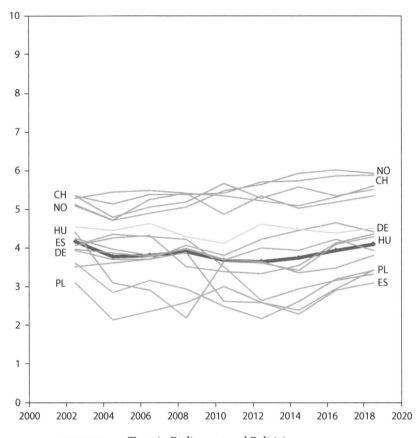

FIGURE 5.2. Trust in Parliament and Politicians, 2002–2019

rounds.[9] Five countries—Switzerland, Norway, the Netherlands, Sweden, and Finland—stand out as having had consistently high levels of political trust.[10] Elsewhere there was more temporal variability in political trust, especially in Southern and Eastern Europe, where average levels of trust were generally lower.

The first column of Table 5.1 summarizes changes in average levels of political trust in each country for which we have ESS data from before and after

9. These tabulations include the 96.7% of ESS respondents who answered both questions. It is clear from Figure 5.1 that these responses shifted in close parallel, insofar as they shifted at all. They are also highly correlated at the individual level (.72). By comparison, the correlations with (and among) the other measures of trust included in all eight ESS rounds range from .35 to .60.

10. Denmark does not appear in Figure 5.2 because it was not represented in ESS round 8. Danes were exceptionally trusting through 2009 (5.9), but somewhat less so thereafter (5.4).

TABLE 5.1. Changes in Political Attitudes in the Wake of the Euro-Crisis, by Country

	Trust in parliament and politicians	Satisfaction with national government	Satisfaction with the way democracy works
Austria	+.30 (.19)	+.44 (.35)	−.11 (.31)
Belgium	−.08 (.06)	−.33 (.14)	−.12 (.04)
Czechia	+.64 (.20)	+1.06 (.21)	+.46 (.14)
Denmark	−.59 (.07)	−.96 (.07)	−.31 (.07)
Estonia	+.27 (.16)	−.01 (.33)	+.38 (.17)
Finland	−.22 (.09)	−1.33 (.24)	−.46 (.17)
France	−.32 (.12)	−.89 (.18)	−.47 (.07)
Germany	+.73 (.09)	+1.31 (.25)	+.59 (.04)
Great Britain	+.03 (.14)	+.01 (.25)	+.19 (.11)
Hungary	+.47 (.47)	+.66 (.62)	+.34 (.37)
Ireland	−.20 (.21)	−.78 (.25)	−.21 (.31)
Italy	−1.03 (.37)	−.17 (.59)	−.49 (.46)
Netherlands	+.31 (.19)	+.70 (.35)	+.28 (.14)
Norway	+1.07 (.09)	+1.10 (.11)	+.91 (.12)
Poland	+.39 (.36)	+1.12 (.43)	+.78 (.31)
Portugal	−.12 (.28)	+1.01 (.61)	+.54 (.52)
Slovakia	+.14 (.41)	−.08 (.72)	+.04 (.36)
Slovenia	−.84 (.21)	−1.01 (.33)	−.82 (.36)
Spain	−1.09 (.12)	−1.63 (.27)	−1.42 (.17)
Sweden	+.41 (.15)	+.09 (.21)	+.41 (.15)
Switzerland	+.54 (.07)	+.98 (.19)	+.78 (.14)
Population-weighted average	+.02 (.11)	+.13 (.17)	+.01 (.11)

Note: Changes from 2002–2007 (ESS rounds 1–3) to 2014–2019 (ESS rounds 7–9) by country (with standard errors clustered by country-round in parentheses). Country-rounds are weighted by population.

the economic crisis. For Europe as a whole, as in Figure 5.2, there is no discernible change in the average level of trust. Some countries recorded substantial declines—a full point on the zero-to-ten scale in Spain and Italy, and only a bit less than that in Slovenia. On the other hand, there were significant increases in trust in other countries, including Norway, Germany, Czechia, and Switzerland.

Hungary and Poland also experienced substantial increases in trust.[11] In Hungary, political trust plummeted from 4.4 in 2002 to 2.2 in 2009, just before the election that returned Victor Orbán to power; but it rebounded to 4.3 over the course of the next decade. In Poland, political trust reached a new high of 3.4 in 2018–2019. In both countries, these increases in public trust in politicians and parliaments coincided with a significant erosion of democratic institutions and norms, underlining the folly of treating citizens' trust in their political leaders as an indicator of the health of a democratic system.

Persistent differences across political systems in levels of public trust in parliaments and politicians presumably reflect long-standing differences in political history and culture. However, when it comes to changes in levels of political trust within specific countries, a surprising amount of variation is accounted for by shifts in economic sentiment. For example, Figure 5.3 shows how changes in political trust in each country in the wake of Europe's economic crisis were related to changes in satisfaction with the national economy over the same period. The strength of the relationship suggests that much of what is captured by fluctuating levels of political trust in surveys has less to do with the political process, specifically, than with changes in the economic climate. In places like Germany, Czechia, and Switzerland, where people became more satisfied with economic conditions, they also became more trusting of parliament and politicians. In places like Spain, Denmark, and Slovenia, where economic disaffection grew, so did political distrust. Of course, distrust is not entirely a reflection of economic conditions; trust in political leaders plummeted even more than economic malaise seemed to warrant in Italy, and it improved even more than economic satisfaction seemed to warrant in Norway. Nonetheless, the strength of the relationship suggests that even significant shifts in political trust may be no more enduring—and no more reflective of the actual quality of political leadership—than fluctuations in national economic moods.[12]

---

11. The standard errors of estimated shifts in political trust in Table 5.1 allow for the possibility of correlated disturbances within each country-round in the ESS data. As a result, fluctuations in average trust within each six-year period produce considerable statistical uncertainty regarding overall trends. Both Hungary and Poland experienced fluctuations of almost a full point or more on the zero-to-ten scale in both the pre-crisis and post-crisis periods.

12. Armingeon and Guthmann's (2014) analysis of Eurobarometer survey data from 2007–2011 documented similarly strong relationships between changing assessments of national economic conditions and changing levels of trust in national parliaments and satisfaction with democracy.

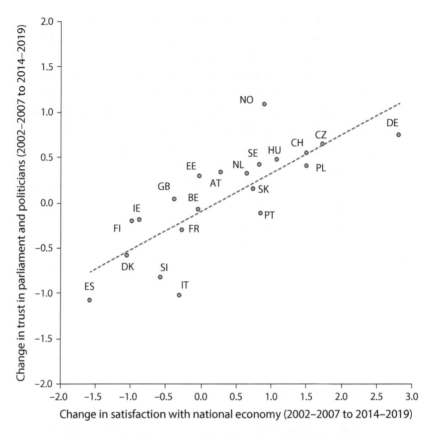

FIGURE 5.3. Satisfaction with the Economy and Political Trust

The strong association between economic satisfaction and political trust is evident not just across countries over time but also across individuals within countries and ESS rounds. Table 5.2 reports statistical analyses relating levels of trust in parliament and politicians to a variety of individual characteristics. The analysis presented in the first column shows that affluent and better-educated people were generally much more trusting than those with less income and education. There is also a significant curvilinear relationship with age: 45-year-olds were more than half a point less trusting than 20-year-olds, but also one-third of a point less trusting than 70-year-olds, other things being equal. The statistical results presented in the second column of Table 5.2 are from an analysis including worldviews and economic satisfaction as additional explanatory factors. They imply that almost half of the relationship between income and trust within countries and ESS rounds

TABLE 5.2. Bases of Public Trust in Parliament and Politicians

	(1)	(2)	2002–2007	2008–2013	2014–2019
Income (percentile/100)	.82	.46	.40	.47	.39
	(.04)	(.04)	(.08)	(.06)	(.05)
Education (years)	.054	.041	.043	.047	.051
	(.005)	(.003)	(.006)	(.005)	(.005)
Age (years)	.061	.037	.028	.042	.046
	(.003)	(.003)	(.004)	(.005)	(.004)
ln(Age)	−2.66	−1.64	−1.15	−1.82	−2.09
	(.15)	(.13)	(.20)	(.21)	(.20)
Female	−.11	−.02	−.05	.02	−.01
	(.01)	(.02)	(.02)	(.03)	(.03)
Religious	1.00	.70	.72	.62	.72
	(.05)	(.04)	(.06)	(.07)	(.08)
Union member	.09	.10	.11	.11	.07
	(.03)	(.02)	(.03)	(.04)	(.03)
Foreign-born	.51	.28	.18	.28	.37
	(.04)	(.03)	(.06)	(.04)	(.04)
Conservative worldview	—	.043	.054	.054	.024
		(.009)	(.011)	(.015)	(.012)
Economic satisfaction	—	.403	.385	.407	.451
		(.011)	(.011)	(.020)	(.011)
Standard error of regression	2.06	1.86	1.83	1.83	1.88
Adjusted R²	.14	.30	.27	.32	.33
N	343,363	343,363	111,718	119,807	111,838

Note: Ordinary least-squares regression parameter estimates (with standard errors clustered by country-round in parentheses). Fixed effects for countries are included in the analyses but not shown. Country-rounds are weighted by population.

is mediated by economic satisfaction. A shift of two standard deviations in economic satisfaction (about 4.8 points on the ten-point scale) is associated with a two-point shift in trust—roughly equivalent to the difference in average trust between the Netherlands and Greece or Finland and Italy. By comparison, the apparent impact of worldviews is quite modest, with conservatives slightly more trusting than liberals.

Separate analyses of attitudes before, during, and after the Euro-crisis (in the third, fourth, and fifth columns of Table 5.2) suggest that the bases of political trust remained largely unaltered by the crisis. The impact of economic satisfaction probably increased slightly, while the impact of worldviews became even smaller. There was also a significant increase in political trust among young people, relative to older cohorts, during the crisis. In the pre-crisis period, 20-year-olds were about 0.4 points more trusting than 45-year-olds with similar social characteristics; during the crisis, that gap shrunk to less than one-fourth of a point before widening again after 2013. Put differently, the temporary decline in political trust during the Euro-crisis affected middle-aged and older Europeans more than young people.

Satisfaction with Government and Democracy

Trust in specific political actors and institutions is just one aspect of citizens' relationships with their political systems. The European Social Survey has also consistently included two broader items tapping respondents' satisfaction with the way their country's government "is doing its job" and with "the way democracy works" in their country. Responses are recorded on scales ranging from zero ("extremely dissatisfied") to ten ("extremely satisfied").

In theory, it is obviously possible to be satisfied with "the way democracy works" in general but dissatisfied with the performance of the incumbent government—or vice versa. Empirically, however, there is a good deal of overlap in people's assessments of the democratic system and its current leaders. At the individual level, the correlation is .62; at the level of country-rounds, it is .88. The structure and correlates of these attitudes are also generally similar. I focus here primarily on satisfaction with democracy, for two reasons. First, this indicator looms larger in concerns about a "crisis of democratic legitimacy" in contemporary Europe. And second, views about how well "democracy works" ought to be (and are, somewhat) less amenable to short-term influences than are assessments of incumbent governments.

The relative stability of satisfaction with democracy is evident from a comparison of the shifts in average assessments of incumbent governments and democracy in each country in the wake of the Euro-crisis. These shifts are summarized in the second and third columns of Table 5.1. As in the case of trust in parliament and politicians, satisfaction with national governments and with the way democracy works were unchanged in Europe as a whole; but satisfaction did increase or decrease substantially in some countries. Gener-

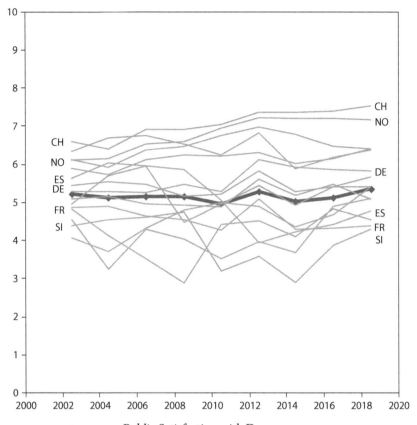

FIGURE 5.4. Public Satisfaction with Democracy, 2002–2019

ally, the two indicators moved in the same direction, but with significantly larger shifts in assessments of incumbent governments. For example, satisfaction with national government performance increased by a full point or more in Germany, Norway, Poland, Czechia, and Portugal, but in most of those countries the corresponding increase in satisfaction with democracy was closer to half a point. Conversely, substantial declines in satisfaction with national government in Spain, Finland, and Slovenia (and to a lesser extent in Denmark, France, and Ireland) were coupled in every case with somewhat smaller declines in satisfaction with democracy.

Figure 5.4 provides a more detailed look at changing levels of satisfaction with democracy from 2002 to 2019 for Europe as a whole and for each of the individual countries participating in all nine ESS rounds. For Europe as a whole, there is no real trend to speak of—average satisfaction fluctuated modestly during the economic crisis but rebounded after 2015, ending up in 2018–2019 just one-tenth of a point higher on the zero-to-ten scale than it had been in 2002–2003. By this measure, at least, the notion of an escalating crisis in public attitudes toward democracy is simply untenable.

The lowest levels of satisfaction with democracy were recorded in Slovenia, Portugal, and Hungary. In Switzerland and Norway, satisfaction was consistently high (never dipping below 6.0) and mostly increasing over time, perhaps due in part to implicit or explicit comparison with countries bound to the EU in the midst of the Euro-crisis. On the other hand, some EU countries also saw significant increases in satisfaction with democracy, especially if they were relatively unscathed by the crisis or made solid economic recoveries. Germany, Poland, and Portugal all saw sustained increases of more than half a point in satisfaction with democracy between the pre- and post-crisis periods.

As with shifts in political trust, shifting national attitudes toward democracy were strongly correlated with changes in the economic climate. Ten of the eleven ESS countries in which economic satisfaction was higher after the Euro-crisis than before—all except Austria—also saw increases in public satisfaction with democracy. Conversely, eight of the ten countries in which economic satisfaction declined also saw declining satisfaction with democracy. While the statistical relationship is far from perfect—Spain, for example, experienced a larger decline in satisfaction with democracy than economic disaffection alone would warrant, while Germany experienced a smaller increase than the improvement in economic satisfaction would suggest—attitudes toward democracy are clearly strongly colored by economic moods.

As in the case of political trust, the individual-level correlates of satisfaction with democracy, summarized in Table 5.3, are consistent with this aggregate-level pattern. Here, too, affluent and (to a lesser extent) better-educated people were much more satisfied with the workings of democracy, and much of the impact of income on attitudes toward democracy was mediated by satisfaction with the state of the economy. Indeed, the apparent impact of economic satisfaction was even larger for satisfaction with democracy than for trust in parliaments and politicians, and this relationship, too, was even stronger after the Euro-crisis than before.

It is worth noting that the European Social Survey measures satisfaction with the national economy, the national government, and the working of democracy in close succession using similar question formats. Thus, there is

TABLE 5.3. Bases of Public Satisfaction with Democracy

	(1)	(2)	2002–2007	2008–2013	2014–2019
Income (percentile/100)	1.01	.58	.47	.64	.47
	(.05)	(.04)	(.07)	(.07)	(.06)
Education (years)	.037	.023	.022	.033	.028
	(.006)	(.005)	(.006)	(.008)	(.007)
Age (years)	.060	.031	.023	.035	.038
	(.004)	(.003)	(.005)	(.005)	(.005)
ln(Age)	−2.64	−1.45	−1.04	−1.56	−1.77
	(.16)	(.13)	(.21)	(.20)	(.21)
Female	−.18	−.08	−.09	−.08	−.04
	(.02)	(.02)	(.03)	(.03)	(.03)
Religious	.91	.54	.51	.52	.53
	(.07)	(.06)	(.09)	(.09)	(.09)
Union member	−.00	.00	.01	.02	.00
	(.03)	(.02)	(.03)	(.04)	(.04)
Foreign-born	.77	.48	.44	.46	.53
	(.04)	(.03)	(.06)	(.05)	(.05)
Conservative worldview	—	.088	.065	.101	.080
		(.011)	(.014)	(.018)	(.021)
Economic satisfaction	—	.481	.481	.482	.553
		(.013)	(.014)	(.016)	(.015)
Standard error of regression	2.30	2.04	2.00	2.04	2.03
Adjusted R²	.12	.30	.29	.31	.35
N	342,512	342,512	111,395	119,590	111,527

Note: Ordinary least-squares regression parameter estimates (with standard errors clustered by country-round in parentheses). Fixed effects for countries are included in the analyses but not shown. Country-rounds are weighted by population.

some reason to worry that the strong correlations among these indicators may be exaggerated by the tendency of inattentive survey respondents to provide consistent responses to superficially similar questions. Fortunately, a different survey, the European Values Survey (EVS), provides independent evidence regarding Europeans' attitudes toward democracy. The 2008 EVS invited respondents to agree or disagree with the statement that "democracy may have problems but it's better than any other form of government."[13] Despite the differences in survey samples and question formats—and despite significant shifts in economic conditions in some countries between 2006–2007 and 2008—there is a strong positive correlation (.54) between satisfaction with the national economy in the 2006–2007 ESS and subsequent enthusiasm for democracy in each country in the 2008 EVS.[14] Clearly, citizens' perceptions of economic conditions have profound effects not only on the popularity of incumbent governments, but also on supposedly more fundamental evaluations of democracy as a political system.

Ideological Polarization

Another factor sometimes cited as an explanation for public frustration with democracy is ideological polarization. In the US, we are told, "polarization and partisan conflict lead to inaction," which in turn contributes to "low evaluations" of politicians and political institutions. More broadly, "severe polarization threatens both governability and social cohesion, and in turn, support for democracy in advanced and developing democracies alike."[15]

Figure 5.5 tracks the extent of ideological polarization in Europe as a whole and country-by-country from 2002 to 2019. "Polarization" here refers to the amount of ideological disagreement within each country, as measured by the standard deviation of ESS respondents' self-placements on the zero-to-ten left-right scale. For Europe as a whole, there was a noticeable uptick in ideological polarization in 2012–2013, as the Euro-crisis deepened; but the overall

13. More than 70% of respondents in Denmark and Norway strongly agreed that democracy is "better than any other form of government," but only 48% in Germany and Italy, 38% in the Netherlands, and 17% in Slovenia did so.

14. By comparison, the correlation between country average levels of economic satisfaction in the 2006–2007 ESS and satisfaction with democracy in the 2008–2009 ESS is .82. The higher correlation is presumably due in part to the similarity of item formats and in part to differences in sampling strategies and biases between the EVS and ESS projects. The correlation between country average levels of economic satisfaction and satisfaction with democracy in the 2006–2007 ESS is even higher, .90, reflecting the additional impact of having the same respondents answer both questions in the same survey.

15. Frank Newport, "The Impact of Increased Political Polarization," Gallup Polling Matters, 5 December 2019, https://news.gallup.com/opinion/polling-matters/268982/impact-increased-political-polarization.aspx. McCoy, Rahman, and Somer (2018: 17).

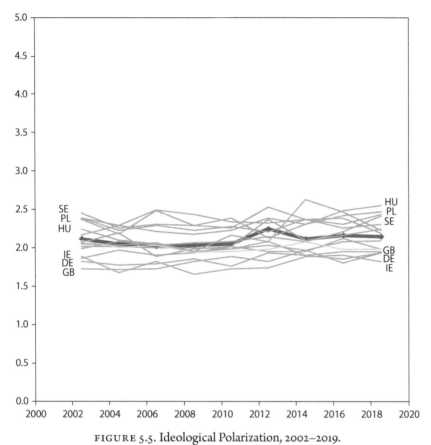

FIGURE 5.5. Ideological Polarization, 2002–2019.

Standard deviations of positions on zero-to-ten left-right scale.

change from 2002 to 2019 was just .03 on the zero-to-ten scale, an increase of less than 2%.

There is little apparent connection between changes in ideological polarization and the changes in satisfaction with democracy recorded in Table 5.1. While the countries with significant decreases in polarization in the aftermath of the Euro-crisis (from 2002–2007 to 2014–2019)—Czechia and the Netherlands—experienced increases in satisfaction with democracy, so did most of the countries with the largest *increases* in polarization over the same period—Portugal, Denmark, Norway, and Great Britain. Conversely, the countries with significant declines in satisfaction with democracy (Spain, Slovenia, Italy, France, and Finland) experienced relatively modest increases in ideological polarization (and in the case of France, a slight *decrease*).

Nor is there much indication in the survey data that high *levels* of ideological polarization erode support for democracy. The countries with notably high levels of polarization include Hungary, Poland, and Slovenia, but also France, Sweden, and, more recently, Norway; overall, there is little relationship between levels of polarization and support for democracy.[16] While polarization may have other ill effects, there is scant evidence here that ideological disagreement per se leads to bad attitudes about democracy.

Of course, ideological polarization is not the only sort of disagreement that might corrode support for democracy. However, tracking polarization in other attitudes tapped consistently in the European Social Survey—including satisfaction with incumbent governments, attitudes toward immigration and European integration, political trust, and satisfaction with democracy—produces trendlines resembling those in Figure 5.5, with overall increases in polarization ranging from just 2% to 5% over the 18 years covered by the ESS data. Neither the Euro-crisis nor the broader evolution of European politics in this period has produced a substantial increase in political disagreement among ordinary Europeans.[17]

Taking to the Streets

One of the most dramatic manifestations of popular political frustration is public protest activity. Governments are rattled, and occasionally toppled, when tens of thousands of people swarm into streets and plazas, in some cases risking violent repression, to demand change. In democratic systems, the risk of violent repression is generally modest and radical regime change is seldom on the agenda. Nonetheless, because protest activity requires significantly more time and commitment than responding to an opinion survey, it may

16. Comparing the extent of ideological polarization in each country in the 2002–2007 European Social Survey rounds and public support for democracy as "the best political system" in the 2008 European Values Survey likewise reveals little overall relationship, although there is a clear cluster of formerly communist countries (Slovenia, Poland, Hungary, Slovakia, and Czechia) combining relatively high levels of polarization and relatively low levels of support for democracy.

17. The linear trend in polarization from 2002 through 2019 amounts to 2.9% for the left-right scale, 1.7% for attitudes toward European integration, 3.7% for immigration opinion, 4.1% for satisfaction with the incumbent government, 4.2% for satisfaction with democracy, and 5.4% for political trust.

shed a different light on the relationship between citizens and their government. What does that light reveal about the state of democracy in contemporary Europe?

Popular impressions of protest activity are likely to be dominated by a few dramatic, well-publicized events. But unconventional political behavior is by no means rare in contemporary Europe. Indeed, according to political scientist Hanspeter Kriesi, "political protest has become an integral part of these countries' way of life: protest behavior is no longer used as a last resort only but is employed with greater frequency, by more diverse constituencies, to represent a wider range of claims than ever before."[18]

A team of scholars led by Kriesi assembled data on more than 30,000 protest events throughout Europe from 2000 to 2015. The events include demonstrations, strikes, blockades, and petitions addressing a wide variety of economic, political, and cultural grievances. Perhaps the most striking feature of these data is how little trace they reveal of the greatest economic crisis in recent European history. The overall number of protest events recorded in the 23 countries included in my analysis increased by just 19% between 2006 and 2008, then leveled off and, after 2012, declined steeply. As Kriesi put it, "From the perspective of Europe as a whole, the great economic crisis did not make much of a difference in terms of protest. If anything, counter-intuitively it contributed to the pacification of protest in the long-run." Protests focusing specifically on economic grievances became more common as the Euro-crisis wore on, but even at their peak in 2012, there were only about 45% more than there had been in 2006—or, for that matter, in 2000—and after 2012, they, too, declined precipitously.[19]

Of course, merely counting protest events may provide little sense of their social and political significance. Kriesi and his colleagues also collected

18. Kriesi (2014: 301).

19. Kriesi et al. (2020). The data are based on semiautomated coding of five million English-language news reports from ten international and local news agencies covering 30 countries, with manual coding of events and event properties in random samples of relevant documents. In addition to weighting the data to reflect the country-specific sampling scheme, I follow Kriesi et al. (chap. 2) in down-weighting reports from news agencies reporting on their own countries (though I do so at the level of individual news reports rather than country-years). The weighted data include 59,822 protest events in the 23 countries included in my analysis. "Economic" protests include those coded by Kriesi et al. as involving "economic claims addressed to public institutions" (30.8% of all protests) or "economic claims addressed to firms/employers" (12.4%).

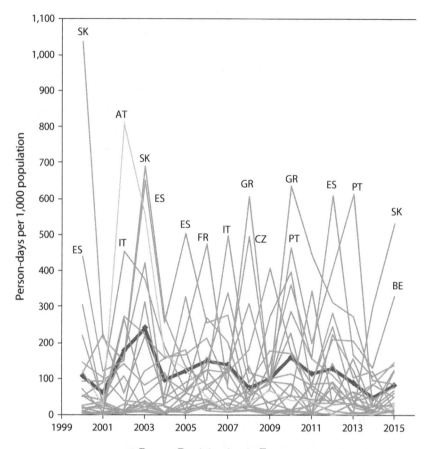

FIGURE 5.6. Protest Participation in Europe, 2000–2015

information on the estimated number of participants in each of these events. Figure 5.6 shows the total number of protest participants (per thousand population) in each year from 2000 through 2015 for Europe as a whole and for individual countries. While the figures on which these trend lines are based are subject to significant vagaries of sampling and measurement, they suggest even more clearly than the simple counts of protest events that there has been no general increase in protest activity in Europe over the course of the 21st century. The continent's busiest single year for protest participation, by this measure, was 2003, with more than 100 million cumulative participants—the equivalent of almost one-fourth of the total population of the 23 countries considered here—in 3,400 protest events. After the onset of the economic crisis, only two years (2010 and 2012) saw even half that many total protesters.[20]

The most substantial wave of protest activity in any single country was not in Greece in the throes of the Euro-crisis, but in Slovakia more than a decade earlier, in 2000. The estimated cumulative number of participants in 96 separate protest events that year exceeded the entire population of the country. Ironically, their primary grievance was an austerity program adopted to qualify Slovakia for membership in the European Union. Slovakia is also the country with the highest average number of protest participants over the entire period from 2000 to 2015, relative to the size of its population, with significant spikes in protest activity not only in 2000 but also in 2003, 2009, and 2015. Spain is just behind, followed by Greece, Portugal, France, and Italy. At the opposite extreme, the countries with the least protest activity over this 16-year period are mostly small Scandinavian and Baltic countries—Finland, Lithuania, Sweden, the Netherlands, Poland, Estonia, and Denmark. In those countries, the cumulative number of protest participants amounted to 30 or 40% of their populations, whereas in Slovakia and Spain the entire populations turned out more than four times over.

What, if anything, do these protests tell us about the state of democracy in contemporary Europe? Dissatisfaction with the democratic process seems to be a necessary but far from sufficient condition for high levels of protest activity. Among the half-dozen countries with the highest levels of satisfaction with democracy, only Switzerland experienced any significant protest activity. But among countries with lower levels of satisfaction there was enormous variation in the prevalence of protest activity, ranging from about 2% of the population per year in Poland, Estonia, and Lithuania to ten times that in Slovakia, Spain, and Greece. In the latter cases, protest was indeed "an integral part of these countries' way of life."

The ambiguous meaning of protest activity is illustrated by France's wave of *gilets jaunes* ("yellow vests") protests beginning in late 2018 (too late to be included in the Kriesi team's data collection). The protests went on for weeks, routinely drawing tens of thousands of citizens into the streets and sometimes devolving into riots; the Interior Ministry estimated that 2,500 protesters and 1,800 police officers were injured. "A crisis of representative democracy

20. The data presented in Figure 5.6 exclude Northern Ireland, which accounted for a considerable share of protest activity for reasons unrelated to the economic crisis.

is unfolding in France," one observer proclaimed. Others called the protests "a symptom of France's dysfunctional democracy" or even "a broader crisis for western democracy." But by the following summer the movement had "run out of steam," with just "a trickle" of protests and "flagging support" in the broader public.[21]

Did the ebbing of protests mean that the crisis of Western democracy was over? President Macron had taken steps to defuse the unrest, calling off an unpopular fuel tax increase and embarking on a "Great National Debate" touted by an enthusiastic political theorist as "the world's biggest 'deliberative democracy' exercise to date." However, the most plausible explanations for the demise of the *gilets jaunes* were an uptick in the economy and infighting among the movement's leaders and participants. According to one, "The old tensions between the right and the left that people had forgotten when they joined the movement have resurfaced." Disagreements about the legitimacy of engaging in violence further divided the protesters. A few months earlier, a sympathetic journalist attempting to account for the appeal of the movement had written, "People were thinking and talking about politics in ways they had never done before." But thinking and talking about politics turned out to be far from sufficient to alleviate the frustrations of democracy.[22]

Political Culture, Institutions, and Disaffection in Italy

Changes in economic mood seem to account for a surprising fraction of the observed changes in democratic attitudes across the countries of Europe in the first two decades of the 21st century. But of course, they do not account for *all* of those changes. One of the most notable outliers, especially when it comes to political trust, was Italy, where the substantial decline in trust in

21. Rachel Donadio, "France's Yellow Vests Are Rebels without a Cause," *Atlantic*, 18 March 2019. Emmanuel Martin, "Opinion: Yellow Vests Are a Symptom of France's Dysfunctional Democracy," *Geopolitical Intelligence Services*, 14 December 2018. Ishaan Tharoor, "France's Protests Mark a Broader Crisis for Western Democracy," *Washington Post*, 4 December 2018. Noemie Bisserbe, "French Protesters Hang Up Their Yellow Vests," *Wall Street Journal*, 16 June 2019.

22. Hélène Landemore, "Can Macron Quiet the 'Yellow Vests' Protests with His 'Great Debate'? Tune In Tomorrow," *Washington Post*, 24 April 2019. Bisserbe, "French Protesters Hang Up Their Yellow Vests." Harrison Stetler, "France's Yellow Vest Movement Comes of Age," *Nation*, 5 February 2019.

parliament and politicians between 2003 and 2013—1.7 points on the zero-to-ten scale—exceeded even the 1.5-point decline in satisfaction with the national economy over the same decade. Thus, Italy is a good place to look for noneconomic bases of bad attitudes toward democracy.

In *The Civic Culture*, a pioneering cross-national study published in 1963, political scientists Gabriel Almond and Sidney Verba characterized Italy as "an alienated political culture." They traced that fact to "centuries of fragmentation and external tyranny" followed by the deep divisions of the Fascist era. "The political culture of Italy does not support a stable and effective democratic system," they concluded; "but these characteristics are quite understandable in the light of her political history."[23]

Following in Almond and Verba's footsteps three decades later, Robert Putnam attributed stark regional differences in the apparent quality of Italian democracy in the 1970s and 1980s to distinct "civic traditions" with even deeper historical roots in the Norman conquest of medieval Sicily and the contrasting "communal republicanism" of northern and central Italy. "Stocks of social capital, such as trust, norms, and networks, tend to be self-reinforcing and cumulative," he wrote, producing impressive path dependence in the civic prerequisites for effective democracy. Conversely, "distrust, shirking, exploitation, isolation, disorder, and stagnation intensify one another in a suffocating miasma of vicious circles."[24]

Putnam's emphasis on "trust, norms, and networks" echoed Almond and Verba's emphasis on the importance of trust as "a generalized resource that keeps a democratic polity operating. Constitution makers have designed formal structures of politics that attempt to enforce trustworthy behavior, but without these attitudes of trust, such institutions may mean little." In particular, they argued, "trust in the political elite—the belief that they are not alien and extractive forces, but part of the same political community—makes citizens willing to turn power over to them."[25] In this respect, among others, they found Italy's civic culture lacking.

The generally low levels of trust in parliament and politicians and dissatisfaction with democracy recorded in Italian survey data over the course of the 21st century might be seen as a reflection of the long-term impact on democratic attitudes of these cultural and historical burdens. However, a more

23. Almond and Verba (1963: 402–403).
24. Putnam (1993: 121–137, 177).
25. Almond and Verba (1963: 490).

proximate influence on contemporary political attitudes would seem to lie in the political turmoil of the 1990s.

For almost half a century following the end of World War II, Italian politics had been dominated by three main parties—the Christian Democrats, the Socialists, and the Communists. The parties' leaders, platforms, and vote shares were remarkably stable. As late as 1987, they won a combined 75% of the popular vote. But in the early 1990s, this stable political system collapsed. In Milan, more than a thousand people, mostly politicians and businessmen, were convicted of bribery or corruption in the wake of the *mani pulite* ("clean hands") investigation. In 1993, longtime Socialist Party leader Bettino Craxi was indicted; he eventually fled the country and died in exile. The once-dominant Christian Democratic Party, too, was mired in scandal, and both parties disbanded in 1994.[26]

The sinking of the traditional party system in an undertow of corruption seems to have had a profound, corrosive impact on Italian politics. A team of Italian scholars found that people who entered the electorate in the immediate wake of the scandals of the early 1990s expressed significantly less trust in institutions, and greater support for populist parties, even 25 years later. "The idea that the people, as opposed to the corrupt elite, are the best part of society took root," a Milan-based journalist observed. "People became convinced that power was intrinsically corrupt, and politicians became convinced that the best way to defeat their opponents was to accuse them of corruption. By embracing this mindset, Italy committed a political suicide."[27]

One of the figures who emerged in the wake of the scandals was Silvio Berlusconi, a bombastic tycoon who led his new political party, Forza Italia, to victory in the 1994 general election. Berlusconi was "thrust to power on the basis that he would break with Italy's dysfunctional politics and that, as a self-made billionaire, he knew how to fix problems." He campaigned on a populist anticorruption platform despite himself being a target of the Milan prosecutors; he was eventually convicted of tax fraud and barred from legislative office for six years.[28]

26. Anna Momigliano, "It's Been 25 Years since Anyone in Italy Trusted the Government," *Foreign Policy*, 12 September 2018.

27. Aassve, Daniele, and Le Moglie (2019). Momigliano, "It's Been 25 Years Since Anyone in Italy Trusted the Government."

28. Roger Cohen, "The Trump-Berlusconi Syndrome," *New York Times*, 14 March 2016.

For two decades, Berlusconi was the most salient point of continuity (one hesitates to say "stability") in the Italian party system. He served nine years as prime minister in three separate stints between 1994 and 2011 and led a center-right coalition in six consecutive elections, alternating in and out of government. The center-left coalition opposing him bore a variety of labels (Alliance of Progressives, The Olive Tree, The Union) and included an evolving variety of parties descended from the old Communist and Socialist parties.

The first round of ESS interviews in Italy was conducted in 2003, halfway through the Berlusconi era and 18 months into his second stint as prime minister. The economy was not yet contracting. The Italian Senate had recently passed a "Berlusconi bill" reducing the legal vulnerability of his business empire to corruption charges, prompting 100,000 protesters to take to the streets of Rome. Meanwhile, the prime minister was busy writing music for "a recording of original ballads, in a syrupy Neapolitan vein." He had not yet likened a German member of the European Parliament to "a concentration camp guard," or encouraged Wall Street to invest in Italy because "we have beautiful secretaries," or argued that "Mussolini never killed anyone," or had his first face lift.[29]

The 2003 ESS data provide a clear indication of the limitations of macrohistorical explanations for bad attitudes toward democracy in Italy. Despite the "suffocating miasma" of feudalism in Sicily and the 20th-century legacy of fascism—and, for that matter, despite the scandal-ridden collapse of the party system just a decade earlier—Italian attitudes toward democracy in 2003 were remarkably unremarkable. Italians' average level of trust in parliament and politicians (4.2) exceeded those in Spain (4.1), France (4.0), Germany (3.9), and several other countries, while their average level of satisfaction with the working of democracy (5.0) was not far below the European average of 5.2. An observer who happened upon Italy in the early years of the 21st century could be forgiven for thinking that the country, under the unlikely leadership of Berlusconi, had escaped its long, vicious cycle of political distrust and disorder.

Berlusconi narrowly lost a bid for reelection in 2006, but he returned to office two years later in a snap election precipitated by the collapse of the

---

29. Associated Press, "'Berlusconi Bill' Passes," *New York Times*, 2 August 2002. Frank Bruni, "Protesters in Rome Accuse Berlusconi of Exploiting His Power," *New York Times*, 15 September 2002. Frank Bruni, "Berlusconi Tries New Field: Tin Pan Alley," *New York Times*, 7 December 2002. Day (2015: 89–90). John Hooper, "Mussolini Wasn't That Bad, Says Berlusconi," *Guardian*, 12 September 2003.

center-left government led by Romano Prodi. As Italy struggled through the economic crisis that followed, and under increasing pressure from European leaders and the IMF to implement reforms, Berlusconi's support in the Chamber of Deputies eroded, and in 2011 he, too, was forced to resign. To form a new government, President Giorgio Napolitano tapped Mario Monti, an economist who had never held elective office. According to one observer, Monti "owed his rise to Italy's highest office to Chancellor Merkel's insistence that he replace the elected, albeit obnoxious" Berlusconi—"not the best of credentials for endearing him to an Italian public skeptical of the German leader's right to decide who ruled their nation." Monti assembled a cabinet of technocrats, appointing himself finance minister, and pushed through a package of tax increases, pension reforms, and other austerity measures.[30]

In the wake of Berlusconi's ouster, the political situation was complicated by another round of major scandals that "astonished even cynical Italians." A study conducted on behalf of Transparency International cited "questionable institutional integrity, weak control mechanisms, biased news media and a social code that condones certain illegalities." The fall of the Berlusconi government and the continuing political turmoil "led to a trail of internal dissension, fragmentation and break up, resulting in new parties and parliamentary groupings." A year after leaving office, Berlusconi announced that he would run again in 2013; but the leader of the right-wing populist Lega Nord (Northern League) announced that his party would not support Berlusconi's bid to become prime minister if their coalition won the election. Monti, the incumbent prime minister, declared that he would not seek election, then reversed course and launched a new parliamentary group and electoral list, Civic Choice. Meanwhile, the Democratic Party organized a new center-left coalition, Common Good, and satirical comedian Beppe Grillo's antiestablishment Five Star Movement, founded in 2009, fielded its own slate of candidates.[31]

30. Varoufakis (2016: 173). Joshua Chaffin and Rachel Sanderson, "Big Two Show Rare Unanimity over Berlusconi," *Financial Times*, 23 October 2011. Patrick Wintour and Larry Elliott, "G20 Leaders Press Italy to Accept IMF Checks on Cuts Programme," *Guardian*, 4 November 2011. Rachel Donadio and Elisabetta Povoledo, "Facing Crisis, Technocrats Take Charge in Italy," *New York Times*, 16 November 2011.

31. Rachel Donadio and Elisabetta Povoledo, "Corruption Rattles Italians' Already Shaky Trust in Politicians," *New York Times*, 17 October 2012. Elisabtta Povoledo, "Lake of Safeguards Enables Italy Corruption, Report Says," *New York Times*, 30 March 2012. Bull and Pasquino (2018: 5); Tarchi (2018).

Perhaps unsurprisingly, this crowded menu of electoral options produced no decisive victor in the 2013 election. The center-left Common Good edged Berlusconi's center-right coalition, 29.6% to 29.2%, while the Five Star Movement was the largest single party with 25.6%. Monti's Civic Choice and its allies won just 10.9%. President Napolitano invited Pier Luigi Bersani, the secretary of the Democratic Party and leader of the Common Good coalition, to form a government; but Bersani ruled out a grand coalition with Berlusconi, the Five Star Movement refused to be a coalition partner, and talks dragged on. Eventually, a split within the Democratic Party forced Bersani to resign as party leader, and Napolitano turned to the party's deputy secretary, Enrico Letta, who had roots in the conservative Christian Democracy and close ties through an uncle to Berlusconi. Letta did what Bersani would not—form a grand coalition including Berlusconi's People of Freedom and Monti's Civic Choice.

The next round of ESS interviews in Italy began just weeks after the advent of the new government in late April 2013. Political trust and satisfaction with democracy were at a low point. Italians' trust in parliament and politicians was almost two points lower in 2013 than it had been a decade earlier, while their satisfaction with democracy was one point lower. No doubt, these declines were in large part a reflection of five years of economic crisis; but the election result and its aftermath may have played a role as well.

Within months, the grand coalition began to fray and its popular support ebbed.[32] Letta survived an attempt by Berlusconi to bring down the government, but he succumbed to internal pressure from Bersani's charismatic young successor as head of the Democratic Party, Matteo Renzi. Less than ten months after taking office, Letta resigned and Renzi took his place. The Vatican newspaper called it "the umpteenth government crisis with reasons and rituals that taste stale," concluding that "the moment has come in which the whole of Italy needs to turn a new leaf, after 20 years in which little of use has been achieved."[33]

---

32. This decline in popular support is evident in the ESS interviews, which were spread out over six months, from mid-June to mid-December. Allowing for demographic differences in the sample from month to month, the estimated linear decline in satisfaction with the government was .10 points per month on the zero-to-ten scale (with a standard error of .06), from 3.0 in June to 2.4 in December.

33. Rachel Donadio, "Split Vote Sends One Clear Message in Italy: No to Austerity," *New York Times*, 25 February 2013. Elisabetta Povoledo, "An Italian Leader and a Political Acrobat," *New York Times*, 28 April 2013. Jim Yardley, "Mutiny Halts Italian Gambit by Berlusconi," *New*

Renzi's governing strategy, according to his chief of staff, was "to give a violent shock to the Italian system." He pushed through a major labor reform loosening restrictions on employers; the move was hailed by Angela Merkel but sparked massive protests by trade unions. He also forced out the heads of Italy's biggest state-owned companies, replacing most of them with women. Some members of his own party joined the Five Star Movement in opposing Renzi's proposal to reform the electoral system to ensure parliamentary majorities, but the prime minister enlisted the support of Berlusconi, who retained his position as the leader of Forza Italia despite having been expelled from the Senate for tax evasion. A constitutional reform that would have reduced the size and power of the Senate was approved by both chambers of parliament but soundly defeated in a public referendum, prompting Renzi to resign as prime minister.[34]

The 2018 election further scrambled the Italian party system. A coalition including Berlusconi's Forza Italia and Lega, the right-wing populist party now claiming national rather than merely regional scope, won 37% of the vote; but Lega, with 17%, turned out to be the senior partner in the coalition. The Five Star Movement under new leader Luigi Di Maio won 33%. According to the *New York Times*, "The results were not just a disconcerting measure of Italy's mood but also a harbinger of the troubles that may yet lay ahead for Europe. Far-right and populist forces appeared to gain more than 50 percent of the vote in Italy, where the economy has lagged, migration has surged and many are seething at those in power."[35]

Di Maio and Lega standard-bearer Matteo Salvini spent several weeks jockeying for control of a new government, each proposing and rejecting a variety of potential coalitions. President Sergio Mattarella offered an "exploratory mandate" to the head of the Senate, then to the head of the Chamber of Deputies, but neither could negotiate an agreement. Finally, when it looked like another caretaker government and new elections might be in the offing, Di Maio and

---

York Times, 2 October 2013. Jim Yardley, "Italy's Prime Minister Announces Resignation amid Party Revolt," *New York Times*, 13 February 2014. Jim Yardley, "A Berlusconi Reminder as Italy Faces Another Unelected Premier," *New York Times*, 16 February 2014.

34. Jane Kramer, "The Demolition Man: Matteo Renzi Is on a Mission to Remake Italy," *New Yorker*, 29 June 2015. Jim Yardley, "In Italy, Matteo Renzi Aims to Upend the Old World Order," *New York Times*, 31 March 2015. Elisabetta Povoledo, "Matteo Renzi Resigns, Ending Italy's 63rd Government in 70 Years," *New York Times*, 7 December 2016.

35. Jason Horowitz, "In Italy Election, Anti-E.U. Views Pay Off for Far Right and Populists," *New York Times*, 4 March 2018.

Salvini agreed to a deal that both had been rejecting for more than two months, an unlikely coalition between their two parties. After two more weeks of negotiations, they agreed that each party's leader would be a deputy prime minister in the new government, with the role of prime minister filled by Giuseppe Conte, a law professor who had been slotted for a cabinet position by the Five Star Movement. However, when news leaked that the finance ministry would go to an economist who had helped draft a guide to abandoning the Euro, global markets tumbled; President Mattarella vetoed the plan and turned to a former director of the IMF, Carlo Cottarelli, to form a caretaker government. But Cottarelli had difficulty recruiting ministers for his new government, and in the meantime Di Maio and Salvini negotiated a reshuffling of cabinet portfolios that revived their coalition. Finally, at the beginning of June—nearly three months after the election—Conte was installed as prime minister. According to the *New York Times*, "The remarkable rise of the populists now leaves Italy's traditional political establishment, left and right, in tatters."[36]

For Italian voters, the tenuous connection between electoral politics and government was nothing new. Since 1992, the country had had 15 governments— one every 20 months—led by eleven different prime ministers. Remarkably, only two of the eleven, Berlusconi and Romano Prodi, reached the office by leading their parties to election victories—and only Berlusconi ever stood for reelection. Most of the rest were party functionaries tapped for leadership after cabinets fell or coalition negotiations soured, and they were gone in their turn by the time of the next election. A few, like Conte, had no prior experience in government, but suited the contentious factions (or the independent-minded president) of the moment.

In some ways, Italian politics since the early 1990s recalls the "kaleidoscopic" politics described by V. O. Key Jr. in parts of the American South in the Jim Crow era. With the Republican Party uncompetitive in the former Confederate states, the nature of politics was largely determined by the structure of the Democratic Party. In states with relatively stable, identifiable factions competing for control, Democratic primaries provided a rough substitute for two-party competition. However, in states without clear factions, "the battle for control of a state is fought between groups newly formed for the particular campaign." With little continuity in leadership, voters are "confronted with new faces, new choices, and must function in a sort of state of nature.... A governor serves his

36. Jason Horowitz, "Italy's Populist Parties Win Approval to Form Government," *New York Times*, 31 May 2018.

tenure—fixed either by constitution or custom—and the race begins anew." Key surmised that "the lack of continuing groups of 'ins' and 'outs' profoundly influences the nature of political leadership," frustrating political accountability and making governments "especially susceptible to individual pressures and especially disposed toward favoritism. . . . The erratic changes in personnel and policy associated with control by a succession of unrelated and irresponsible factional groups make the consideration, much less the execution, of long-term governmental programs difficult."[37]

The "kaleidoscopic" quality of Italian politics may help to account for three significant differences in political attitudes between Italy and the rest of Europe. First, Italians expressed significantly less interest in politics than other Europeans. In response to a question in the European Social Survey, 46% of Europeans claimed to be "very interested" or "quite interested" in politics, while 19% said they were "not at all interested." In Italy, the corresponding proportions were 33% "very interested" or "quite interested" and 30% "not at all interested." For many people, attempting to follow the complex vicissitudes of Italian politics may be about as interesting as watching a sporting event with arcane rules and no fixed team colors.

Second, Italians' low level of political interest seems to reinforce their low level of political trust. While political trust is positively correlated with political interest throughout Europe, that correlation is even stronger in Italy than elsewhere; the average level of trust among people who said they were "not at all interested" in politics was just 2.5 on the zero-to-ten scale, almost 1.5 points less than the corresponding average among people who said they were "very interested" or "quite interested." While familiarity generally seems to breed at least a modicum of trust in parliament and politicians, distrust is a default posture for many Italians uninterested in politics.[38]

Third, political attitudes in Italy seem to be even more sensitive to economic fluctuations than elsewhere in Europe. The strong cross-national correlations between shifts in economic satisfaction and changes in political trust (in Figure 5.3) and in satisfaction with democracy suggest that economic conditions significantly color assessments not only of incumbent performance,

---

37. Key (1949: 303–306).

38. The corresponding difference for all of Europe is 1.1 points. Satisfaction with democracy also varies with political interest, though not as strongly. While lack of interest in politics may be a consequence as well as a cause of political distrust, Italians' average level of interest was distinctly higher in 2013—a low point in political trust—than in other years.

but also of the trustworthiness of parliaments and politicians and the workings of democracy. That seems to be even more true in Italy than elsewhere. The overall relationship between satisfaction with the economy and political trust was about 20% stronger in Italy than elsewhere in Europe, while the relationship between satisfaction with the economy and satisfaction with democracy was almost 15% stronger.

The strength of the connection between economic and political attitudes helps to account for the fact that Italians' enthusiasm for democracy rebounded after 2013, despite the seeming chaos in the political system. After seven years of economic crisis, growth resumed in 2015 and accelerated modestly in 2016 and 2017. The cumulative gain in real GDP per capita between 2013 and 2019 amounted to nearly 5%—hardly a boom, but a significant improvement. Political trust increased somewhat from 2013 to 2017, and increased still further by 2018–2019, regaining most of the ground lost between 2003 and 2013. Satisfaction with democracy rebounded even more sharply, reaching the highest level on record in 2018–2019. For the moment, democratic disaffection had ebbed significantly. However, in a system with considerable instability in party alignments and highly uncertain connections between elections and government, it seems likely that the inevitable next round of economic frustrations will once again tend to discredit not only specific incumbent leaders but also the political system.

The electoral reform advocated by Matteo Renzi would have bolstered political accountability by guaranteeing a parliamentary majority for the largest party grouping. But with the failure of the 2016 constitutional referendum, and in the face of significant opposition from smaller parties, the final product was a mixed system with the share of first-past-the-post seats reduced to just 37%. As we have seen, in its first trial in 2018, the new system failed to produce a parliamentary majority, with the center-right coalition getting 42% of the seats in the Chamber of Deputies, the Five Star Movement getting 36%, and the center-left coalition getting 19%. The result was "weeks of confusing backroom negotiations that have made serious people despair and markets tremble," finally resulting in the unlikely pairing of the antiestablishment Five Star Movement and the right-wing populist Lega under a new prime minister with no experience in government.[39]

39. Giada Zampano, "Italian Parliament Approves Controversial Electoral Law," Politico, 28 October 2017. Rachel Donadio, "Italy's Populist Victory Is Both Tragedy and Farce," Atlantic, 23 May 2018.

Within a year, this unlikely coalition was unraveling. A prominent business journalist observed, "Whatever hopes there were that a radically unconventional government might jolt Italy out of its economic torpor have mostly given way to bitter resignation that, in this country, nothing ever seems to change." Conte, the inexperienced prime minister, warned the contending coalition partners "that if they didn't stop paralyzing the government, and derailing sensitive financial negotiations with the European Union, with their perpetual bickering, political point scoring and media propaganda, he would walk and bring the government down with him." The right-wing populist Salvini, who had been gaining in national popularity, called Conte's bluff, announcing "that he'd had enough of his coalition government" and wanted "full powers." But Salvini's hopes for an early election were dashed when the Five Star Movement instead reached a new coalition agreement with the mainstream center-left Democratic Party, allowing Conte to continue as prime minister.[40]

Just as the new coalition was getting off the ground, former prime minister Renzi announced that he would leave the Democratic Party, which he once led, to form a new party. He viewed himself as the left's main hope of forestalling Salvini's rise to power. Although Renzi remained in the governing coalition for more than a year, he grew increasingly frustrated with Conte's leadership and with the government's inept handling of the Covid-19 pandemic. In early 2021, he withdrew his support, triggering yet another government crisis. This time the president turned to Mario Draghi, the economist who had famously pledged that the European Central Bank would do "whatever it takes to preserve the euro," to assemble a broad national unity government. Pro-European elites were heartened by the prospect of competent leadership—and by the sidelining, for the moment, of right-wing populism. But in the context of contemporary Italian political history, this was yet another precarious improvisation with little basis in any expressed will of the people.[41]

40. Peter S. Goodman, "Italy's Biggest Economic Problem? It's Still Italy," *New York Times*, 9 August 2019. Jason Horowitz and Elisabetta Povoledo, "Italy's Prime Minister Delivers Ultimatum to Warring Coalition Partners," *New York Times*, 3 June 2019. Anna Momigliano, "Italy's Parliament Backs Rail Link as National League Party Comes Out on Top," *New York Times*, 7 August 2019. Jason Horowitz, "Italy's Most Powerful Populist Rules from the Beach," *New York Times*, 8 August 2019. Jason Horowitz, "New Government Takes Shape in Italy, Sidelining Salvini and the Hard Right," *New York Times*, 28 August 2019.

41. Jason Horowitz, "Dueling Matteos Battle for the Future of Italy," *New York Times*, 17 November 2019. Jason Horowitz, "Italy Looks to Mario Draghi to Solve Crisis, to Delight of

Attempting to explain the 2018 election and its aftermath to American readers, a seasoned observer of Italian politics wrote that "Italy's election results and this populist coalition have sprung from a crisis of both Italy's and Europe's making, one that combines homegrown political disarray, corruption, and miscalculations along with the complexities of Eurozone economics."[42] That seems like a fair assessment. But what was the role of ordinary citizens in the vicissitudes of Italian democracy? They were not in any obvious sense responsible for the rampant corruption of an entire generation of political leaders across the ideological spectrum, or for the fragmenting and destabilizing features of their country's electoral system, or for the structural vulnerability of the Italian economy to the reverberating shocks of the Great Recession. No doubt they were sometimes short-sighted, self-interested, and susceptible to demagoguery; but that hardly distinguishes them from people in other times and places. For the most part, they were victims rather than perpetrators of dysfunctional politics and government. Under the circumstances, their political distrust and frustration are hardly surprising.

Summary

In the midst of the Euro-crisis, many observers expressed concern that economic disaffection and the politics of austerity would corrode public confidence not only in incumbent leaders, but also in political institutions and democracy itself. Political scientist Armin Schäfer, for example, worried, "As the financial crisis puts strains on national budgets, the dissatisfaction with the way democracy works is likely to be exacerbated. . . . Even worse is that income inequality will increase as austerity measures begin to work—and citizens' faith in democratic politics is likely to erode further as a result."[43]

In one sense, these concerns proved to be well-founded. Public trust in politicians and parliaments, assessments of national governments, and satisfaction with the way democracy works all declined in times and places where economic disaffection increased. However, the political frustrations stemming from Europe's economic crisis were, for the most part, modest in magnitude and of short duration. As we have seen, Europeans overall were just as trusting

---

Pro-E.U. Politicians," *New York Times*, 2 February 2021. Jason Horowitz, "Renzi's Power Play Is a 'Masterpiece.' He'll Be the First to Tell You," *New York Times*, 9 February 2021.

42. Donadio, "Italy's Populist Victory Is Both Tragedy and Farce."

43. Schäfer (2013: 16).

of politicians and parliaments, just as satisfied with the performance of their national governments, and just as sanguine about the working of democracy after the Euro-crisis as they had been before.

Nor is there any evidence here of Foa and Mounk's "significant generational reversal" in attitudes toward the political system. Europeans born after World War II have generally expressed somewhat lower levels of satisfaction with democracy than earlier cohorts. However, the only perceptible decline in satisfaction with democracy (and other indicators show similar patterns) in the wake of the Euro-crisis was among people born in the late 1980s and early 1990s—the youngest cohort in the pre-crisis surveys. That decline merely brought their views into line with those of people born in the preceding five decades, which rebounded virtually completely after the Euro-crisis. If anything, there has been a very slight *increase* in satisfaction with democracy among younger cohorts compared to their elders. Meanwhile, people too young to have been included in the pre-crisis surveys expressed even more satisfaction with democracy in 2014–2019 than their predecessors had at the same age. Whether they, too, will fall into line with previous cohorts as they become older remains to be seen; but even if they do, the result will hardly represent a crisis for European democracy.[44]

44. Foa and Mounk (2016: 8).

6

The Populist "Wave"

THE WIDESPREAD PERCEPTION of a contemporary "crisis of democracy" has been stoked, in significant part, by a global "populist explosion." While populism as a political style is neither new nor intrinsically antidemocratic, such prominent figures as Hugo Chavez in Venezuela, Recep Tayyip Erdoğan in Turkey, Jair Bolsonaro in Brazil, Narendra Modi in India, and Donald Trump in the United States have combined populist rhetoric and antidemocratic behavior to varying degrees. In 2016, political scientist Pippa Norris declared that "authoritarian populism is rising across the West." In Europe, right-wing populist parties gained ground in such seemingly unlikely locales as Finland and Sweden, while new populist parties rose to prominence in Germany, Italy, and Spain. Five months after the UK's stunning Brexit vote and just weeks after Trump's election in the US, a *Newsweek* cover story warned that "Europe's Populist Revolt Is Spreading."[1]

The image of a populist "wave" was ubiquitous in discussions of these developments. According to the *Washington Post*'s Adam Taylor, "The global wave of populism . . . turned 2016 upside down." When some observers suggested that setbacks in France and elsewhere the following year provided "a rebuttal of claims that a right-wing populist wave is sweeping through Europe," Norris countered that "the wave of populist nationalism" is "hardly finished." *Time* added that "the wave to come . . . may well spill over into the rest of the world."[2]

---

1. Pippa Norris, "It's Not Just Trump. Authoritarian Populism Is Rising Across the West. Here's Why," *Washington Post*, 11 March 2016. Josh Lowe, Owen Matthews, and Matt McAllester, "Why Europe's Populist Revolt Is Spreading," *Newsweek*, 23 November 2016.

2. Adam Taylor, "The Global Wave of Populism That Turned 2016 Upside Down," *Washington Post*, 19 December 2016. Kim Sengupta, "French Election Result Shows Right-Wing Populist

Even when they disagreed about the precise amplitude and implications of Europe's populist wave, commentators were in impressive agreement regarding the forces propelling it. A key factor in most accounts was the Euro-crisis and the rigid economic policies of the European Union. The thesis of John Judis's popular book *The Populist Explosion* was conveyed by its subtitle: *How the Great Recession Transformed American and European Politics*. In a book entitled *What Is Populism?*, political theorist Jan-Werner Müller asked, "Why might Europe have become particularly vulnerable to populist actors since the mid-1970s or so, and in recent years in particular? Some answers might seem obvious: a retrenchment of the welfare state, immigration, and, above all in recent years, the Eurocrisis." In *Foreign Affairs*, Michael Bröning echoed this assessment. "Two core issues lie at the root of today's rising populism," he wrote, "the challenge of migration and the lingering euro crisis." In the *New York Times*, Steven Erlanger and Alison Smale added that "the issues that have animated the [far-right populist] movements—slow economies, a lack of jobs, immigration—are not going anywhere."[3]

My aim in this chapter is to assess the nature and significance of right-wing populism in contemporary Europe. First, I analyze the bases of support for right-wing populist parties, focusing particularly on factors that have loomed large in scholarly and journalistic interpretations of the populist "wave"— economic distress, antipathy to immigration and the EU, distrust of political elites, and so on. Then I track the prevalence of right-wing populist sentiment over time and across countries. Rather remarkably, given the common understanding of populism in contemporary Europe, the overall prevalence of right-wing populist sentiment turns out to be essentially constant since the turn of the century. In particular, the fallout from the Great Recession and the Euro-crisis did nothing at all to "fuel the flames" of right-wing populist sentiment.

But then, why have parties appealing to right-wing populist sentiment been flourishing in so many parts of Europe? One answer is that they haven't, mostly. The impression of a "populist wave" is largely a product of selective focus on particular cases in which right-wing populist parties surged at the

Wave Is Not Sweeping Europe," *Independent*, 24 April 2017. Pippa Norris, "So Is the Wave of Populist Nationalism Finished? Hardly," *Washington Post*, 17 May 2017. Ian Bremmer, "The Wave to Come," *Time*, 11 May 2017.

3. Judis (2016). Müller (2016: 96). Michael Bröning, "The Rise of Populism in Europe: Can the Center Hold?," *Foreign Affairs* Snapshot, 3 June 2016. Steven Erlanger and Alison Smale, "After French Vote, Mainstream Europe Breathes a Sigh of Relief," *New York Times*, 24 April 2017.

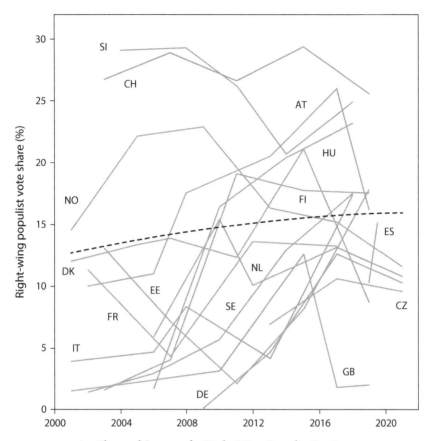

FIGURE 6.1. Electoral Support for Right-Wing Populist Parties, 2001–2021

polls, with much less attention to instances of stable or declining electoral support. A tabulation by Norris and Ronald Inglehart put the average vote share of European populist parties in the 2010s at 12.4%. That was a substantial increase over the 5% or 6% those parties attracted in the first decades after World War II, but a surprisingly modest increase over the 10% or 11% they received in the 1980s and 1990s.[4]

Figure 6.1 provides a qualitatively similar picture on a more compressed time scale. It charts electoral support for 16 right-wing populist parties from 2001 to 2021. While there are some spectacular jumps in vote shares during this period, the overall picture is certainly not of a continent-wide wave of popular support for these parties; the average vote share represented by the

4. Norris and Inglehart (2019: 9).

heavy dashed line increased by just a few percentage points over the 20-year period.[5]

In any case, and more importantly, insofar as electoral support for these parties has indeed grown, the change is due not to increased demand for right-wing populism among ordinary Europeans, but to the increased ability and willingness of populist entrepreneurs to mobilize and cater to that demand. The populist "wave," such as it is, reflects changes in the behavior of political elites, not shifting public opinion.

Bases of Support for Right-Wing Populist Parties

Scholars of populism have explored a variety of potential explanations for the willingness of some European voters to support right-wing populist parties. Some have devoted significant effort to explicating and measuring specific populist attitudes, though comparative research along these lines has been hampered by a paucity of consistent survey data across countries and, especially, over time.[6] Others have focused on broader social characteristics and attitudes, such as "people's feelings of attachment to their local communities" or "the backlash against the Silent Revolution." One early study found that immigration was a more consistent source of support for seven right-wing populist parties in Western Europe than economic disaffection or political elitism and corruption. A more recent study attributed support for populist parties to retrospective voting against mainstream parties, with the choice of specific challenger parties influenced by views about EU integration, austerity, and immigration.[7]

Here, I relate support for right-wing populist parties to seven potential explanatory factors introduced in previous chapters—conservative ideology, conservative worldviews, anti-EU sentiment, anti-immigrant sentiment, distrust of parliaments and politicians, dissatisfaction with "the way democracy works in [country]," and dissatisfaction with "the present state of the economy in [country]." Together, these factors capture the most prominent themes in

---

5. The dashed line in Figure 6.1 represents the quadratic trend in overall support for these 16 parties in 93 elections, from 12.6% in 2001 to 16.0% in 2021.

6. See, for example, Abts and Rummens (2007); Van Hauwaert and Van Kessel (2018); Wettstein et al. (2020); Moffitt (2020).

7. Fitzgerald (2018: 3); Norris and Inglehart (2019: 87–94); Ivarsflaten (2008); Hobolt and Tilley (2016).

discussions of the "populist wave" in contemporary Europe, as well as broader concerns about a potential "crisis of democracy."

My analysis of support for right-wing populist parties focuses on 16 examples—the Freedom Party of Austria (FPÖ), Freedom and Direct Democracy (SPD, and its predecessor, Dawn) in Czechia, the Danish People's Party (DPP), the Conservative People's Party in Estonia, True Finns in Finland, France's National Front (after 2018, National Rally), the Alternative for Germany (AfD), the United Kingdom Independence Party (UKIP) in Great Britain, Jobbik (Movement for a Better Hungary), Lega (formerly Lega Nord) in Italy, the Party for Freedom (PVV) in the Netherlands, the Progress Party in Norway, the Slovenian Democratic Party (SDS), Vox in Spain, Sweden Democrats (SD), and the Swiss People's Party (SPP).[8] These parties are by no means identical in their platforms and appeals, but all have been cited as examples of the populist "wave" in contemporary Europe, and all tap into varying combinations of right-wing ideology, nationalism, antipathy to immigration and the European Union, and political and economic disaffection.[9] *Left*-wing populism, as exemplified by Podemos in Spain, has made less headway in contemporary Europe and is beyond the scope of my analysis.

I measure support for these 16 right-wing populist parties using responses to two questions in the European Social Survey. The first simply asked respondents which party they voted for in their country's most recent parliamentary election.[10] Overall, about two-thirds of respondents in 2014–2019 reported having voted. Among those who did, average vote shares for the 16 right-wing populist parties considered here ranged from a bit less than 5% for Freedom

---

8. Some other plausibly comparable parties, including Vlaams Belang in Belgium, People's Party Our Slovakia, and the Slovenian National Party, are excluded because there are not enough adherents represented in the European Social Survey to permit reliable statistical analysis.

9. Based on experts' ratings of party platforms, Inglehart and Norris (2016: 44) classified five of these parties—Danish People's Party, True Finns, National Front, Jobbik, and Sweden Democrats—as "Populist-Left" rather than "Populist-Right." However, as we shall see, conservative ideology was at least mildly—and in most cases quite strongly—related to support for all of these parties. For an unusually careful discussion of issues in classifying "populist radical right parties," see Mudde (2007: 11–59).

10. In France, the question referred to the first of two election rounds. In Germany's mixed electoral system, the ESS included separate questions focusing on votes for candidates and parties; I count respondents as AfD supporters if they named the party in response to either question.

and Direct Democracy in Czechia and the Conservative People's Party in Estonia to a little more than 20% for the Slovenian Democratic Party and the Swiss People's Party.

Comparing these reported votes with actual election returns reveals a significant underreporting of support for right-wing populist parties in the ESS data. This is a common failing of political surveys, reflecting some combination of sampling problems and differential nonresponse, either because the sorts of people who support right-wing populist parties are less likely to participate in surveys or because they are reluctant to express their support for these parties. Nonetheless, the correlation between reported and actual support across parties and elections is quite strong (.90), suggesting that the surveys provide a reasonably good accounting of the bases of support for right-wing populist parties. In order to minimize the impact of misreporting, I weight the survey data from each country-round to accurately reflect the proportion of right-wing populist voters, other voters, and nonvoters in the most recent election.[11]

ESS also asked respondents whether they "feel closer" to any particular political party. This measure captures contemporaneous identification with right-wing populist parties among both voters and nonvoters. In most countries, only about half the survey respondents reported feeling close to any particular party; thus, the proportions of respondents categorized as identifying with right-wing populist parties are generally lower than the proportions who reported voting for those parties, ranging from less than 5% of the eligible electorate in Germany, Czechia, and Great Britain to 11% in Austria, 12% in Denmark, and 18% in Switzerland.

The statistical analyses reported in Table 6.1 document the bases of electoral support for each of the 16 right-wing populist parties considered here. In most of these cases, the most important factors in accounting for right-wing populist electoral support were conservative ideology and anti-immigrant sentiment. However, the relative importance of these two factors varied considerably from place to place. For example, Jobbik in Hungary, the Slovenian

---

11. Valentim (2021: Table A1) reported that surveys conducted as part of the Comparative Study of Electoral Systems underrepresented overall support for "radical right parties" by 20%. The corresponding underrepresentation in the ESS data of support for the 16 right-wing populist parties analyzed here is likewise 20% overall, and 23% in the 2014–2019 surveys. Figure A1 in the Appendix provides a more detailed comparison of surveys and election returns for these cases.

TABLE 6.1A. Bases of Electoral Support for Right-Wing Populist Parties, 2014–2019

	Austria (Freedom Party)	Czechia (Freedom and Direct Democracy)	Denmark (Danish People's Party)	Estonia (Conservative People's Party)
Conservative ideology	.284	.050	.092	.064
	(.022)	(.018)	(.024)	(.026)
Conservative worldview	−.093	−.024	−.007	.008
	(.031)	(.044)	(.051)	(.047)
Anti-EU sentiment	.083	.039	.087	.029
	(.015)	(.021)	(.028)	(.020)
Anti-immigrant sentiment	.216	.121	.248	.147
	(.021)	(.029)	(.042)	(.025)
Political distrust	.082	.069	.033	.067
	(.020)	(.025)	(.031)	(.027)
Dissatisfaction with democracy	.071	−.027	−.000	.055
	(.018)	(.024)	(.031)	(.027)
Economic dissatisfaction	−.013	.005	.034	−.034
	(.021)	(.027)	(.030)	(.027)
Pseudo-R²	.31	.06	.22	.13
N	4,168	3,616	1,179	3,297

Note: Probit regression parameter estimates (with standard errors in parentheses). Fixed effects for survey rounds are included in the analyses but not shown. Eligible voters post-stratified by vote choice.

TABLE 6.1B. Bases of Electoral Support for Right-Wing Populist Parties, 2014–2019

	Finland (True Finns)	France (National Front)	Germany (Alternative for Germany)	Great Britain (UK Independence Party)
Conservative ideology	.011	.116	.166	.083
	(.013)	(.018)	(.021)	(.024)
Conservative worldview	−.025	−.111	−.089	.009
	(.027)	(.037)	(.038)	(.038)
Anti-EU sentiment	.107	.064	.075	.067
	(.016)	(.016)	(.016)	(.021)
Anti-immigrant sentiment	.205	.241	.167	.155
	(.018)	(.022)	(.028)	(.021)
Political distrust	.081	.088	.119	.054
	(.019)	(.026)	(.026)	(.026)
Dissatisfaction with democracy	.028	.054	.101	.086
	(.018)	(.021)	(.021)	(.026)
Economic dissatisfaction	−.019	−.002	.002	−.025
	(.017)	(.025)	(.021)	(.025)
Pseudo-R²	.16	.28	.39	.24
N	3,901	3,101	5,507	4,278

Note: Probit regression parameter estimates (with standard errors in parentheses). Fixed effects for survey rounds are included in the analyses but not shown. Eligible voters post-stratified by vote choice.

TABLE 6.1C. Bases of Electoral Support for Right-Wing Populist Parties, 2014–2019

	Hungary (Jobbik)	Italy (Lega)	Netherlands (Party for Freedom)	Norway (Progress Party)
Conservative ideology	.229	.259	.100	.234
	(.018)	(.017)	(.021)	(.019)
Conservative worldview	−.180	.094	.000	−.006
	(.043)	(.041)	(.037)	(.032)
Anti-EU sentiment	.025	.020	.046	−.010
	(.016)	(.015)	(.018)	(.020)
Anti-immigrant sentiment	−.008	.097	.212	.256
	(.022)	(.021)	(.026)	(.028)
Political distrust	.097	.019	.171	.066
	(.022)	(.020)	(.029)	(.025)
Dissatisfaction with democracy	.183	−.018	.054	.040
	(.024)	(.021)	(.028)	(.024)
Economic dissatisfaction	.033	−.087	.023	−.001
	(.026)	(.021)	(.027)	(.023)
Pseudo-R^2	.23	.27	.25	.25
N	2,649	2,241	3,775	3,349

Note: Probit regression parameter estimates (with standard errors in parentheses). Fixed effects for survey rounds are included in the analyses but not shown. Eligible voters post-stratified by vote choice.

TABLE 6.1D. Bases of Electoral Support for Right-Wing Populist Parties, 2014–2019

	Slovenia (Slovenian Democratic Party)	Spain (Vox)	Sweden (Sweden Democrats)	Switzerland (Swiss People's Party)
Conservative ideology	.327	.301	.100	.322
	(.022)	(.035)	(.019)	(.023)
Conservative worldview	−.031	−.030	−.021	.134
	(.044)	(.069)	(.037)	(.040)
Anti-EU sentiment	−.030	.001	.075	.101
	(.017)	(.033)	(.021)	(.019)
Anti-immigrant sentiment	.057	.156	.326	.169
	(.023)	(.042)	(.028)	(.028)
Political distrust	.036	.107	.049	.051
	(.024)	(.036)	(.028)	(.028)
Dissatisfaction with democracy	.016	.034	.105	.063
	(.024)	(.033)	(.024)	(.026)
Economic dissatisfaction	.043	.042	.054	.025
	(.023)	(.037)	(.024)	(.025)
Pseudo-R^2	.26	.31	.35	.32
N	1,852	983	4,048	2,090

Note: Probit regression parameter estimates (with standard errors in parentheses). Fixed effects for survey rounds are included in the analyses but not shown. Eligible voters post-stratified by vote choice.

Democratic Party, Lega in Italy, Vox in Spain, and the Swiss People's Party all seem to have been fueled much more by conservative ideology than by anti-immigrant sentiment, while the reverse was true for True Finns, Sweden Democrats, the Danish People's Party, and the National Front in France.

Similar cross-national variation appears in the relative importance of the other explanatory factors in Table 6.1. Antipathy to further European integration was a substantial source of support for right-wing populist parties in Finland, Switzerland, Denmark, Austria, Sweden, and Germany, among other places, but not in Slovenia, Norway, Spain, or Italy. Distrust of political elites contributed significantly to electoral support for the Party for Freedom in the Netherlands, the Alternative for Germany, Vox in Spain, and Jobbik in Hungary, while dissatisfaction with democracy was strongly associated with voting for Jobbik, the Sweden Democrats, the Alternative for Germany, and UKIP; but neither of these factors had any apparent impact in Italy, Denmark, or Slovenia.

Table 6.2 reports parallel analyses of identification with right-wing populist parties based on the "feeling closer" measure in the ESS questionnaire.[12] The results generally resemble those for electoral support in Table 6.1, except that conservative ideology seems to have loomed even larger in identification than in voting behavior, while political distrust and democratic disaffection seem to have mattered somewhat less for identification than for voting behavior. Here, too, there is cross-national variation, with ideology standing out as the dominant factor in Hungary, Italy, Slovenia, and Spain and anti-immigrant sentiment primarily propelling identification with right-wing populist parties in Finland, Denmark, Sweden, and Great Britain.

While the specific bases of support for right-wing populist parties varied from country to country, and between electoral support and identification, the general family resemblance among these parties is clear from the statistical results. Figure 6.2 summarizes the impact of key explanatory factors across all 16 countries.[13] Overall, the most important factors in accounting for both

12. Respondents who reported feeling closer to a party were asked how close they felt to that party: not at all close, not close, quite close, or very close. I employ ordered probit models to analyze the full range of ordinal responses for each party.

13. I summarize the impact of each factor on support for right-wing populist parties by averaging the 16 country-specific estimated effects in Table 6.1 or 6.2. Incremental support is calculated for someone on the cusp of voting for or identifying with a right-wing populist party. The probit regression specification implies that the corresponding impact on people with typical (much lower) probabilities of supporting a right-wing populist party would be smaller.

TABLE 6.2A. Bases of Identification with Right-Wing Populist Parties, 2014–2019

	Austria (Freedom Party)	Czechia (Freedom and Direct Democracy)	Denmark (Danish People's Party)	Estonia (Conservative People's Party)
Conservative ideology	.321 (.021)	.097 (.025)	.114 (.025)	.106 (.024)
Conservative worldview	−.167 (.029)	.073 (.051)	−.042 (.046)	−.017 (.037)
Anti-EU sentiment	.082 (.016)	.143 (.024)	.106 (.026)	.013 (.017)
Anti-immigrant sentiment	.137 (.020)	.008 (.032)	.229 (.038)	.145 (.021)
Political distrust	.007 (.018)	.008 (.024)	.035 (.032)	.043 (.022)
Dissatisfaction with democracy	.016 (.017)	−.021 (.026)	−.028 (.029)	.023 (.021)
Economic dissatisfaction	−.005 (.019)	.032 (.029)	.028 (.030)	.026 (.020)
Pseudo-R²	.21	.09	.17	.10
N	5,782	6,289	1,337	4,994

Note: Probit regression parameter estimates (with standard errors in parentheses). Additional response thresholds and fixed effects for survey rounds are included in the analyses but not shown. Eligible voters post-stratified by vote choice.

TABLE 6.2B. Bases of Identification with Right-Wing Populist Parties, 2014–2019

	Finland (True Finns)	France (National Front)	Germany (Alternative for Germany)	Great Britain (UK Independence Party)
Conservative ideology	.056 (.017)	.224 (.019)	.190 (.024)	.117 (.025)
Conservative worldview	−.032 (.030)	−.034 (.035)	.015 (.046)	.009 (.035)
Anti-EU sentiment	.119 (.019)	.037 (.015)	.077 (.018)	.074 (.023)
Anti-immigrant sentiment	.183 (.022)	.192 (.019)	.118 (.025)	.189 (.022)
Political distrust	.017 (.021)	.040 (.020)	.095 (.023)	.082 (.028)
Dissatisfaction with democracy	.006 (.021)	.047 (.018)	.105 (.024)	.047 (.022)
Economic dissatisfaction	−.005 (.019)	.038 (.020)	−.025 (.019)	−.037 (.023)
Pseudo-R²	.12	.23	.26	.19
N	5,229	5,136	7,364	6,047

Note: Probit regression parameter estimates (with standard errors in parentheses). Additional response thresholds and fixed effects for survey rounds are included in the analyses but not shown. Eligible voters post-stratified by vote choice.

TABLE 6.2C. Bases of Identification with Right-Wing Populist Parties, 2014–2019

	Hungary (Jobbik)	Italy (Lega)	Netherlands (Party for Freedom)	Norway (Progress Party)
Conservative ideology	.289	.293	.123	.342
	(.027)	(.020)	(.022)	(.024)
Conservative worldview	−.083	.028	−.016	−.021
	(.040)	(.035)	(.036)	(.034)
Anti-EU sentiment	.021	.041	.053	.026
	(.016)	(.016)	(.017)	(.020)
Anti-immigrant sentiment	.005	.071	.177	.211
	(.023)	(.019)	(.024)	(.028)
Political distrust	−.011	−.004	.121	.016
	(.023)	(.017)	(.027)	(.027)
Dissatisfaction with democracy	.182	−.033	.024	.004
	(.024)	(.018)	(.026)	(.026)
Economic dissatisfaction	.039	−.036	.068	.018
	(.025)	(.019)	(.024)	(.023)
Pseudo-R²	.21	.21	.18	.24
N	4,504	4,358	4,864	3,924

Note: Probit regression parameter estimates (with standard errors in parentheses). Additional response thresholds and fixed effects for survey rounds are included in the analyses but not shown. Eligible voters post-stratified by vote choice.

TABLE 6.2D. Bases of Identification with Right-Wing Populist Parties, 2014–2019

	Slovenia (Slovenian Democratic Party)	Spain (Vox)	Sweden (Sweden Democrats)	Switzerland (Swiss People's Party)
Conservative ideology	.327	.338	.137	.381
	(.021)	(.039)	(.020)	(.022)
Conservative worldview	−.022	−.106	−.014	.103
	(.037)	(.068)	(.036)	(.032)
Anti-EU sentiment	−.025	.007	.057	.074
	(.015)	(.030)	(.022)	(.016)
Anti-immigrant sentiment	.082	.107	.245	.172
	(.021)	(.048)	(.031)	(.021)
Political distrust	−.035	.079	.034	.014
	(.022)	(.040)	(.030)	(.019)
Dissatisfaction with democracy	.015	.031	.114	.003
	(.021)	(.028)	(.024)	(.019)
Economic dissatisfaction	.017	.037	.070	−.004
	(.020)	(.034)	(.023)	(.019)
Pseudo-R²	.19	.25	.27	.24
N	3,521	1,490	4,558	3,450

Note: Probit regression parameter estimates (with standard errors in parentheses). Additional response thresholds and fixed effects for survey rounds are included in the analyses but not shown. Eligible voters post-stratified by vote choice.

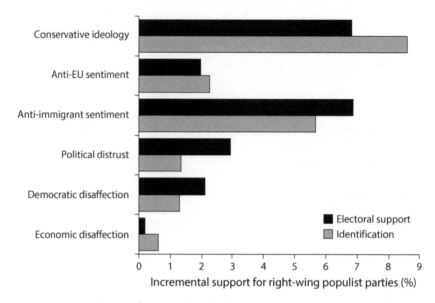

FIGURE 6.2. Bases of Support for Right-Wing Populist Parties, 2014–2019.

Estimated maximum incremental support attributable to a one-point shift on each zero-to-ten scale (based on statistical analyses reported in Tables 6.1 and 6.2).

electoral support and identification with right-wing populist parties were conservative ideology and anti-immigrant sentiment. Anti-EU sentiment, political distrust, and dissatisfaction with democracy also had substantial effects on support for right-wing populist parties in most countries, though their apparent effects were somewhat less consistent and generally less powerful.

By comparison, dissatisfaction with economic conditions was much less strongly and consistently related to support for right-wing populist parties. Indeed, Sweden and the Netherlands are the only places in which economic disaffection seems to have contributed substantially to identification with right-wing populist parties, while associations between economic disaffection and electoral support for these parties were even more modest. The relative unimportance of economic disaffection in fueling support for populist parties casts doubt on any simple interpretation of right-wing populism in contemporary Europe as a response to economic distress.[14]

14. I find even less support for Kavanagh, Menon, and Heinze's (2021) claim, based on the same ESS data, that poor health contributed to support for right-wing populist parties. Adding the ESS measure of subjective health to the analyses reported in Table 6.1 produces parameter

Another notable departure from conventional wisdom regarding the bases of support for right-wing populist parties is that people with conservative worldviews were generally slightly less likely than those with more liberal worldviews to express support for populist parties, other things being equal. In one sense, the qualifier "other things being equal" makes this surprising result more apparent than real. People with conservative worldviews were somewhat more likely to express anti-immigrant sentiment, right-wing ideological views, and anti-EU sentiment, all of which contributed to support for right-wing populist parties.[15] As a result, they were more likely, overall, to support right-wing populist parties. But even if we regard those sentiments as byproducts, in part, of more basic conservative worldviews, the strength of the resulting relationship was very modest. Among 2014–2019 ESS respondents eligible to vote in the most recent national election, the probability of reporting having voted for a right-wing populist party increased from 7.7% in the lowest (most liberal) quartile of worldviews to 11.6% in the highest (most conservative) quartile—a 4% gap. The corresponding gap in electoral support for right-wing populist parties between voters in the top and bottom quartiles of left-right ideology was 18%, and between those in the top and bottom quartiles of anti-immigration sentiment, 22%.

Why did "authoritarian" tendencies not loom larger in support for right-wing populist parties? Perhaps people who valued security and conformity were less likely than others with comparable grievances to turn to the unconventional remedy of an antiestablishment party.[16] It may be telling in this regard that the strongest positive association between conservative worldviews and support for a right-wing populist party, both in raw terms

---

estimates that are negligible in magnitude and quite plausibly zero in 11 of the 15 countries. The only two countries in which poor health was positively related to electoral support for right-wing populist parties are the Netherlands and Norway. In Hungary and Spain, poor health seems to have *depressed* support for right-wing populist parties by about the same amount.

15. In the post-stratified sample of eligible voters, conservative worldviews were only moderately correlated with anti-immigration sentiment (.29), and even less correlated with conservative ideology (.15), support for European integration (.11), and political trust (.04).

16. In a detailed analysis of the impact of "authoritarianism" on voting behavior in Western Europe, Tillman (2021: 121) suggested that identification with "traditional sources of authority" might make voters with authoritarian values less likely to support "'outsiders'" with "little or no history of participation in governance and lacking a historical core of supporters." He added that authoritarians' "higher needs for order and aversion to change" might likewise make them less likely to abandon previous partisan attachments.

and after taking other explanatory factors into account, was for the Swiss People's Party—the most established of these parties and the most experienced in government.[17]

One other specific grievance that looms large in discussions of populism is a perception of elite unresponsiveness to the views of ordinary citizens. Political scientist Wendy Rahn and colleagues argued that flare-ups of support for populist candidates in the United States (including Pat Buchanan, Ross Perot, and Donald Trump) have been stimulated in part by "representation gaps" between conventional party elites and citizens, resulting in public perceptions that "existing political parties are not responding to the desires of large sections of the electorate." Political scientists Lea Elsässer and Armin Schäfer made a related argument for Europe, citing research on class-biased responsiveness as "a real foundation" for perceptions of unresponsiveness among the less-well-off and showing that those perceptions contributed to support for right-wing populist parties.[18]

Elsässer and Schäfer's analysis was based on two questions included in recent European Social Survey rounds tapping concerns about political voice. One asked whether "the political system in [country] allows people like you to have a say in what the government does." The other asked whether "the political system in [country] allows people like you to have an influence on politics." There is considerable variation across countries in levels of perceived unresponsiveness, from a high of almost 8 on a zero-to-ten scale in Italy and Slovenia to a low of under 5 in Switzerland.[19] However, there is little indication that high levels of perceived unresponsiveness generated support

17. The overall correlation between conservative worldviews and electoral support for right-wing populist parties was .05; the corresponding correlation for the Swiss People's Party was .21. The correlation was .12 for Vox in Spain, .08 for Lega in Italy, and even weaker elsewhere. In Hungary, the correlation between conservative worldviews and support for Jobbik was *negative* (−.08), presumably due to competition for conservatives' support from the more established Fidesz.

18. Oliver and Rahn (2016: 194); Rahn and Lavine (2018); Elsässer and Schäfer (2018).

19. The format of these items changed from ten-point numerical scales in ESS round 7 to five-point labeled scales in rounds 8 and 9. Simply transposing the five-point responses to a ten-point scale produces roughly similar distributions, except that the average level of perceived unresponsiveness is nearly half a point higher in the latter format, mostly because very few people chose the highest labeled response, "a great deal." My tabulations include fixed effects for ESS rounds to take account of these differences, as well as differences in political contexts across the three rounds. (Normalizing the responses in each format separately would not materially alter the results reported here.)

for right-wing populist parties. While those parties attracted substantial support in the countries with the greatest perceived unresponsiveness (Italy, Slovenia, and Hungary), they attracted as much or more support in the countries with the *least* perceived unresponsiveness (Switzerland, Norway, and Denmark); the overall correlation between average levels of perceived unresponsiveness in each country and aggregate electoral support for right-wing populist parties is −.39.[20]

Elsässer and Schäfer focused on individual citizens rather than countries, incorporating perceived unresponsiveness along with conservative ideology, attitudes toward immigrants, and other explanatory factors in statistical analyses of right-wing populist voting. Their analyses differed from those reported in Tables 6.1 and 6.2 in a variety of ways—including a somewhat larger set of parties and a range of demographic control variables, but excluding some of the attitudinal factors incorporated in my analyses, including anti-EU sentiment and satisfaction with democracy. Another important difference is that they pooled survey responses from 15 countries, obscuring differences in the bases of support for different right-wing populist parties.[21]

Simply incorporating perceived unresponsiveness as an additional explanatory factor in analyses paralleling those reported in Table 6.1 produces little evidence that it contributed to support for right-wing populist parties. The estimated effects are generally small, and more often negative than positive; the average estimated effect is almost exactly zero. The few countries in which perceived unresponsiveness did seem to boost electoral support for right-wing populist parties—the Netherlands, Finland, and Switzerland—were all among the most responsive political systems in Europe, as judged by their citizens; and even in those places, there was no discernible relationship between perceived unresponsiveness and identification with those parties. In short, there is little reason to think that perceived unresponsiveness per se

20. This surprising negative correlation is due in part to the fact that the six countries without significant right-wing populist parties all had higher-than-average levels of perceived unresponsiveness. Excluding those countries produces a smaller but still negative correlation, −.27.

21. Elsässer and Schäfer classified right-wing populist parties on the basis of expert ratings of "anti-establishment and anti-elite rhetoric" and "views on democratic freedoms and rights" (primarily in the social and cultural domain), *relative to other parties in the same country*. Their explanatory variables, in addition to perceived unresponsiveness, included measures of immigration sentiment and trust in institutions, self-placements on the left-right scale, measures of unemployment and income insecurity, and demographic variables.

has been an important factor in generating support for right-wing populist parties in Europe.[22]

A Reservoir, Not a Wave: The Stability
of Right-Wing Populist Sentiment

The analyses reported in Tables 6.1 and 6.2 focus on support for 16 specific right-wing populist parties in the aftermath of the Euro-crisis. While the bases of these parties' appeals differ in some important ways, the general pattern is sufficiently consistent to suggest that *right-wing populist sentiment* is a meaningful phenomenon across contemporary Europe. Focusing on this combination of political attitudes, rather than on the specific aspects of populism that happen to be most salient in particular countries at particular times, makes it possible to track *potential* support for right-wing populist parties in general, and also to examine when and how that potential support is translated into actual support for right-wing populist parties.

My measure of right-wing populist sentiment is comprised of the seven separate factors listed in Tables 6.1 and 6.2—conservative ideology, conservative worldviews, anti-immigrant sentiment, anti-Europe sentiment, political distrust, democratic disaffection, and economic disaffection. In combining these factors, I weight each by its average estimated impact on electoral support (from Table 6.1) and identification (from Table 6.2) with the 16 right-wing populist parties included in my analysis.[23] Thus, the overall measure reflects the extent to which the attitudes of any given survey respondent would incline her to support a typical contemporary European right-wing populist party.

22. Not surprisingly, perceived unresponsiveness was correlated with political distrust (.52) and dissatisfaction with democracy (.45), so it may be that the impact of unresponsiveness was subsumed by those factors. Omitting them from the statistical analyses bolsters the apparent impact of perceived unresponsiveness, producing significant positive relationships in 8 of 16 countries. However, the average estimated impact of perceived unresponsiveness remains modest, and these analyses account less well for right-wing populist voting, suggesting that perceived unresponsiveness does not fully capture the impact of political distrust and dissatisfaction with democracy. Moreover, perceived unresponsiveness has no apparent impact on identification with right-wing populist parties even when political distrust and dissatisfaction with democracy are omitted from the analyses.

23. The summary measure is a weighted average of conservative ideology (.3648), *liberal* worldviews (.0394), anti-EU sentiment (.0998), anti-immigration sentiment (.2952), political distrust (.1005), dissatisfaction with democracy (.0803), and economic dissatisfaction (.0200).

One important advantage of this approach is that it provides a meaningful measure of populist *sentiment* even in countries where no right-wing populist party has gained significant political traction. Similarly, since all of the explanatory factors related to support for right-wing populist parties in Tables 6.1 and 6.2 were also measured in four of the six earlier ESS rounds, the measure facilitates temporal comparisons of populist sentiment stretching back to 2004, unconfounded by fluctuations in the presence or attractiveness of right-wing populist parties in specific countries. In total, this approach provides a plausible, consistent measure of right-wing populist sentiment for almost 275,000 survey respondents in 23 European countries over 15 years.[24]

Figure 6.3 shows the average level of right-wing populist sentiment in each of the seven relevant ESS rounds for Europe as a whole and for each of the 15 countries represented consistently in the surveys.[25] Remarkably, the figure shows a slight *decline* in right-wing populist sentiment across Europe between 2004 and 2019. Indeed, there was a slight decline even during the Euro-crisis, with a further decline thereafter, the total amounting to one-fourth of a point on the zero-to-ten scale. The familiar specter of a "populist wave" sweeping contemporary Europe is, at least when it comes to overall public opinion, wholly illusory.

Some countries did experience increases in right-wing populist sentiment during and after the Euro-crisis. The largest of these, amounting to three-fourths of a point, was in Slovakia. Right-wing populist sentiment also increased by half a point in Ireland and 0.3 points in Spain and Italy, with smaller increases in Hungary, Czechia, Poland, and Slovenia.[26] A striking fact about

24. To maximize the effective sample size, I substitute neutral values for data missing due to scattered item nonresponse. However, I exclude respondents from the first and fifth ESS rounds, which did not include the item on European integration. With these exclusions, the index of right-wing populist sentiment is available for 274,955 survey respondents in ESS rounds 2, 3, 4, 6, 7, 8, and 9 (2004–2009 and 2012–2019).

25. The tabulations for Europe as a whole weight each country by population. They include countries in each survey round even if those countries are missing in other rounds. However, in order to avoid having the average skewed by which countries happen to be included in each round, I calculate the averages based on a pooled regression analysis that also includes fixed effects for countries.

26. The post-crisis data for Slovakia are from a single survey fielded in the summer and fall of 2019, a year after the murder of a prominent journalist fueled mass demonstrations and the resignation of Prime Minister Robert Fico. In Greece, right-wing populist sentiment increased by one-third of a point between 2005 and 2009, but there are no subsequent ESS data from that country.

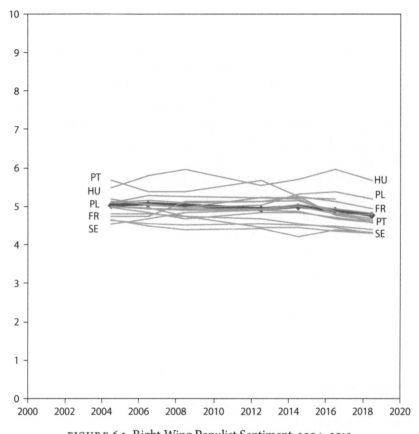

FIGURE 6.3. Right-Wing Populist Sentiment, 2004–2019

these shifts in sentiment is that they bear little apparent relationship to economic experiences. While Spain and Italy were hard hit by the Euro-crisis, all the other countries in which right-wing populist sentiment increased were among Europe's most *successful* economies over this period. Conversely, two of the largest *decreases* in right-wing populist sentiment were in countries that experienced little or no economic growth, Norway and Portugal.[27] Clearly, shifts in right-wing populist sentiment in specific countries were mostly *not* attributable to economic distress.

27. The largest increases in real income per capita between 2007 and 2017 were in Poland (38%), Lithuania (31%), Ireland (31%), Slovakia (25%), Hungary (16%), and Czechia (15%). Real incomes declined by 8% in Italy and 2% in Finland, were stagnant in Spain and Norway, and increased by just 2% in Portugal.

The "Populist Explosion" Reflects Supply, Not Demand

If right-wing populist sentiment—as measured by public attitudes toward immigrants, European integration, political elites, and the like—has not increased in most of Europe, how are we to account for the increase in electoral support for right-wing populist parties evident in Figure 6.1? In some cases, these parties have emerged or gained ground in places that *have* experienced increases in right-wing populist sentiment. But remarkably, for Europe overall, there is essentially *no relationship* between the level of right-wing populist sentiment in any given country and the vote share garnered by right-wing populist parties. In Figure 6.4, countries are arrayed along the horizontal axis based on their average level of right-wing populist sentiment in the 2014–2019 ESS data, from Sweden, Germany, Norway, and Switzerland at the low end (with average sentiment ranging from 4.3 to 4.5) to Italy, Czechia, Slovakia, and Hungary at the high end (with average sentiment ranging from 5.5 to 5.8). The vertical axis shows the average level of support for right-wing populist parties in parliamentary elections conducted in each country during the same period.

The mildly negative relationship between right-wing populist sentiment and vote shares, represented by the dotted summary line in Figure 6.4, hinges on my classification of specific parties, which is subject to debate.[28] However, it is clear from the figure that, by any plausible assessment, the overall relationship between sentiment and vote shares is remarkably weak. The countries in which right-wing populist parties won more than 15% of the total vote in this period include Hungary and Italy, with among the highest level of right-wing populist sentiment in Europe, but also Switzerland, Sweden, and Norway, with among the lowest levels.

The striking discrepancy between *potential* and *actual* support for right-wing populist parties appears equally clearly at the individual level. Figure 6.5 shows the overall distribution of right-wing populist sentiment in Europe in 2014–2019; survey respondents from each country-round are weighted in proportion to the adult populations of their countries. Although the distribution

28. In Slovakia, the right-wing People's Party Our Slovakia (L'SNS) garnered 8% of the parliamentary vote in 2016, but it was only represented by the "other" response in ESS data until 2019, when just 35 respondents reported having voted for the party. The much larger party SMER-Social Democracy has drifted to the right in recent years, but even in 2019 its supporters were drawn primarily from the left (69% reported positions left of the midpoint on the ESS left-right scale).

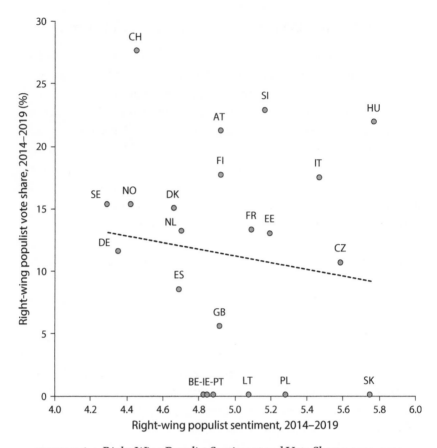

FIGURE 6.4. Right-Wing Populist Sentiment and Vote Shares, 2014–2019

of populist sentiment covers virtually the full range of the zero-to-ten scale, most respondents fell near the middle of the scale, between 4 and 6.[29] However, 10% had scores above 6.6 on the ten-point scale, 5% had scores above 7.2, and the most extreme 1% had scores above 8.3.

The overall distribution of sentiment in Figure 6.5 represents roughly 785 million actual or potential voters in 43 parliamentary elections. The shading in the figure divides them into three groups. The dark bars at the bottom show the distribution of right-wing populist sentiment among the 5,197 ESS respondents who reported voting for a right-wing populist party in the most recent

29. The interquartile range of the population-weighted distribution runs from 4.06 to 5.79.

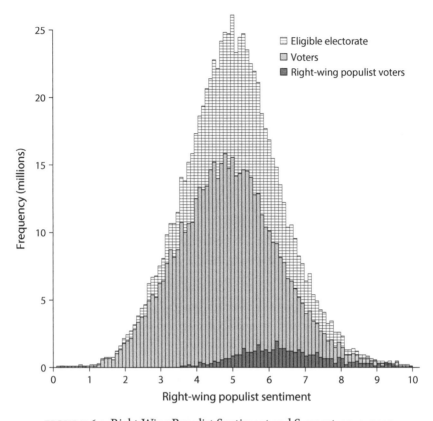

FIGURE 6.5. Right-Wing Populist Sentiment and Support, 2014–2019

election; they represent roughly 42 million right-wing populist voters.[30] The medium gray bars stacked above them represent 64,230 ESS respondents (and 475 million Europeans) who voted for other parties, while the lightest hatched bars at the top of the figure represent 34,418 ESS respondents (and 268 million people) who did not vote. Roughly three-fourths of those who did not support right-wing populist parties *could* have done so; the rest lived in places with no significant right-wing populist party on the ballot.[31]

30. To compensate for the underreporting of right-wing populist support in the surveys, I weight survey respondents in each ESS country-round to match the actual proportions of right-wing populist voters, other voters, and nonvoters in the most recent election; I exclude survey respondents who reported being ineligible to vote.

31. The countries represented in ESS rounds 7–9 where right-wing populist parties did *not* garner significant public support were Belgium, Ireland, Lithuania, Poland, Portugal, Slovakia, and (in rounds 7 and 8 only) Spain.

It is clear from Figure 6.5 that the relationship between populist sentiment and actual support is remarkably hit-or-miss. People who reported voting for these parties were, not surprisingly, more likely than not to express at least somewhat populist views. (The median level of populist sentiment among supporters of right-wing populist parties was 6.2.) But even extreme populist *sentiment* was far from sufficient to produce populist *support*, even in countries with viable populist parties. As political scientist Cas Mudde noted more than a decade ago, "Populist radical right attitudes might be more prevalent and intense within the electorates of populist radical right parties, but they are very widespread within the electorates as a whole. As a consequence, the relationship between populist radical right attitudes and the support for populist radical right parties is far from perfect."[32]

The implication, as Mudde went on to note, is that the success of populist parties in particular times and places depends much less on public opinion than on elite politics:

Most of the macro-level processes [posited by scholars as bases of populist support] affect European countries in roughly similar ways. . . . Hence, the macro-level explanations cannot account for the striking differences in populist radical right electoral success between countries with fairly similar breeding grounds. . . . In other words, the demand-side might explain why and which people constitute the *potential* electorate of populist radical right parties, but they do not (necessarily) explain why and who actually *votes* for these parties.[33]

Perhaps the most important lesson to be drawn from Figure 6.5 is that, even in countries where right-wing populist parties have made significant headway, they have not come anywhere close to fully exploiting their political potential. An optimist might conclude that mainstream political elites are still very good at marginalizing right-wing populist parties and co-opting their potential supporters. A pessimist might worry that populist parties have only begun to tap the deep reservoir of right-wing populist sentiment in contemporary Europe. In either case, it seems clear that the future of right-wing populism will hinge primarily on the ability and willingness of political elites to mobilize or defuse

---

32. Mudde (2007: 222). Wouter Van der Brug and his colleagues (2005: 547) likewise noted the limited mobilization of "potential voters" by populist parties.

33. Mudde (2007: 230).

populist sentiment, not on any substantial shifts in the prevalence of that sentiment.

One factor contributing to the translation of sentiment into votes is the existence and strength of right-wing populist party organizations. In Sweden, for example, whether Sweden Democrats had an organizational presence in a community "had a substantial effect on its results in the national election and on the probability of gaining representation in local councils." The strength of party organizations is partly a reflection of favorable opinion; but there is good reason to suppose that it is also a catalyst for mobilizing favorable opinion and translating it into right-wing populist votes.[34]

My aim here is not to provide a full-scale analysis of the "supply-side" factors facilitating or inhibiting the electoral success of right-wing populist parties. However, in order to underline and elucidate the surprising irrelevance of right-wing populist sentiment in accounting for that success, it will be helpful to consider in a bit more detail the shifting electoral fortunes of a few of Europe's most prominent right-wing populist parties. Their rise (and in one case, fall) will illustrate some of the ways in which populist entrepreneurs, mainstream political elites, and the structure of political institutions affect the conversion of public opinion into votes.

The End of "The Spanish Exception"

Spain is one of the best places in contemporary Europe to observe the rise of right-wing populism. As we saw in Chapter 3, the Spanish economy and society were buffeted by the Euro-crisis and by austerity measures adopted under pressure from the Troika. Yet the country produced surprisingly little right-wing populism. This so-called Spanish exception to the global "wave" of populism was much remarked upon. "No electorally viable movement in Spain espouses a nativist, xenophobic, or anti-globalization platform," a 2017 article in *Foreign Affairs* noted. "Indeed, far-right or populist parties in Spain have been unable to get more than one percent of the vote in most recent elections; the Spanish Parliament is one of very few in Europe in which these parties have no representation." Earlier that year, a detailed report from a Spanish think-tank had offered a variety of explanations for "The Spanish Exception," including "relatively favourable attitudes to immigration and globalization," "the lack of a strong, common Spanish national identity," the ties of right-wing parties

---

34. Erlingsson, Loxbo, and Öhrvall (2012: 817); Loxbo and Bolin (2016).

to the legacy of the Franco regime, and the structural disadvantage faced by small parties in the Spanish electoral system, which employs proportional representation, but with an average of just seven deputies elected per district. The report concluded that "it is difficult to imagine an extreme right-wing, xenophobic, anti-globalisation and/or anti-EU party gaining a foothold in Spain in the foreseeable future."[35]

When Vox surged at the polls two years later, gaining just such a foothold, another report in *Foreign Affairs* attempted to explain "The End of the Spanish Exception." It attributed Vox's success to "a far more momentous shift: the stunning implosion of the center-right People's Party (PP), the Spanish right's home for the last 30 years." The author acknowledged "the broader malaise gripping many Western establishment parties," but concluded that "ultimately, the PP's implosion is a uniquely Spanish story." Prime Minister Mariano Rajoy had failed to head off a chaotic referendum on Catalan independence in 2017, provoking a constitutional crisis and the imposition of direct rule in the recalcitrant province. Rajoy suffered another major setback the following spring when a 1,687-page National Court ruling was handed down in the sprawling Gürtel scandal, convicting prominent former PP officials of fraud, accepting bribes, and money laundering, and placing the party itself at the center of a long-running "network of institutionalized corruption." A week later, Rajoy narrowly lost a no-confidence vote in the Spanish parliament—a first in the country's post-Franco history—and was replaced as prime minister by Pedro Sánchez of the center-left Socialist Workers' Party (PSOE).[36]

Interpreting Vox's rise as a direct result of the PP's fall is probably too simplistic. Spanish opinion polls show PP's support falling for two years (from 36% in late 2016 to 22% in late 2018) before Vox ever got off the ground. Most of those defections seem to have been to the Citizens party, a pro-European center-right party with roots in Catalonia. Only after Citizens also began to

35. Omar G. Encarnación, "The Spanish Exception: Why Spain Has Resisted Right-Wing Populism," *Foreign Affairs*, 20 July 2017. Carmen González-Enriquez, "The Spanish Exception: Unemployment, Inequality and Immigration, but No Right-Wing Populist Parties," Working Paper 3/2017, Real Instituto Elcano, 14 February 2017.

36. Sam Edwards, "The End of the Spanish Exception? Far-Right Populism Has Finally Conquered Spain, but the Real Shift Lies Elsewhere," *Foreign Affairs*, 12 June 2019. Raphael Minder, "Spain's Prime Minister, Mariano Rajoy, Is Ousted in No-Confidence Vote," *New York Times*, 1 June 2018.

TABLE 6.3. Voting Behavior of Right-Wing Populist Sympathizers in Spain

	2015 survey (2011 election)	2017 survey (2016 election)	2019–2020 survey (November 2019 election)
Eligible voters with right-wing populist sentiment greater than 6			
Vox	—	—	32.8% (48.1%)
People's Party (PP)	45.7% (73.4%)	37.0% (63.3%)	22.0% (32.2%)
Socialist Workers (PSOE)	8.6% (13.8%)	5.0% (8.6%)	4.9% (7.2%)
Citizens (Ciudadanos)	—	6.6% (11.4%)	3.0% (4.3%)
Other (Podemos, etc.)	8.0% (12.8%)	9.8% (16.7%)	5.5% (8.1%)
Didn't vote	24.8%	25.5%	18.2%
Not ascertained	12.9%	16.1%	13.7%
N	312 [17.7%]	225 [12.6%]	213 [14.7%]
Eligible voters with right-wing populist sentiment between 5 and 6			
Vox	—	—	10.6% (17.6%)
People's Party (PP)	32.1% (49.5%)	25.5% (43.0%)	21.6% (36.2%)
Socialist Workers (PSOE)	14.4% (22.3%)	10.4% (17.6%)	12.0% (20.0%)
Citizens (Ciudadanos)	—	11.3% (19.0%)	4.9% (8.2%)
Other (Podemos, etc.)	18.2% (28.2%)	12.2% (20.5%)	10.7% (17.9%)
Didn't vote	19.0%	20.9%	24.9%
Not ascertained	16.3%	19.6%	15.3%
N	526 [30.5%]	502 [28.8%]	365 [23.7%]

Note: Party shares of reported votes cast in parentheses; populist shares of ESS samples in brackets.

slide did Vox support rise above 2%, and the two parties' subsequent poll movements were near-mirror-images of each other.[37]

The voting behavior reported by Spain's right-wing populist sympathizers in recent European Social Survey rounds, summarized in Table 6.3, sheds some light on these shifts. The top panel of the table focuses on people with right-wing populist sentiment above 6—the top 20% of the overall European distribution shown in Figure 6.5—while the bottom panel focuses on the next 28% of the distribution, people with scores between 5 and 6. Before Vox appeared on the scene in 2018, the most promising right-wing populist supporters, in the top panel, overwhelmingly supported the People's Party, if they voted at all. After Citizens started competing nationally in 2013, it attracted some

37. These figures are drawn from the Politico "poll of polls" compilation, https://www.politico.eu/europe-poll-of-polls/spain/.

support from this group, but PP retained the support of more than 60% of those who voted, while another one-fourth supported leftist (PSOE or Podemos) or other parties.

The emergence of Vox in 2019 marked a sea change, cutting PP support in this group by half while also drawing significant support away from Citizens and other parties.[38] However, its impact on the much larger group of Spaniards with less extreme right-wing populist sympathies, in the bottom panel of Table 6.3, seems to have been rather different. In that group, the rise of Citizens in the 2016 election was fueled by roughly proportional net shifts from PP, PSOE, and other parties, while Vox's support in 2019 came mainly at the expense of Citizens, leaving PP still with a strong plurality. Nonetheless, given the size of the two groups, Vox's overall support in 2019 depended almost as much upon the modest support it drew from the less extreme right-wing populist sympathizers in the bottom panel of Table 6.3 as on the much stronger support it drew from the smaller group of more extreme sympathizers in the top panel.

The paradox of Vox's rise is that it coincided with a significant decline in right-wing populist sentiment in Spain as the Euro-crisis ebbed. In 2015, the proportion of potential right-wing populist supporters in the Spanish electorate was typical of Europe—18% had summary scores greater than 6, while another 30% had summary scores between 5 and 6. By 2019–2020, these proportions had fallen to just 15% and 24%. Over the same period, the average level of economic disaffection declined by two full points on the ESS zero-to-ten scale. Perhaps as a result, distrust of politicians declined by 0.7 points and dissatisfaction with democracy by 0.8 points, despite the Gürtel scandal. Anti-immigration sentiment, already low by European standards, declined by half a point, reaching one of the lowest levels anywhere in Europe. Anti-EU sentiment declined only slightly over this period; but then, the analyses reported in Tables 6.1 and 6.2 suggest that it was not a significant factor in support for Vox, anyway.

38. Spain held two general elections in 2019. Prime Minister Sánchez, struggling to hold together the coalition that had ousted Rajoy in 2018, called a snap election held in late April. His party won a clear plurality, but he was unable to form a governing coalition, resulting in a second election in November. The election returns were generally similar, except that PP and Vox both gained support at the expense of the Citizens party, whose vote share fell from 15.9% in April to 6.8% in November. Round 9 ESS interviews in Spain began the day after the November election, and the 2019 votes reported in Table 6.3 refer to that election.

In an influential dissection of Vox's rise, journalist and historian Anne Applebaum described "its macho, cinematic Spanish nationalism," encapsulated in the slogan "Make Spain Great Again." While outlining the party's ties to other right-wing populist parties in Europe and elsewhere, she seemed to accept the view of observers in Madrid that "it was the Catalan secession crisis, beginning in 2017, that really put Vox into the center of Spanish politics."[39]

Although the European Social Survey has not included questions tapping nationalist sentiment, a survey conducted in 2019 by Madrid's Centro de Investigaciones Sociológicas provides some evidence that it was indeed a significant factor in explaining support for Vox. However, a much more important factor was conservative ideology, which also appears as the most important factor, by far, in support for Vox in Tables 6.1 and 6.2—twice or three times as important as anti-immigrant sentiment, for example.[40]

It is, of course, possible that Spanish nationalism and immigration may become even more salient political issues in the future, providing opportunities for Vox to expand upon its existing support. In the meantime, however, even the "implosion" of the People's Party in the wake of the Catalan crisis and the Gürtel scandal did not provide a sufficient opening for Vox to supplant PP among conservative voters, beyond the relatively small share of extreme right-wing populist sympathizers represented in the top panel of Table 6.3.

The electoral rise of Podemos on the left and Vox on the right has disrupted what was an unusually stable two-party system. From the 1980s through 2011, PSOE and PP together garnered at least 65%—and sometimes as much as 80%—of the vote in nine successive elections; in the November 2019 election, they netted just less than half. Yet the Spanish party system retains a good deal of structure. On the left, PSOE and Podemos combined to win 41–44% of the vote and 44–47% of the seats in four elections from 2015 through 2019; on the right, PP, Citizens, and Vox combined to win 43–46% of the vote and 42–47% of the seats. In its first national campaigns, in 2015 and 2016, Podemos came close to toppling PSOE as the top vote-getter on the left, but it has since settled

39. Anne Applebaum, "Want to Build a Far-Right Movement? Spain's Vox Party Shows How," *Washington Post*, 2 May 2019.

40. Turnbull-Dugarte, Rama, and Santana (2020). The survey (CIS 3248) was conducted shortly after the April 2019 election. The question tapping nationalist sentiment asked whether "you feel more Spanish than [region]" or vice versa. The reported estimated impact of nationalist sentiment on support for Vox was only slightly smaller than that of left-right ideology; however, the range of the ideology variable was ten times as large and its standard deviation was almost five times as large.

into a distinctly secondary role, netting just half as many votes and even fewer seats. Vox did not come quite as close to toppling PP in 2019, but it has remained within striking distance in subsequent polls.

In a pure two-party system, either party's governing failures, scandals, and unpopular candidates almost invariably benefit the other. With the emergence of Podemos and Vox, contemporary Spain has significant competition within as well as between the left and right. The Spanish electoral system, in which most deputies are elected in provinces with fewer than ten seats, creates significant pressure for these parties to appeal to relatively broad swaths of the political left and right, respectively, in order to win parliamentary representation.

While Vox in 2019 seems to have competed successfully with the People's Party for the support of the relatively narrow segment of the Spanish electorate with strong right-wing populist sympathies (in the top panel of Table 6.3), its future as a major force in Spanish politics will hinge on making further inroads in the wider segment of the right with weaker populist sympathies (in the bottom panel of the table). Thus, just as its rise to prominence paradoxically corresponded with a *decline* in right-wing populist sentiment in Spain following the Euro-crisis, its prospects for winning real power will paradoxically depend on transcending the limited intrinsic appeal of right-wing populism in contemporary Spain.

The "New Populist Playbook" in Italy

If Vox's rise in Spain primarily reflected an opportunistic response to the governing failures of the People's Party, what about the even more heralded rise of Lega in Italy? Since the early 1990s, Lega Nord had been a minor regional party on the fringes of the Italian political system. But in 2018, having unofficially shed its regional designation, the party won 17.4% of the vote in a fragmented parliamentary election field, narrowly besting the latest incarnation of Silvio Berlusconi's party, Forza Italia, for primacy in their center-right coalition. Almost three months of byzantine private and public negotiation eventually produced an unlikely government pairing Lega and the eccentric populist Five Star Movement, with the political neophyte Giuseppe Conte as prime minister.

Lega's electoral breakout was widely interpreted as reflecting a groundswell of right-wing populist sentiment in Italy. In the months after the election, the party and its leader, Deputy Prime Minister Matteo Salvini, continued to gain in popularity. Polls showed support for Lega doubling, from 16% on the eve of the 2018 election to 32% six months later. By July 2019, 37% of Italians said they intended to vote for Lega in the next election, while support for the Five Star Movement had collapsed from 34% to 16%. The *Guardian* told readers that Salvini "pulled Italy to the far right" by stoking "anti-immigrant panic." According to the *New Statesman*, "Salvini has not just won the hard right mainstream; he is realigning the Italian politics along his chosen dividing lines." The *New York Times* put Italy "on the front lines of a nationalist resurgence in Europe."[41]

Ironically, by the time these pieces were published, right-wing populist sentiment in Italy was already waning. The average level of right-wing populist sentiment in the ESS data fell from 5.6 in late 2017 to 5.2 in early 2019, while the proportion of eligible voters with summary right-wing populist scores above 6 fell from 39% to 31%. Antipathy to immigration fell by 0.5 points on the zero-to-ten scale in the year after the 2018 election; support for European integration increased by 0.4 points, while trust in politicians and parliament increased by 0.9 points and satisfaction with democracy increased by more than a full point. While the salience of right-wing populism in media portrayals of Italian politics was skyrocketing, its hold on Italian public opinion was slipping significantly.

A detailed profile of Salvini's "New Populist Playbook" by journalist Rachel Donadio described how he succeeded in transcending his eroding base of right-wing populist sentiment. "Salvini's formula has been to combine tough 'us versus them' talk on immigration and emotional, yet vague, defenses of national identity with an Italian-everyman relatability," she wrote.

> His popularity has allowed him to transcend his party, the right-wing League, and become the face of Italy, eclipsing the prime minister in the public imagination. . . . Salvini's social-media feeds are a window into the brain, or the stomach, of the average Italian . . . a canny combination of genuine personal charisma and extreme calculation. . . . Salvini's focus on migrants isn't just about immigration. It's a fluid frame that easily and quickly expands into vaguer and more emotional questions of national

41. Alexander Stille, "How Matteo Salvini Pulled Italy to the Far Right," *Guardian*, 9 August 2019. David Broder, "How Italy's Separatist Northern League Went National," *New Statesman*, 24 October 2018. Katrin Bennhold, "'Italy First,'" *New York Times*, 12 June 2019. Poll figures are drawn from the Politico "poll of polls" compilation, https://www.politico.eu/europe-poll -of-polls/italy/.

identity, race, and belonging. . . . The near-total control Salvini exercises over his party and its message makes it extremely difficult to pin him down. How far to the right is he, exactly? Would he moderate if he became prime minister? . . . What are his views on race? What about the euro? What does he believe in, exactly, beyond his own will to power? . . . He is the man of the moment for a social-media age when outrage runs high, attention spans low, and historical memory lower.

"They wanted change," Donadio concluded of Salvini's supporters, "and he seemed like change. Some were waiting for a strongman, others for a leader. And, well, when they looked out on the horizon, Salvini was the only one they could see."[42]

Of course, poll support based on charisma, social media buzz, and a shortage of alternatives can be ephemeral. Support for Lega peaked at 37% in July 2019, just before Salvini provoked a government breakup in a failed attempt to force an early election. Over the next 30 months, Lega's standing in the polls steadily eroded to just 18%. Much of that support seemed to have shifted to another party on the right, Fratelli d'Italia (Brothers of Italy), which rose from 7% to 20%, eclipsing the much-diminished Five Star Movement and rivalling the center-left Democratic Party. The press proclaimed that "the Brothers of Italy are on a roll," and polls showed the party's leader, Giorgia Meloni, rivalling Salvini for leadership of the Italian right. "Meloni's strategy has been to position her party as the true right," according to one account, "while simultaneously offering a softer message to attract those who might otherwise be turned off by her links to fascism."[43]

Italy provides more fertile ground than Spain for right-wing populists. Even after the erosion of right-wing populist attitudes between the 2017 and 2019 ESS readings, 31% of the Italian electorate expressed significant right-wing populist sentiment (with summary scores above 6, in the top panel of Table 6.4), while another 25% expressed milder right-wing populist sympathies (with summary scores between 5 and 6, in the bottom panel of the table); the corresponding proportions in Spain were just 15% and 24%. Still, even in Italy there is not enough "true right" for both Salvini and Meloni to thrive—especially when both together win less than half of the votes cast by right-wing

42. Rachel Donadio, "The New Populist Playbook," *Atlantic*, 5 September 2019.

43. "The Brothers of Italy Are on a Roll," *Economist*, 12 December 2020. Hannah Roberts, "Sister of Italy," *Politico*, 13 March 2020.

TABLE 6.4. Voting Behavior of Right-Wing Populist Sympathizers in Italy

	2017 survey (2013 election)	2018–2019 survey (2018 election)
Eligible voters with right-wing populist sentiment greater than 6		
Lega	5.9% (8.6%)	27.0% (38.6%)
Five Star Movement	19.7% (28.4%)	25.0% (35.8%)
People of Liberty/Forza Italia	13.8% (20.0%)	9.7% (13.9%)
Brothers of Italy	4.3% (6.2%)	4.3% (6.2%)
Democratic Party	11.8% (17.0%)	1.5% (2.2%)
Other (La Destra, Altro, etc.)	13.8% (19.9%)	2.3% (3.3%)
Didn't vote	13.6%	12.9%
Not ascertained	17.1%	17.4%
N	913 [39.1%]	784 [30.6%]
Eligible voters with right-wing populist sentiment between 5 and 6		
Lega	2.5% (3.8%)	11.4% (17.0%)
Five Star Movement	21.2% (32.2%)	36.7% (54.8%)
People of Liberty/Forza Italia	11.0% (16.8%)	6.1% (9.2%)
Brothers of Italy	2.9% (4.3%)	2.3% (3.4%)
Democratic Party	19.5% (29.6%)	9.1% (13.6%)
Other (La Destra, Altro, etc.)	8.9% (13.2%)	1.3% (2.0%)
Didn't vote	12.9%	12.8%
Not ascertained	21.2%	20.2%
N	569 [23.0%]	630 [24.6%]

Note: Party shares of reported votes cast in parentheses; populist shares of ESS samples in brackets.

populists, and only about one-fifth of the votes cast by marginal right-wing populist sympathizers, as they did in 2018. Sustained right-wing populist success in Italy will probably depend on the further erosion of Berlusconi's more traditional right, represented by Forza Italia, and of the iconoclastic Five Star Movement as well.

No political system unerringly translates citizens' attitudes into proportional governing clout, and that is especially true of Italy's fluid multiparty system. In Spain, Vox's 15% of the vote in the November 2019 election merely made it the second-largest opposition party. In Italy, Lega's 17% of the vote in the 2018 election vaulted Salvini into the unlikely position of deputy prime minister, and from there into "the face of Italy, eclipsing the prime minister in the public imagination." It was a remarkable political ride, but hardly a reliable measure of the strength of right-wing populism among ordinary Italians. While right-wing populist sentiment remains stronger in Italy than almost anywhere else in Europe, the translation of that sentiment into real political power will hinge crucially on the complex vagaries of Italian party politics.

Britain's "Leap in the Dark"

If Lega illustrates the potential for right-wing populist entrepreneurs to thrive in a system of fluid, multiparty politics, the rise and fall of the United Kingdom Independence Party (UKIP) illustrates the opportunities and difficulties facing populist entrepreneurs in more stable majoritarian systems. UKIP never succeeded in winning real political power, or even in winning the support of a plurality of Britons with right-wing populist sympathies. Nonetheless, it played a significant role in injecting right-wing populist demands into a previously unresponsive British political system, catalyzing the chain reaction of pressures that would eventually precipitate the momentous "leap in the dark" of Britain's withdrawal from the European Union.

UKIP had existed for years on the margin of British politics, never winning as much as 5% of the vote. But under the leadership of "eye-catching media performer" Nigel Farage, the party registered growing support in local elections in 2013 and 2014 and—rather ironically, given its anti-EU stance—won the 2014 European Parliament elections with 27.5% of the vote. In a General Election the following spring, UKIP won 12.6% of the vote. In the British first-past-the-post system, that support translated into just one seat in Parliament. Nonetheless, reelected Conservative Prime Minister David Cameron, who had once dismissed UKIP as "fruitcakes and loonies," was clearly nervous about the party's growing support, and about the appeal within his own party of its opposition to the European Union and immigration.[44]

The statistical analyses of voting behavior and identification in Tables 6.1 and 6.2 indicate that the bases of UKIP's support were very much in keeping with the common pattern for right-wing populist parties: conservative ideology, political distrust, antipathy to European integration, and, above all, anti-immigrant sentiment. But it would be a mistake to suppose that the party's dramatic rise marked an increase in those views in the British public. Indeed, right-wing populist sentiment in Britain was remarkably stable from 2006 to

44. Alex Hunt, "UKIP: The Story of the UK Independence Party's Rise," BBC News, 21 November 2014.

2014, even as UKIP soared in the polls. The average level of right-wing populist sentiment declined slightly over this period, from 5.3 to 5.2, while the proportion of respondents with high levels of right-wing populist sentiment remained steady at 25%.

This stability confirms political scientist Matthew Goodwin's 2014 observation that "underlying social change had already created a large reservoir of potential radical right voters long before Nigel Farage and UKIP even started to campaign." Goodwin continued, "Only now—through an articulate and effective campaigner—are these underlying conflicts once again being mobilized by UKIP into British politics, much as they have been for over twenty years in other EU Member States."[45]

While it is easy to attribute any party's success to "an articulate and effective campaigner," detailed analysis of fluctuations in UKIP support over this period provide statistical evidence that its rise was significantly fueled by "disproportionate attention" from the British media—attention that was not itself contingent on the party's standing in the polls. Just as media fascination with Donald Trump helped fuel his march to the Republican nomination in the US in 2016, the British media seem to have played a critical role in amplifying Farage's populist message.[46]

In the face of UKIP's rise and divisions within his own party, Cameron had pledged to hold a referendum on the UK's role in the European Union if the Tories remained in power. After the 2015 election, he struck a deal with Brussels providing more favorable terms for continued EU membership, then scheduled a June 2016 referendum posing "one of the biggest decisions this country will face in our lifetimes: whether to remain in a reformed EU or to leave." The prime minister made his own position clear, arguing that "Britain will be safer, stronger and better off by remaining in a reformed EU" and warning that leaving would be a "leap in the dark."[47]

According to press reports, "Cameron called the referendum as a calculated gamble, aimed at silencing the Eurosceptics in his own party for a generation.

45. Matthew Goodwin, "Explaining the Rise of the UK Independence Party," https://eu .boell.org/sites/default/files/uploads/2014/06/ukip_eu.pdf.

46. Murphy and Devine (2020). On Trump and the media, see Sides, Tesler, and Vavreck (2018: chap. 4).

47. Laura Kuenssberg, "EU Referendum: Cameron Sets June Date for UK Vote," BBC News, 20 February 2016. Rowena Mason, Nicholas Watt, Ian Traynor, and Jennifer Rankin, "EU Referendum to Take Place on 23 June, David Cameron Confirms," Guardian, 20 February 2016.

Yet he had underestimated the backing Vote Leave would receive on his own backbenches; and reckoned without the charismatic and popular former mayor of London, Boris Johnson, becoming its figurehead." A divisive referendum campaign produced a narrow but momentous majority in favor of "Brexit." "The prime minister's team were left shocked and distraught," while Farage crowed that the British public had given "two fingers up" to Westminster and pro-EU elites.[48]

In the wake of the Brexit vote, "Cameron promptly resigned, and the new Conservative Prime Minister, Theresa May, adopted other Farage policies—stating not only that 'Brexit must mean Brexit,' but also that immigration must be reduced and criticizing liberal cosmopolitan 'citizens of nowhere.' The Conservative Party went UKIP-lite. UKIP's vote slumped after Farage stood down as leader, feeling, like many former voters, that the party's main task was complete."[49] Indeed, opinion polls showed electoral support for UKIP falling almost as soon as the Brexit referendum votes were counted—from 17% to 4% by the time of the next General Election a year later.[50] In that election, the party polled just 1.8% of the vote.

Table 6.5 tracks the voting behavior of right-wing populist sympathizers in Great Britain before and after the Brexit vote. One important takeaway from these tabulations is that, throughout this period, UKIP never won the votes of more than a sliver of its potential supporters. Even at the height of its electoral success, in 2015, a substantial plurality of those with strong right-wing populist sympathies and an even larger plurality of those with weaker right-wing populist sympathies were voting Conservative. Some of this support was no doubt tactical, reflecting recognition of the severe disadvantage facing UKIP in winning parliamentary representation in a first-past-the-post electoral system, even by comparison with more geographically concentrated minor parties. But clearly, there was also a good deal of heterogeneity in the partisan loyalties of Britain's right-wing populist sympathizers. Not only the EU, but other aspects of the right-wing populist agenda as well, crosscut Britain's existing partisan alignment without, at least immediately, displacing it. Indeed, among the less extreme right-wing populist sympathizers in the

48. Heather Stewart, Rowena Mason, and Rajeev Syal, "David Cameron Resigns after UK Votes to Leave European Union," *Guardian*, 24 June 2016.

49. Eatwell and Goodwin (2018: 285).

50. These figures are drawn from the Politico "poll of polls" compilation, https://www.politico.eu/europe-poll-of-polls/united-kingdom/.

TABLE 6.5. Voting Behavior of Right-Wing Populist Sympathizers in Great Britain

	2014–2015 survey (2010 election)	2016–2017 survey (2015 election)	2018–2019 survey (2017 election)
Eligible voters with right-wing populist sentiment greater than 6			
UK Independence Party	6.1% (9.4%)	21.5% (34.0%)	3.2% (5.1%)
Conservative Party	33.4% (51.8%)	28.3% (44.8%)	39.1% (62.5%)
Labour Party	12.5% (19.3%)	8.4% (13.2%)	13.4% (21.4%)
Other (Lib Dem, etc.)	12.6% (19.5%)	5.0% (7.9%)	6.8% (10.9%)
Didn't vote	29.6%	28.9%	33.2%
Not ascertained	5.9%	8.0%	4.3%
N	577 [24.7%]	313 [15.9%]	387 [16.7%]
Eligible voters with right-wing populist sentiment between 5 and 6			
UK Independence Party	1.3% (2.1%)	12.1% (18.7%)	1.6% (2.3%)
Conservative Party	29.6% (47.6%)	29.1% (45.0%)	38.3% (55.2%)
Labour Party	18.2% (29.2%)	15.6% (24.1%)	20.0% (28.8%)
Other (Lib Dem, etc.)	13.2% (21.2%)	7.9% (12.2%)	9.5% (13.7%)
Didn't vote	31.7%	29.3%	24.3%
Not ascertained	6.0%	6.0%	6.2%
N	687 [31.5%]	577 [29.7%]	597 [27.0%]

Note: Party shares of reported votes cast in parentheses; populist shares of ESS samples in brackets.

bottom panel of Table 6.5, even the conventional left-wing Labour Party alone easily outpolled UKIP.

Perhaps for that reason, the largest share of UKIP's net gain in support between 2010 and 2015 seems to have come from the Liberal Democrats and other minor parties, not from Tories or Labour supporters. Cameron's efforts during the 2015 campaign to straddle the issue of Britain's role in Europe were sufficient to maintain the Tories' substantial plurality among right-wing populist sympathizers, notwithstanding growing support for UKIP. After the Brexit referendum, as his successors aligned the Conservative Party forthrightly in opposition to Europe, the party gained even more support at the expense of UKIP, but it made no significant dent in the substantial number of right-wing populist sympathizers who continued (or reverted to) supporting Labour, the Liberal Democrats, or other parties. That pattern helps to account for the fact that the Conservatives lost seats in the 2017 election despite increasing their overall vote share by more than five percentage points—they were winning additional votes that had mostly been wasted, anyway.

One other crucial point worth noting in the tabulations reported in Table 6.5 is the substantial *decline* in right-wing populist sympathies in Britain over this period. The average level of right-wing populist sentiment, which had held steady at 5.2 for the preceding decade, fell to 4.8 between 2014–2015 and 2016–2017, while the share of the electorate with high scores plunged from 25% to 16%. These shifts reflected significant increases in support for European integration and trust in politicians, and an even more significant decline (more than 0.8 points on the zero-to-ten scale) in anti-immigrant sentiment. The shock of the Brexit vote seems to have dented long-standing right-wing populist sentiment in Britain, just as Theresa May and her colleagues were pressing ahead to implement the supposed public demand for "UKIP-lite."

Having resigned as UKIP leader immediately after the Brexit referendum, Farage cofounded a rival Brexit Party in late 2018. As bitter Brexit negotiations dragged on, that party picked up much of the support that had been lost by UKIP, winning another round of European Parliament elections and briefly reaching 20% in polls in the summer of 2019. However, its fortunes reversed when opposition to May within the Conservative Party finally boiled over and she was ousted as prime minister, replaced by populist firebrand Boris Johnson. In the subsequent General Election, the rejuvenated Conservatives won 43.6% of the vote and an outright majority of seats in Parliament, while the Brexit Party won just 2% of the vote and no seats. A year later, with the Tories seemingly in firm control of its putative constituency, the Brexit Party changed its name to Reform UK, and within a few months, Farage retired from politics.

As political scientists Pippa Norris and Ronald Inglehart have written,

The story behind Britain's momentous decision to withdraw from the European Union after more than 40 years of membership, and the historical legacy of UKIP in this process, rests ultimately on "supply-side" factors in Westminster politics—including the critical role of contingent historical events and key decisions made by leading politicians. David Cameron chose for strategic reasons, not personal convictions, to hold a referendum on EU membership—hoping to secure his authority over his recalcitrant backbenchers and to see off UKIP. Yet rather than proving a major threat to the electoral fortunes of the Conservative Party, like many related fringe parties, UKIP has remained a marginal force in British politics. It lost its raison d'etre once the Conservative Party pledged to Leave but also, like many fringe parties, it was unable to overcome the many logistical, financial, and organizational obstacles facing small parties contesting seats in Majoritarian electoral systems.[51]

UKIP did little or nothing to increase right-wing populist sentiment in Britain, or even to capitalize on an increase in right-wing populist sentiment. There *was* no increase in right-wing populist sentiment in Britain. What UKIP did, as successful right-wing populist parties elsewhere have done, was to draw on the reservoir of right-wing populist sentiment that exists to a greater or lesser degree in every contemporary democracy. The success of these parties depends on the existence of right-wing populist sentiment, but even more on the strategic opportunities offered by political systems and on the skill of political entrepreneurs in exploiting those opportunities. As the authors of a detailed study of UKIP's rise put it, "The potential for a political insurgency of this kind has existed for a long time."[52]

Summary

Much commentary on contemporary populism has attributed increasing support for right-wing populist parties to shifts in public attitudes stemming from "the challenge of migration and the lingering euro crisis." According to political scientist Benjamin Moffitt, for example,

> The effects of the Global Financial Crisis drag on, the Eurozone sovereign-debt crisis continues to threaten the very existence of the European Union, and more broadly, it is alleged that we are suffering from a crisis of faith in democracy, with political party membership falling dramatically and citizens finding themselves more and more disillusioned with mainstream politics. . . . A prolonged global financial downturn, rising unemployment in a number of areas and a loss of faith in perceived elite projects like the European Union are helping fuel the flames. Wherever there are dissatisfied citizens who feel as if their voice is not being heard, there is space for populists to appeal to "the people."[53]

---

51. Norris and Inglehart (2019: 395).
52. Ford and Goodwingg (2014: 271).
53. Bröning, "The Rise of Populism in Europe: Can the Center Hold?" Moffitt (2016: 1, 159–160).

Some of the factual premises underlying Moffitt's analysis of populism seem, based on the evidence presented here, to be unfounded. Overall, Europeans had no less appetite for further European integration after the global financial crisis than they had before its onset. Their trust in politicians and parliaments was no lower, and they were no less satisfied with the working of democracy. In one respect, however, Moffitt was quite right: "Wherever there are dissatisfied citizens who feel as if their voice is not being heard, there is space for populists to appeal to 'the people.'"

What the purveyors of the notion of a "populist explosion" overlook is that there are *always* dissatisfied citizens in democracies, and thus there is *always* "space for populists to appeal to 'the people.'" To suppose that this is a novel state of affairs is naively Panglossian. On the other hand, to suppose that a reservoir of right-wing populist sentiment is enough to constitute a crisis of democracy is unduly alarmist. As the preeminent scholar of contemporary populism, Cas Mudde, has written, "Far from being an aberration, the attitudes and ideological features of the populist radical right are fairly widespread in contemporary European societies. . . . Provocatively stated, the real question is not why populist radical right parties have been so successful since the 1980s, but why so *few* parties have profited from the fertile breeding ground available to them."[54]

The evidence presented in this chapter provides considerable support for Mudde's view. On the one hand, Figure 6.3 shows that right-wing populist sentiment has been "fairly widespread in contemporary Europe" through the first two decades of the 21st century, though slightly *less* so recently than before the Euro-crisis. On the other hand, Figure 6.5 shows that only a sliver of that sentiment has, so far, been translated into actual support for right-wing populist parties. The real threat of a "populist explosion" is that political elites will harness the ubiquitous dissatisfactions of democratic politics in support of antidemocratic rule. So far, that mostly hasn't happened. But *could* it happen?

54. Mudde (2016: 3, 11).

7

Democracy Erodes from the Top

THE RISE OF RIGHT-WING populist parties has debased European politics in some important ways, perhaps most importantly by normalizing xenophobia and the scapegoating of immigrants. However, the notion that European democracy is in crisis involves more than that. Lurking in the background is a deeper worry about the fundamental stability of liberal democratic systems.

That concern stems from a conviction that citizens' bad attitudes—anti-immigrant, anti-EU, antiestablishment, perhaps even antidemocracy—will lead, one way or another, to autocracy. Roberto Stefan Foa and Yascha Mounk's influential account of "democratic deconsolidation" illustrates this quasi-logic with a series of quick jump-cuts:

> Approval ratings for the continent's leading politicians stand at record lows, and citizens have grown deeply mistrustful of their political institutions. Far-right populist parties, such as France's National Front or the Sweden Democrats, have risen from obscurity to transform the party system of virtually every Western European country. Meanwhile, parts of Central and Eastern Europe bear witness to the institutional and ideological transformations that might be afoot: In Poland and Hungary, populist strongmen have begun to put pressure on critical media, to violate minority rights, and to undermine key institutions such as independent courts.[1]

A subsequent book-length analysis by Mounk runs the same movie in reverse, from "electoral dictatorships" back to populist backsliding stemming from electoral support for "extremists":

> In Russia and Turkey, elected strongmen have succeeded in turning fledgling democracies into electoral dictatorships. In Poland and Hungary,

---

1. Foa and Mounk (2016: 15–16).

populist leaders are using that same playbook to destroy the free media, to undermine independent institutions, and to muzzle the opposition. More countries may soon follow. In Austria, a far-right candidate nearly won the country's presidency. In France, a rapidly changing political landscape is providing new openings for both the far left and the far right. In Spain and Greece, established party systems are disintegrating with breathtaking speed. Even in the supposedly stable and tolerant democracies of Sweden, Germany, and the Netherlands, extremists are celebrating unprecedented successes.[2]

In much the same vein, political scientists Roger Eatwell and Matthew Goodwin cited Hungarian leader Victor Orbán's social conservatism and attacks on democratic institutions as grounds for worry that populism may "presage the collapse" of liberal democracy:

> Some [radical-right parties], like Victor Orbán's governing Fidesz in Hungary or the Law and Justice party in Poland, are clearly right-wing socially, arguing that rampant liberals have been obsessed with expanding the rights of minority groups and promoting multiculturalism, placing the nation's religious values and traditional family life under threat. Given that Orbán has also attacked key groups such as the judiciary and free media as part of his attempt to create an "illiberal democracy," it is hardly surprising that many commentators are worried that this form of politics may presage the collapse of liberal-democratic freedoms and rights.[3]

Regardless of whether the path is traced forward or backward, the frightening route from "supposedly stable and tolerant democracies" to "the collapse of liberal-democratic freedoms and rights" runs squarely through Hungary and Poland, where "populist leaders" have indeed endeavored "to destroy the free media, to undermine independent institutions, and to muzzle the opposition." Thus, any attempt to assess the nature and magnitude of Europe's crisis of democracy must carefully consider how and why these two countries' democratic systems have suffered such significant erosion.

In this chapter, I focus on these two key instances of democratic backsliding in contemporary Europe, and specifically on the connection between right-wing populist sentiment, political leadership, and the erosion of democ-

---

2. Mounk (2018: 2–3).
3. Eatwell and Goodwin (2018: 72).

racy. By sketching the evolution of public opinion, electoral politics, and government in these countries in the first decades of the 21st century, I hope to shed light on the nature and severity of threats to liberal democracy elsewhere in Europe.

Quantifying the Erosion of Democracy

There is a broad gray area between democracy and dictatorship. No one doubts that democracy died in Weimar Germany when Adolf Hitler seized power, or in Chile when military aircraft bombed Salvador Allende's presidential palace. But the real threats to democracy in contemporary Europe are of a different order. Indeed, in their influential account *How Democracies Die*, political scientists Steven Levitsky and Daniel Ziblatt classified both Hungary and Poland as "mildly authoritarian regimes," but were notably more sanguine about the state of democracy in Europe than in the US: "Although European democracies face many problems, from weak economies to EU skepticism to anti-immigrant backlash, there is little evidence in any of them of the kind of fundamental erosion of norms we have seen in the United States."[4]

Efforts to quantify the functioning of democracy are inevitably crude. Nonetheless, it is worth reviewing what they suggest about the severity and timing of democratic backsliding in contemporary Hungary and Poland. Figure 7.1 tracks estimates of the state of liberal democracy in these two countries from 2001 through 2021. The estimates, from the Varieties of Democracy (V-Dem) project, are based on annual ratings by country experts.[5] For purposes

---

4. Levitsky and Ziblatt (2018: 188, 205).

5. Data and documentation are available from the V-Dem website, https://www.v-dem.net/. The figure shows each country's scores on the "liberal democracy index" in version 12 of the V-Dem data. According to the project codebook, "The liberal principle of democracy emphasizes the importance of protecting individual and minority rights against the tyranny of the state and the tyranny of the majority. The liberal model takes a 'negative' view of political power insofar as it judges the quality of democracy by the limits placed on government. This is achieved by constitutionally protected civil liberties, strong rule of law, an independent judiciary, and effective checks and balances that, together, limit the exercise of executive power. To make this a measure of liberal democracy, the index also takes the level of electoral democracy into account." As for electoral democracy, "The electoral principle of democracy seeks to embody the core value of making rulers responsive to citizens, achieved through electoral competition for the electorate's approval under circumstances when suffrage is extensive; political and civil society organizations can operate freely; elections are clean and not marred by fraud or systematic irregularities; and elections affect the composition of the chief executive of the country. In

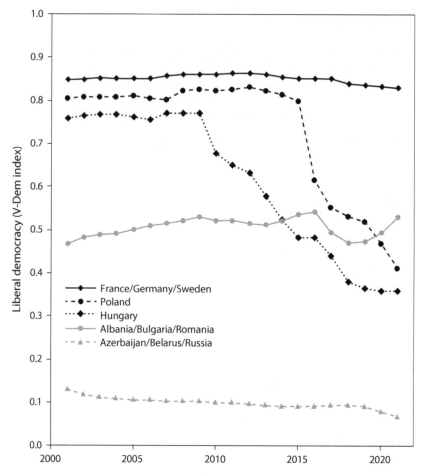

FIGURE 7.1. Democratic Backsliding in Hungary and Poland, 2001–2020.

V-Dem annual assessments of "Liberal Democracy."

of comparison, the figure shows parallel assessments for some typical high-functioning European democracies (France, Germany, and Sweden), some intermediate cases (Albania, Bulgaria, and Romania), and some unambiguously authoritarian systems (Azerbaijan, Belarus, and Russia).[6]

between elections, there is freedom of expression and an independent media capable of presenting alternative views on matters of political relevance."

6. According to the V-Dem data, Romania experienced a significant increase in liberal democracy over the two decades represented in Figure 7.1, while Russia and, to a lesser extent, Bulgaria and Belarus experienced declines.

According to the V-Dem assessments, Hungary and Poland in the first decade of the 21st century were already slightly less democratic than the established liberal democracies of Western Europe; but they were a good deal closer to those models than to countries like Bulgaria and Romania, much less to Belarus and Russia. In Hungary, a substantial, sustained decline in liberal democracy began in 2010 and only began to level off after 2018. In Poland, the decline was later but even more rapid, with a precipitous drop in the perceived quality of liberal democracy in 2016 followed by further significant decline thereafter. By 2021, both countries looked much more like "mildly authoritarian regimes," as Levitsky and Ziblatt put it, than like model liberal democracies. Even with due allowance for the difficulty of assessing something as elusive as the quality of liberal democracy, clearly the cumulative erosion of democracy in these cases was substantial.

How did these declines in democratic functioning come about? What maladies of public opinion and electoral behavior contributed to them? And what do they portend for the rest of Europe?

Public Opinion and the Erosion of Democracy in Hungary

In the first 15 years after the fall of communism, Hungary seemed closer than any other formerly communist country to evolving into a stable two-party system. Parliamentary elections in 1998 and 2002 had seen the Hungarian Socialist Party (MSZP) and the conservative Hungarian Civic Alliance (Fidesz) alternate in power following successive close divisions of votes and of seats in the National Assembly. In the next election, in April 2006, the vote was even closer, 41.6% for Fidesz and 41.4% for MSZP; but the Socialists won a near-majority of seats in the National Assembly (186 of 386) and renewed their governing coalition with a smaller liberal party, the Alliance of Free Democrats.[7]

At that point, Hungary looked like a decidedly conventional parliamentary democracy. For the first time in the country's postcommunist history, a governing party had succeeded in winning reelection. Moreover, the party system seemed to be consolidating, with the two major parties, one on the left and

7. Until 2012, the Hungarian electoral system was a mixed-member system with 176 members of the National Assembly elected in single-member districts, 140 (later, 146) elected in multi-member districts with territorial party lists, and 70 (later, 64) selected from national party lists to achieve proportional representation (with a 5% threshold). The vote shares quoted here reflect the combined votes from single-member and multimember districts.

the other on the right, having increased their combined share of the vote from 57% in 1998 to 83% in 2006. An electoral alliance between the right-wing nationalist Hungarian Justice and Life Party and a new Christian nationalist party, Jobbik (officially, the Movement for a Better Hungary), garnered just 1.9% of the vote.

The statistical analysis reported in the first column of Table 7.1 sheds light on the bases of electoral support for Fidesz in the 2006 parliamentary election.[8] The explanatory factors included in this analysis are the same as in Table 6.1, which focused on electoral support for right-wing populist parties across 16 European countries. The key finding is that the most important basis of support for Fidesz in 2006, by far, was conservative ideology. That is hardly surprising, since Fidesz was the largest conservative party in the Hungarian party system. What is more surprising is that there was very little connection between support for Fidesz and the variety of other factors associated with support for right-wing populist parties in Chapter 6. Neither antipathy to the EU nor opposition to immigration nor distrust of politicians and parliament played significant roles in support for Fidesz at this point. (Dissatisfaction with democracy did, but that may be a reflection in the 2006–2009 surveys of subsequent events rather than a contemporaneous source of support.) In short, Fidesz in 2006 seems to have been a thoroughly conventional conservative opposition party, at least as judged by the bases of its appeal to ordinary Hungarians.

This seeming normalcy was thrown out of kilter five months after the 2006 election with the leaking of an audio recording of Prime Minister Ferenc

---

8. The analysis is based on recalled votes of people surveyed in ESS round 3, fielded from November 2006 through January 2007, and round 4, fielded in February–April 2009. There is always reason to be concerned about the accuracy of self-reported voting behavior in surveys, especially here, since 20% to 25% of the survey respondents who reported voting declined to say which party they voted for. The reported votes overstate support for Fidesz by 7.2 percentage points in the 2006–2007 survey and by 13.3 percentage points in the 2009 survey. The Appendix provides a more detailed analysis of discrepancies between survey vote shares and actual vote shares for the major parties, in and out of government, in Hungary and Poland. Support for all these parties is generally exaggerated in the ESS data (by an average of about 15%, with support for minor parties correspondingly underestimated). Variation in support across parties and elections is quite reliably reflected in the surveys; the overall correlation between reported and actual vote shares (for Fidesz and MSZP in five elections in Hungary and Law and Justice and Civic Platform in four elections in Poland) is .92. Nonetheless, in order to minimize any distorting effect of misreported support, I weight ESS respondents in Tables 7.1 through 7.4 to accurately reflect the numbers of Fidesz and Law and Justice voters, other voters, and nonvoters.

TABLE 7.1. Bases of Electoral Support for Fidesz, 2006–2018

	2006–2009 surveys (2006 election)	2012–2013 survey (2010 election)	2015–2017 surveys (2014 election)	2019 survey (2018 election)
Conservative ideology	.470 (.028)	.265 (.024)	.172 (.016)	.157 (.022)
Conservative worldview	−.021 (.042)	.183 (.043)	.149 (.038)	.020 (.059)
Anti-EU sentiment	−.017 (.016)	−.037 (.017)	.004 (.015)	.093 (.023)
Anti-immigrant sentiment	.034 (.022)	.042 (.022)	.072 (.021)	.146 (.034)
Political distrust	−.003 (.023)	−.043 (.022)	−.055 (.019)	−.112 (.028)
Dissatisfaction with democracy	.047 (.022)	−.074 (.023)	−.160 (.021)	−.186 (.029)
Economic dissatisfaction	.038 (.024)	.042 (.024)	−.023 (.023)	−.118 (.032)
Pseudo-R^2	.34	.17	.22	.39
N	2,253	1,338	2,308	1,148

Note: Probit regression parameter estimates (with standard errors in parentheses). Fixed effects for survey rounds are included in the analyses but not shown. Self-reported voters post-stratified by vote choice.

Gyurcsány addressing a private meeting of MSZP officials. "We screwed up," Gyurcsány told his comrades. "Not a little, a lot. No European country has done something as boneheaded as we have. Evidently, we lied throughout the last year-and-a-half, two years. . . . We lied in the morning, we lied in the evening."[9] Gyurcsány's obscenity-laced admission of deceit and manifest contempt for the electorate triggered a wave of antigovernment protests lasting more than a month. Clashes between protesters and police resulted in hundreds of injuries. Opposition leaders called for Gyurcsány's resignation, and independently

9. "We Lied to Win, Says Hungary PM," BBC News, 18 September 2006. Gyurcsány posted a full transcript of his remarks on his website, suggesting to some that he had authorized the leak "to emphasize the need for tough reforms" in advance of local elections.

TABLE 7.2. Bases of Identification with Fidesz before and after Hungary's 2010 Election

	2006–2007	2009	2012–2015	2017–2019
Conservative ideology	.452	.468	.259	.181
	(.032)	(.031)	(.028)	(.018)
Conservative worldview	.128	−.063	.135	.083
	(.052)	(.064)	(.035)	(.036)
Anti-EU sentiment	.018	−.016	.063	.057
	(.022)	(.021)	(.017)	(.014)
Anti-immigrant sentiment	−.044	.017	−.000	.059
	(.029)	(.029)	(.019)	(.021)
Political distrust	−.045	−.053	−.136	−.157
	(.027)	(.029)	(.019)	(.019)
Dissatisfaction with	.033	.030	−.183	−.169
democracy	(.025)	(.028)	(.020)	(.020)
Economic dissatisfaction	.049	−.010	.005	−.135
	(.029)	(.031)	(.019)	(.025)
Pseudo-R^2	.26	.26	.27	.34
N	1,433	1,355	3,283	2,930

Note: Ordered probit regression parameter estimates (with standard errors in parentheses). Multiple response thresholds and fixed effects for survey rounds are estimated but not shown. Eligible voters post-stratified by vote choice.

elected president Laszlo Solyom urged the National Assembly to oust him, but he survived a public vote of confidence by a 207–165 margin.[10]

Interviews for the Hungarian portion of ESS round 3 were conducted from November 2006 through January 2007, in the midst of the turmoil sparked by the Gyurcsány scandal. The statistical analysis reported in the first column of Table 7.2 details the bases of identification with Fidesz in this key period. As in Table 7.1, the most important factor by far in accounting for support for Fidesz was conservative ideology. Here, unlike in Table 7.1, conservative worldviews also seemed to play a significant role. However, these results parallel those in Table 7.1 in indicating that common sources of support for right-wing

10. Daniel McLaughlin, "150 Injured as Hungarians Riot over PM's Lies," *Guardian*, 19 September 2006. Craig S. Smith, "Clashes Disrupt Hungary's Celebration of Anti-Soviet Revolt," *New York Times*, 24 October 2006.

populist parties elsewhere in Europe—anti-EU sentiment, anti-immigrant sentiment, and political distrust—were still not important bases of support for Fidesz. Despite the extraordinary political situation, identification with Fidesz was driven by conventional conservatism rather than by right-wing populist sentiment.

The political crisis touched off by the Gyurcsány scandal was long-lasting. The efforts of right-wing opposition parties—notably, Fidesz and Jobbik—to mobilize opposition to the government exacerbated long-standing social divisions. The Hungarian Guard, a uniformed offshoot of Jobbik founded "to safeguard Hungarian culture and traditions," emerged in 2007. The group's black vests and boots and red and white kerchiefs reminded some Hungarians of the Arrow Cross Party, Nazi collaborators in World War II. "The widely debated question here," one reporter wrote, "is whether the group is a significant or marginal one, and whether it could ultimately prove to be dangerous."[11]

The second column of Table 7.2 documents the bases of identification with Fidesz in the next round of the ESS, in 2009. Notwithstanding the increasing polarization of Hungarian politics, the pattern of support in 2009 was mostly unchanged from 2006–2007. One important shift is that conservative worldviews, which were positively related to identification with Fidesz in the midst of the 2006 protests, no longer attracted people to the party, perhaps because Jobbik became an increasingly appealing alternative home for people with a penchant for order and tradition.[12] Another is that economic dissatisfaction, which probably contributed to identification with Fidesz in 2006–2007, ceased to do so in 2009.[13] Thus, if anything, the bases of support for Fidesz came to look even more conventional in 2009 than they had in 2006–2007, and even less like the typical bases of support for Europe's right-wing populist parties.

11. Nicholas Kulish, "Hungarian Extremists Reflect Discontent, and Add to It," *New York Times*, 24 October 2007.

12. The relationship between worldviews and partisan attachments and voting behavior in Hungary was probably also skewed by the historical association between the Hungarian Socialist Party (MSZP) and the Hungarian Social Workers' Party (MSZMP), which ruled the country during the communist era. Some people who associated the MSZMP with security and tradition may have supported the left-wing MSZP rather than Fidesz or Jobbik.

13. It seems odd to find no effect of economic disaffection on support for a major opposition party. However, this nonfinding may reflect the fact that most Hungarians, regardless of political leanings, were dissatisfied with the state of the economy by 2009. The average level of dissatisfaction on the ESS zero-to-ten scale increased from 7.0 in 2006–2007 to 8.2 in 2009.

In the next parliamentary election, in 2010, popular disaffection stemming from the Gyurcsány scandal upended the Hungarian party system. The governing MSZP lost more than half its popular support (winning just 20.3% of the vote) and more than two-thirds of its seats in the National Assembly. The big winners were the right-wing parties that had spearheaded the protests of 2006 and subsequent opposition efforts. Jobbik won 16.5% of the vote, making it a not-so-distant third in strength behind the faltering MSZP. Meanwhile, the largest opposition party, Fidesz, won 53.1% of the vote (up from 41.6% in 2006) and, crucially, as it turned out, 263 seats—a bare two-thirds majority—in the National Assembly.

In May 2007, a member of the European parliament affiliated with Fidesz had described an "extraordinarily deep cleavage" in Hungarian society defined by "qualitatively different and mutually exclusive visions of justice, of good and evil, of the country's past, and, ultimately of the 'good life'" on the left and the right. He ascribed the political crisis stemming from Prime Minister Gyurcsány's leaked audio recording to the fact that "a Hungarian prime minister with a parliamentary majority is utterly secure in power; there is no way of removing him or her as long as that majority remains in place. This effectively relieves the prime minister of all responsibility towards society; it is for all practical purposes a semi-democratic system."[14]

When Hungarian voters replaced the discredited MSZP with Fidesz in 2010, the shoe was on the other foot—it was Fidesz's prime minister who was "utterly secure in power" and effectively relieved "of all responsibility towards society." Orbán's room to maneuver was significantly increased by the fact that Fidesz's razor-thin two-thirds majority in the National Assembly allowed him to amend the constitution. According to Hungarian political scientist Béla Greskovits,

> FIDESZ's landslide victory at the 2010 parliamentary elections was a foregone conclusion, whereas the fact that the party acquired two-thirds of the mandate was accidental and is best explained by the Hungarian electoral system. However, it is partly due to this accident that the FIDESZ government could move ahead so fast in rolling back Hungarian democracy by using its overwhelming legislative power to infuse all the democratic institutions with authoritarian and illiberal "checks and balances." A far from

14. György Schöpflin, "Democracy, Populism, and the Political Crisis in Hungary," *Eurozine*, 7 May 2007.

complete list of changes includes softening up the legal and procedural constraints of legislation and government; far reaching centralization within the units of public administration; increasing exposure of civil servants to political pressures; stripping the parliamentary opposition off [sic] its remaining opportunities to influence political decisions; serious restrictions of media freedom; and the repeated modification of the electoral law in favor of the incumbent.[15]

The new government engineered the adoption of a declaration retroactively designating the election outcome as a "voting booth revolution" and the beginning of a new political community: "The National Assembly declares that a new social contract was laid down in the April general elections through which the Hungarians decided to create a new system: the National Cooperation System." As Hungarian legal scholar András Pap noted,

The idea of creating a new political community (or even the adoption of a new constitution) was not part of the political campaign in the elections. . . . The ideological declarations in the new Constitution create the impression that these values were actually expressed in the "voting-booth revolution." This retroactive argument logically cannot hold water, due to the very fact that the campaign did not include it.[16]

The statistical analysis presented in the second column of Table 7.1 sheds light on the bases of electoral support for Fidesz in the crucial 2010 election that brought the party to power.[17] It suggests that support for Fidesz was

---

15. Greskovits (2015: 34).

16. Pap (2018: 50–51, 68).

17. This analysis is based on data from 2012–2013 ESS interviews. Given the momentous implications of the election result, there is more than usual reason to worry that an analysis of recalled votes two years after the election may misconstrue the bases of support for Fidesz. However, the analysis presented in Table 7.1 is quite consistent with one based on the round 5 ESS interviews conducted in October and November 2010, six months after the April election and before the government's amended media law and new constitution. The round 5 survey did not tap attitudes toward European integration, but an otherwise-parallel analysis suggests that support for Fidesz in the 2010 election was grounded primarily in conservative ideology (a probit parameter estimate of .237 with a standard error of .022), with modest effects for conservative worldviews (.049 with a standard error of .050), anti-immigrant sentiment (.040 with a standard error of .028), and economic disaffection (.046 with a standard error of .029) and substantial *negative* effects for political distrust (−.118 with a standard error of .026) and dissatisfaction with democracy (−.148 with a standard error of .027). The overstatement of electoral

probably less strongly grounded in conservative ideology than it had been in 2006, with conservative worldviews playing a more important role. The apparent impact of dissatisfaction with democracy reversed, presumably because Fidesz was now in power, while anti-EU and anti-immigrant sentiment still had little or no effect on the party's electoral support. Clearly, the voters who handed Fidesz the keys to Hungarian democracy in 2010 were not motivated by the same impulses driving support for right-wing populist parties in other parts of Europe. And while it may be tempting to interpret the apparent impact of conservative worldviews as reflecting their allegiance to a distinctive vision "of justice, of good and evil, of the country's past, and, ultimately of the 'good life,'" that interpretation is undercut by the fact that identification with Fidesz as late as 2009 was utterly unrelated to conservative worldviews. People with conservative worldviews—unlike ideological conservatives—mostly seem to have gravitated to Fidesz *after* it came to power, not before.

The next major step in the erosion of Hungarian democracy likewise came after, not before, an election. That election, conducted under the new constitution and electoral law stemming from the "new social contract" of 2010, was held in April 2014. An international election-monitoring group reported that it was "efficiently administered and offered voters a diverse choice following an inclusive candidate registration process," but that Fidesz "enjoyed an undue advantage because of restrictive campaign regulations, biased media coverage and campaign activities that blurred the separation between political party and the State." The ruling party also benefited significantly from gerrymandering, and from the enfranchisement of more than half a million ethnic Hungarians living outside the country, 95% of whom voted for Fidesz.[18]

Despite this "undue advantage," Fidesz's vote share in the 2014 election (in combination with its longtime coalition partner, the Christian Democratic People's Party) declined from 53.1% in 2010 to 44.5% in 2014—just a few points higher than before the Gyurcsány scandal, and hardly a rousing popular endorsement of Hungary's "new social contract." Nonetheless, a few months

---

support for Fidesz is similar in both surveys—11.2 percentage points in 2010 and 10.0 percentage points in 2012–2013—and not unlike previous surveys conducted while the party was still in opposition.

18. Office for Democratic Institutions and Human Rights, Limited Election Observation Mission Final Report, 11 July 2014, https://www.osce.org/odihr/elections/hungary/121098. Kim Lane Scheppele, with Miklós Bánkuti and Zoltán Réti, "Legal but Not Fair (Hungary)," 13 April 2014, https://krugman.blogs.nytimes.com/2014/04/13/legal-but-not-fair-hungary/.

after the election, Orbán took further steps to consolidate what he now famously referred to as an "illiberal" democracy in Hungary. "The Hungarian nation is not simply a group of individuals," Orbán said,

> but a community that must be organized, reinforced and in fact constructed. And . . . the new state that we are constructing in Hungary is an illiberal state, a non-liberal state. It does not reject the fundamental principles of liberalism such as freedom and I could list a few more, but it does not make this ideology the central element of state organization, but instead includes a different, special, national approach.[19]

According to Pap,

> "Hungarian illiberal democracy" is neither a construct of constitutional philosophy nor a principle of constitutional design. . . . Despite the political mantra used by Orbán's party of the legitimating force of a parliamentary supermajority being based on a single event of popular vote, the Hungarian model of illiberal democracy cannot be equated with the unfettered freedom of a parliamentary majority to do as it pleases. Rather, it is a tool to channel, define and dominate general political discourse and to provide a discursive framework for political identification and ideologically biased yet divergent and ad hoc legislation.[20]

In the next election, in April 2018, Orbán and Fidesz campaigned primarily on the issues of immigration and foreign meddling. The result was a modest increase in the Fidesz plurality, from 44.5% in 2014 to 48.6%. As in 2014, the party won 133 seats, just enough to have a two-thirds majority in the reconfigured National Assembly. The Hungarian Socialist Party, now in electoral alliance with the "green" party Dialog for Hungary, sunk from 26.2% of the vote in 2014 to just 11.6% in 2018. By default, the right-wing populist party Jobbik (whose vote share increased slightly, from 20.3% to 21.1%) became the largest opposition party. Hungary was in effect a one-and-a-half-party system, with both the one and the half on the right side of the ideological spectrum.

ESS conducted additional rounds of interviews in Hungary in 2012, 2015, 2017, and 2019, as the country steadily descended into the "mildly authoritarian regime" described by Levitsky and Ziblatt and depicted in Figure 7.1. The third and fourth columns of Tables 7.1 and 7.2 document the bases of support for

19. Pap (2018: 59).
20. Pap (2018: 59–60).

Fidesz in these surveys. Those bases of support were, in some respects, markedly different from the patterns observed earlier. Some of the changes reflect the simple fact that Fidesz was now in power rather than in opposition. Dissatisfaction with Hungarian democracy and with the state of the economy, which had registered at least sporadically as sources of support for Fidesz in opposition, became increasingly strongly *negatively* associated with support for Fidesz in power. Distrust of political elites, which never seems to have contributed even slightly to support for Fidesz, also became an increasingly strong marker of opposition. Presumably these changes reflected the natural tendency of incumbent party supporters to approve—and for opponents to disapprove—of how the political system is working. However, the nature and magnitude of these shifts were especially striking in the context of significant erosion of liberal democracy under Fidesz.

Conservative worldviews became a stronger and more consistent predictor of support, and especially of electoral support, for Fidesz after the party's rise to power. Was that because Orbán as prime minister had a louder megaphone for his nationalist rhetoric? The shift did not represent any overall change in the distribution of worldviews in Hungary; the average level of conservatism stood at 5.2 or 5.3 across nine successive ESS waves, while extreme attitudes on both sides of the spectrum were slightly *less* frequent under Fidesz than they had been earlier.

Two other aspects of the statistical results presented in Tables 7.1 and 7.2 significantly undercut conventional understandings of the rise of Fidesz and its broader relevance for the contemporary crisis of democracy in Europe. First, contrary to the notion of democracy succumbing to ideological polarization, the impact of conservative ideology on support for Fidesz *declined* substantially over time—by almost 50% between the 2006–2009 surveys, when the party was in opposition, and subsequent surveys conducted after it began to entrench itself in power. This was not simply a matter of the party expanding its appeal to broader segments of Hungarian society; indeed, electoral support for Fidesz was only modestly higher, and identification with the party was somewhat lower, in the later surveys than it had been in 2006 and 2009.

The other notable finding in Tables 7.1 and 7.2 is that the factors contributing to support for right-wing populist parties elsewhere in Europe (and indeed, for Jobbik in Hungary) only began to contribute significantly to support for Fidesz well after the party embarked on remaking Hungary as an "illiberal democracy." Antipathy to the EU did not begin to register as a significant factor in identification with Fidesz until 2012, and in electoral support not until 2018. Anti-immigrant sentiment, which had played little or no role in earlier support for the party, became increasingly important after the refugee crisis of 2015–2016—and even then, it seemed to matter much more for voting behavior than for identification with Fidesz. While it is possible that the party attracted new support from Hungarians with right-wing populist sentiments, it seems more likely that Orbán's escalating anti-EU and anti-immigrant rhetoric inspired people who were already Fidesz supporters to express attitudes consistent with that rhetoric.[21]

As Greskovits observed, Orbán's "illiberal state building" advanced "in an almost surreptitious way via adoption of a patchwork of worldwide existing legal and institutional 'worst practices' to gradually weaken democracy."[22] It amounted to a substantial assault on what Levitsky and Ziblatt referred to as the "guardrails" of democracy. But it was not an assault that had much to do with the populist sentiment roiling much of the rest of contemporary Europe. Nor does it seem to have been strongly ratified, much less initiated, by ordinary Hungarians.

Poland Learns from Hungary's Example

The erosion of democracy in Poland reveals some striking similarities to events in Hungary. While scholars sometimes write, metaphorically, of regional "waves" or "contagions" of democracy or autocracy, it is often difficult to pin down the specific processes by which developments in one country affect others. In this case, historical and cultural parallels between the two countries are suggestive, while simply eyeballing the trends in expert ratings of the quality of liberal democracy in Hungary and Poland in Figure 7.1 reinforces the impression that these were not unrelated instances of democratic backsliding. But even more conclusively, we have the testimony of the key figure in the erosion of Polish democracy, Law and Justice party chairman Jaroslaw Kaczynski. "You have given an example," Kaczynski told his Hungarian counterpart Orbán, "and we are learning from your example."[23]

21. On the tendency of partisan loyalties to shape citizens' policy preferences, see (for example) Lenz (2012).

22. Greskovits (2015: 30).

23. Patrick Kingsley, "As West Fears the Rise of Autocrats, Hungary Shows What's Possible," *New York Times*, 10 February 2018.

The relevance of the Hungarian example rested in part on similarities between the two countries' party systems. The first parliamentary election in postcommunist Poland, in 1991, featured 111 parties, 29 of which earned representation in the Sejm. But subsequent elections produced a marked consolidation, with most voters gravitating to Solidarity Electoral Action (AWS), the political successor to the communist-era Solidarity trade union, or to the Democratic Left Alliance, a conglomeration of smaller social democratic parties.

AWS won the 1997 election, but the resulting government was hamstrung by high unemployment, corruption scandals, and the defection of a key coalition partner. In the run-up to the 2001 election, the flagging AWS was further weakened by the emergence of new parties appealing to its former adherents—most notably, the center-right Civic Platform (PO) and conservative Law and Justice Party (PiS). The election produced a landslide for the Democratic Left Alliance, while AWS won less than 6% of the vote and no seats. With the disintegration of AWS, the center and right of the Polish party system were once again fragmented, with five parties winning between 8% and 13% of the vote, including Civic Platform (12.7%), the agrarian nationalist party Self-Defense (10.2%), Law and Justice (9.5%), and the conservative Catholic (and anti-EU) League of Polish Families (7.9%).

Despite its electoral dominance, the Democratic Left Alliance fared no better in government than AWS had. It, too, was plagued by high unemployment and corruption scandals. Prime Minister Leszek Miller resigned in 2004, and a new party leader emerged just four months before the next election in September 2005 election. But shuffling the deck chairs could not prevent an electoral collapse; the party's vote share fell to just 11.3%, as voters flocked in roughly equal numbers to Law and Justice (27.0%) and Civic Platform (24.1%).

The two winning parties, with 51% of the popular vote and 63% of the seats in the Sejm, were expected to form a governing coalition, but negotiations broke down over the distribution of key cabinet portfolios. Instead, Law and Justice formed a minority government supported by two minor parties (and, later, formal coalition partners), Self-Defense and the League of Polish Families.

The 2005 election, and the subsequent failure of the two leading parties to form a governing coalition, inaugurated a decade of relatively stable competition between the Law and Justice party and Civic Platform. The coalition government led by Law and Justice was derailed by a major corruption scandal involving the Self-Defense party leader, resulting in early parliamentary elections in 2007. Unlike its two predecessors in government, AWS and the Democratic Left Alliance, Law and Justice weathered the political storm, even increasing its vote share from 27% in 2005 to 32.1% in 2007. However, Civic Platform capitalized on the scandal, and the collapse of Self-Defense, by winning 41.5% of the vote and a substantial plurality of seats in the Sejm. With no other party winning as much as 15% of the vote, Civic Platform leader Donald Tusk recruited the Polish People's Party as a junior partner in a new coalition government.

Poland under Civic Platform survived the early stages of the Euro-crisis in good economic shape, and the next election in 2011 marked a first in modern Polish electoral history: the incumbent government was reelected. Civic Platform's vote share was down slightly, from 41.5% to 39.2%, but Law and Justice's vote share also declined slightly, from 32.1% to 29.9%. The once-dominant Democratic Left Alliance won just 8.2% of the vote. Tusk, now eight years into his party leadership, announced that Civic Platform would continue its governing coalition with the Polish People's Party. Poland, it seemed, was becoming an increasingly conventional parliamentary democracy, albeit with its major parties representing the political center and right.

The bases of electoral support for Law and Justice in this period are detailed in the first three columns of Table 7.3. In 2005, as Law and Justice vied with Civic Platform to exploit the collapse of the Democratic Left Alliance, the party relied primarily on conservative ideology and worldviews. Anti-EU sentiment was a modest factor in support for Law and Justice, while anti-immigrant sentiment had no effect. Political distrust and dissatisfaction with democracy were negatively related to support for Law and Justice, though that relationship presumably reflects the fact that the party was governing Poland by the time of the 2006 ESS interviews. In the 2008–2015 surveys, after Civic Platform returned to power in 2007, political distrust, dissatisfaction with democracy, and economic disaffection were all notably higher among Law and Justice supporters. Anti-EU sentiment continued to play a modest role in reported electoral support for Law and Justice, while anti-immigrant sentiment also began to register as a significant factor in the party's support; but the main driving forces throughout this period were conservative ideology and, to a lesser extent, conservative worldviews.

The first column of Table 7.4 reports the results of a parallel analysis of identification with the Law and Justice party from 2008 through 2013. It is striking here that, while Law and Justice was winning almost one-third of the

TABLE 7.3. Bases of Electoral Support for Law and Justice Party, 2005–2015

	2006 survey (2005 election)	2008–2009 survey (2007 election)	2012–2015 surveys (2011 election)	2016–2019 surveys (2015 election)
Conservative ideology	.218	.218	.252	.245
	(.021)	(.021)	(.016)	(.018)
Conservative worldview	.174	.111	.157	.165
	(.047)	(.044)	(.035)	(.036)
Anti-EU sentiment	.038	.043	.020	.031
	(.019)	(.018)	(.014)	(.014)
Anti-immigrant sentiment	−.018	.048	.048	.138
	(.024)	(.026)	(.017)	(.020)
Political distrust	−.054	.042	.059	−.109
	(.023)	(.026)	(.019)	(.019)
Dissatisfaction with democracy	−.034	.060	.072	−.118
	(.021)	(.023)	(.018)	(.018)
Economic dissatisfaction	.030	.069	.051	−.013
	(.022)	(.024)	(.019)	(.022)
Pseudo-R^2	.12	.13	.20	.33
N	1,076	1,181	2,358	2,153

Note: Probit regression parameter estimates (with standard errors in parentheses). Fixed effects for survey rounds are included in the analyses but not shown. Eligible voters post-stratified by vote choice.

parliamentary votes in this period, only about 8% of Poles reported feeling "close" to the party.[24] This more stringent definition of support produces an even clearer picture of the bases of the Law and Justice party's appeal. That appeal was grounded first and foremost in conservative ideology, and to a lesser extent in conservative worldviews. Dissatisfaction with the economy was important as well—not surprisingly, since Law and Justice was Poland's primary opposition party throughout this period. Antipathy to immigrants

24. Part of the discrepancy in percentages reflects the fact that only 64% of Poles in these surveys reported voting. But even in absolute numbers, more than twice as many respondents in these three ESS rounds reported voting for Law and Justice (1,044) as reported feeling "close" to the party (436).

TABLE 7.4. Bases of Identification with Law and Justice Party before and after Poland's 2015 Election

	2008–2013	2015 (pre-election)	2016–2017	2018–2019
Conservative ideology	.275	.313	.261	.358
	(.018)	(.029)	(.031)	(.036)
Conservative worldview	.108	.173	.147	.162
	(.031)	(.048)	(.049)	(.051)
Anti-EU sentiment	.023	−.022	.057	.033
	(.015)	(.020)	(.019)	(.022)
Anti-immigrant sentiment	.017	.016	.043	.081
	(.016)	(.032)	(.028)	(.030)
Political distrust	−.008	−.011	−.171	−.157
	(.017)	(.027)	(.025)	(.030)
Dissatisfaction with democracy	.026	.043	−.112	−.083
	(.016)	(.028)	(.030)	(.034)
Economic dissatisfaction	.083	.038	−.021	−.053
	(.018)	(.029)	(.029)	(.041)
Pseudo-R²	.15	.18	.28	.33
N	5,026	1,493	1,566	1,295

Note: Ordered probit regression parameter estimates (with standard errors in parentheses). Multiple response thresholds and fixed effects for survey rounds are estimated but not shown. Eligible voters post-stratified by vote choice.

and to the EU had no significant impact on identification with the party; nor did political distrust or dissatisfaction with democracy.

In the spring of 2015, when ESS round 7 interviews in Poland got underway, it looked like Civic Platform might win a third consecutive term. But support for the party dropped precipitously that summer "when several government officials were caught making profane and impolitic comments on illegal wiretaps"—a striking echo of the events leading to the demise of MSZP in Hungary.[25] On Election Day, in late October, Civic Platform's vote share fell to 24.1%, while the Law and Justice party's share surged to 37.6%. The latter

25. As ESS fieldwork stretched from April through the summer, Poles' average distrust of politicians and parliament increased significantly, by .16 points per month on the zero-to-ten scale. Dissatisfaction with the economy increased at a similar rate.

figure was enough to secure 235 of 460 seats in the Sejm, making Law and Justice the first party in Poland's postcommunist era to win an absolute majority of seats. In stark contrast, the Democratic Left Alliance, now merged with several other parties in a United Left, won less than 8% of the votes and thus, under Poland's electoral rules, no parliamentary representation.[26]

In light of subsequent developments, it is essential to note that the 2015 election outcome was not a popular ratification of an even mildly authoritarian program. According to a BBC News analyst,

> Law and Justice won big because they offered simple, concrete policies for the many in Poland that feel untouched by the country's impressive economic growth. It offered higher child care benefits and tax breaks for the less well-off. After eight years in office many Poles had grown weary of the governing centrist Civic Platform's unfulfilled promises, scandals and what was perceived by some to be an aloof attitude. Law and Justice also stuck with its winning formula of presenting a more moderate face than its rather combative leader Jaroslaw Kaczynski. That moderate face belongs to Beata Szydlo, a 52-year-old miner's daughter and avid reader, who will become the country's next prime minister.[27]

A subsequent scholarly assessment echoed this account, noting that Law and Justice "softened its image. It placed signs of authoritarian leanings as well as controversial personalities (including Jaroslaw Kaczynski himself) out of public view. Running on the slogan 'Good Change,' PiS leaders called for compassionate conservatism, and sought to offer undecided voters an alternative to the 'boring' PO."[28]

The ESS round 7 interviews provide an invaluable record of popular support for the Law and Justice party on the eve of its return to power five months later. The bases of identification with the party in that survey are detailed in the second column of Table 7.4. They provide little evidence of popular enthusiasm for an authoritarian turn. Perhaps most obviously, less than 12% of Poles reported feeling close to the Law and Justice party in spring 2015—fewer than

26. Rick Lyman, "Right-Wing Party Roars Back in Polish Elections," *New York Times*, 25 October 2015. Dorota Bartyzel and Piotr Skolimowski, "Poland Hands Unprecedented Ballot Win to Conservative Party," Bloomberg, 25 October 2015.

27. Adam Easton, "Poland Elections: Conservatives Secure Decisive Win," BBC News, 26 October 2015.

28. Fomina and Kucharczyk (2016: 60–61).

identified with the Swiss and Danish People's Parties, and just half the level of identification with Fidesz in Hungary on the eve of its 2010 triumph. Law and Justice identifiers were distinguished primarily by conservative ideology and conservative worldviews—the same factors that had predicted identification with the party for almost a decade, though the impact of conservative world-views seems to have increased in 2015. Dissatisfactions with democracy and with the economy contributed only modestly to identification with Law and Justice, while the main drivers of support for populist parties elsewhere in Europe seem to have had remarkably little traction; neither anti-EU sentiment nor anti-immigrant sentiment nor distrust of political elites contributed to identification with Law and Justice.

Notwithstanding the limited breadth of popular support for Law and Justice, Poland's new leaders did not hesitate to translate their parliamentary majority into an assault on checks and balances modeled on Orbán's in Hungary. Within two months of the election, the Sejm passed a law reorganizing the Constitutional Court, and early the next year it passed a law initiating the process of giving the government full control of state radio and television. Later, the formerly independent National Council of the Judiciary was packed with party loyalists, and Polish judges were prohibited from implementing rulings by the European Court of Justice. Poland, like Hungary, was consolidating an "illiberal democracy."[29]

In the wake of these moves, a new grassroots organization called the Committee for the Defense of Democracy (KOD) organized a string of successful antigovernment protests. Kaczynski denounced the participants as "Poles of the worse sort," but opinion polls recorded more favorable views of KOD than of any political party, including Law and Justice. Moreover, "many who said that they now backed the KOD also said that they had voted for Law and Justice. . . . Apparently some PiS voters supported many PiS election pledges but were not prepared for the party's dismantling of Poland's democratic institutions."[30]

As in Hungary, the electoral response to the Law and Justice party's power grab was mixed. In 2019 parliamentary elections, Law and Justice's vote share increased by six percentage points, but the party lost seats and control of the

29. Laurent Pech and R. Daniel Kelemen, "If You Think the U.S. Is Having a Constitutional Crisis, You Should See What Is Happening in Poland," *Washington Post*, 25 January 2020.

30. Fomina and Kucharczyk (2016: 63–64).

Senate. In the 2020 presidential election, incumbent Andrzej Duda won 51% of the runoff vote—virtually identical to the 51.5% he had won five years earlier.

In the ESS data, the proportion of Poles who said they felt close to the Law and Justice party gradually increased from 11% in 2015 to 17% in 2018–2019. At the same time, the bases of that support, summarized in the third and fourth columns of Table 7.4, shifted in ways that parallel the shift in support for Fidesz in Hungary. Although conservative ideology and worldviews remained the most important bases of identification with the Law and Justice party, antipathy to immigrants now began to register as a significant factor in support for the party—a signal, perhaps, of increasing openness to nationalist appeals of the sort that seemed to be working for Orbán in Hungary. In addition, Poles who felt close to the Law and Justice party now reported significantly greater levels of satisfaction with democracy and trust in parliament and politicians. Presumably, these attitudes were both a cause and an effect of identification with the Law and Justice party. One way or another, the former Law and Justice supporters who were "not prepared for the party's dismantling of Poland's democratic institutions" were now, apparently, gone.

Bases of Public Acquiescence to Democratic Backsliding

In a comparative analysis of 20th-century breakdowns of democracy, political scientist Nancy Bermeo noted that "ordinary people generally were guilty of remaining passive when dictators actually attempted to seize power." While they "generally did not polarize and mobilize in support of dictatorship, they did not immediately mobilize in defense of democracy either." With due allowance for the significant distinction between "dictatorship" and the "mildly authoritarian regimes" considered here, the same might be said of contemporary Hungary and Poland. While there has certainly been some mobilization of opposition to the ruling parties in both countries, neither has faced massive resistance; indeed, both have enjoyed substantial public support. As political scientist Milan Svolik has observed, "The so-called 'authoritarian populists' appear to be truly popular."[31]

The acquiescence of ordinary Hungarians and Poles to the erosion of democracy has not been much remarked upon. Is it merely a product of government propaganda and escalating restrictions on independent media? A reflection of emotional appeals to national identity? Government largesse to key

31. Bermeo (2003: 222, 235); Svolik (2019: 21).

TABLE 7.5. Subjective Well-Being in Hungary before and after the 2010 Election of Fidesz

	2002–2007	2009	2010–2015	2017–2019	Δ 2009 to 2019
Satisfaction with the economy	3.37 (.04)	1.70 (.05)	3.45 (.03)	4.78 (.04)	+3.04 (.08)
Satisfaction with the national government	3.53 (.05)	1.81 (.07)	3.84 (.04)	4.54 (.05)	+2.70 (.10)
Trust in parliament and politicians	3.47 (.04)	2.19 (.06)	3.56 (.03)	4.19 (.05)	+2.10 (.09)
Satisfaction with democracy	4.15 (.04)	2.89 (.08)	4.35 (.04)	4.68 (.05)	+1.64 (.11)
State of health services	3.43 (.04)	3.78 (.08)	3.76 (.03)	3.85 (.05)	−.03 (.10)
State of education	4.70 (.04)	4.50 (.07)	4.76 (.03)	4.87 (.05)	+.34 (.10)
Satisfaction with life as a whole	5.56 (.05)	5.23 (.08)	5.76 (.03)	6.29 (.04)	+.95 (.10)

Note: Average values (with standard errors in parentheses).

segments of the electorate?[32] While each of these factors is probably relevant, the ESS survey data strongly suggest that there is more to it than that.

Table 7.5 summarizes public opinion in Hungary in four distinct periods: (1) from 2002 through 2007, under the MSZP (Socialist) government; (2) in 2009, on the eve of Fidesz's electoral breakthrough; (3) in the first five years of democratic backsliding under Orbán; and (4) in the 2017 and 2019 ESS rounds. The entries are average responses for the entire population, not just Fidesz supporters. The final column shows changes in public sentiment from 2009, the year before Orbán's election, to 2019.

These data document a remarkable transformation of the social and political climate of Hungary. Average satisfaction with the economy increased by three points on the zero-to-ten scale between 2009 and 2019, a massive

32. Quentin Ariès, "Europe's Failure to Protect Liberty in Hungary," *Atlantic*, 29 December 2019. Una Hajdari, "The Demagogue's Cocktail of Victimhood and Strength," *Atlantic*, 31 December 2019. Gergely Szakacs, "As Polls Tighten, Hungary's Orban Steps Up Pre-Election Spending," Reuters, 4 February 2021.

improvement. Satisfaction with the national government improved almost as much. Trust in parliament and politicians increased by more than two points, and even satisfaction with "the way democracy works in Hungary" increased dramatically. Perhaps most impressively, the average level of satisfaction with "life as a whole nowadays" increased by almost a full point on the ten-point scale. Moreover, by every one of these indicators, life in Hungary continued to improve over the course of Orbán's tenure.[33]

Hungarians' subjective well-being was at a low ebb in 2009, more than two years into the crisis set off by the Gyurcsány scandal and just months after the government accepted a humiliating €15 billion bailout from the EU, IMF, and World Bank.[34] But even if they took the earlier, less dire years of MSZP rule as a psychological baseline, Hungarians would have considered themselves significantly better off—economically, socially, and politically—under Fidesz, and increasingly so as Orbán became more entrenched.

Poland in the spring of 2015, five months before the election that brought the Law and Justice party to power, was not in a crisis comparable to Hungary's in 2009. The various indicators of subjective well-being in the 2015 ESS data, reported in the second column of Table 7.6, are roughly comparable to the average levels from the previous decade reported in the first column of the table. Nonetheless, the two surveys conducted since Jaroslaw Kaczynski began to follow Viktor Orbán's example of "illiberal" entrenchment show improvements in well-being smaller in magnitude but similar in flavor to those in Hungary under Orbán. Here, too, the most striking improvement—1.7 points on the zero-to-ten scale from 2015 to 2019—was in satisfaction with the economy. Here, too, satisfaction with the government increased almost as much, while trust in parliament and politicians and satisfaction with democracy also increased by a full point each. Unlike in Hungary, ratings of the state of health services and education also improved markedly, though satisfaction with life as a whole remained essentially unchanged.

Of course, these improvements in social conditions were unevenly distributed. Nonetheless, public contentment was widespread and multifaceted. In

33. The rates of improvement under Fidesz range from .02 points per year for satisfaction with democracy to .20 points per year for satisfaction with the economy.

34. Kate Connolly and Ian Traynor, "Hungary Receives Rescue Package, with Strings Attached," *Guardian*, 29 October 2008. "Hungary Offered a Tripartite Bailout—with Strings," *Forbes*, 29 October 2008, https://www.forbes.com/2008/10/29/hungary-imf-aid-markets-economy-cx_vr_1029markets7.html#4ae90d1c3404.

TABLE 7.6. Subjective Well-Being in Poland before and after the 2015 Election of the Law and Justice Party

	2002–2013	2015 (pre-election)	2016–2017	2018–2019	Δ 2015 to 2019
Satisfaction with the economy	3.86 (.02)	4.05 (.05)	4.84 (.05)	5.76 (.06)	+1.72 (.08)
Satisfaction with the national government	3.21 (.02)	3.07 (.05)	4.04 (.07)	4.64 (.07)	+1.57 (.09)
Trust in parliament and politicians	2.63 (.02)	2.40 (.05)	2.93 (.05)	3.43 (.06)	+1.03 (.08)
Satisfaction with democracy	4.47 (.02)	4.37 (.06)	4.66 (.06)	5.41 (.07)	+1.04 (.09)
State of health services	3.64 (.02)	3.44 (.06)	3.91 (.06)	4.25 (.06)	+.81 (.08)
State of education	5.35 (.02)	5.41 (.06)	5.69 (.06)	6.03 (.06)	+.62 (.09)
Satisfaction with life as a whole	6.61 (.02)	6.94 (.06)	7.14 (.05)	7.06 (.05)	+.12 (.08)

Note: Average values (with standard errors in parentheses).

Pew Research Center surveys, for example, 85% of Poles in 2019 approved of their country's transitions to a market economy and to a multiparty system— both substantial increases from 2009. Two-thirds said that "ordinary people have benefited" a great deal or a fair amount from the transitions, a 26-point increase from 2009. The corresponding shifts in Hungary were similar in magnitude.[35]

By all these measures, ordinary Hungarians and Poles flourished, even as expert observers recorded substantial declines in the quality of their democracies. Under the circumstances, it is hardly surprising that most people seemed

35. Ghodsee and Orenstein (2021: 125–129). From 2009 to 2019, approval of the change to a multiparty system increased from 70% to 85% in Poland and from 56% to 72% in Hungary. Approval of the change to a market economy increased from 71% to 85% in Poland and from 46% to 70% in Hungary. Perceptions that ordinary people benefited from these changes increased from 42% to 68% in Poland and from 17% to 41% in Hungary. Comparable data from other postcommunist countries generally revealed less contentment with the results of the economic and political transitions from communism, and little or no improvement in the decade following the Euro-crisis.

to accommodate themselves—after the fact—to Orbán's and Kaczynski's "illiberal" entrenchments. And even if they were less troubled by the erosion of checks and balances than democratic theorists might wish, it is very hard to see them as active proponents of authoritarianism, much less as its primary agents. They went about their political lives in much the way that democratic citizens generally do, focusing primarily on their own economic and social well-being and judging their political leaders accordingly.[36]

Lessons for Europe?

Is populism a threat to the "supposedly stable and tolerant democracies" of contemporary Europe? My brief summary of the course of democratic backsliding in Hungary and Poland suggests that it is probably a mistake to extrapolate from these cases to other parts of Europe where right-wing populist parties have established a foothold. For one thing, Fidesz in Hungary and the Law and Justice party in Poland were not typical right-wing populist parties. Indeed, the evidence from surveys conducted on the eve of their rise to power suggests that the bases of their popular support had rather little in common with "the far right" in Austria or France or "extremists" in Sweden or Germany.

One obvious point of difference is that both Viktor Orbán in Hungary and Jaroslaw Kaczynski in Poland had extensive histories as mainstream conservative political leaders. In a 2012 lecture, a leading scholar of populism cited Orbán and Kaczynski, along with Silvio Berlusconi in Italy, as illustrations of the fact that "the main threats to liberal democracy have come from the political mainstream rather than the political extremes." The Global Populism Database, which provides content analyses of speeches by political leaders in many countries, characterized Orbán's rhetoric as "somewhat populist" in 2010–2014 and 2014–2018, but "not populist" in his previous stint as Hungary's prime minister in 1998–2002. Kaczynski's rhetoric was likewise classified as "not populist" when he served as prime minister in 2006–2007.[37] These assessments, as well as contemporaneous accounts of the key election campaigns in Hungary in 2010 and Poland in 2015, raise significant doubts about whether

36. On the ubiquity of so-called retrospective voting, even in the fraught political climate of the Great Depression, see Achen and Bartels (2016: chaps. 5–7). On material bases of support for autocratic regimes, see Rosenfeld (2021).

37. Mudde (2013: 15). Kirk A. Hawkins et al., The Global Populism Database, https://populism.byu.edu/Pages/Data.

ordinary Hungarians and Poles were really voting for populism, much less for autocracy, when they handed power to their "populist leaders."

First and foremost, these voters seemed to be voting *against* discredited incumbent parties. There is a strong tendency in democratic politics for incumbent parties to lose support over time.[38] Perhaps the Poles who preferred "good change" to "boring" incumbency in 2015 should have been wary of the Law and Justice party's authoritarian proclivities. The initiatives it had pursued the last time it held power, in 2006–2007, included attempts to ban marches by pro-gay activists and to bolster political control of journalists and prosecutors. But that had been eight years earlier, with a mostly different cast of characters, and in the context of a coalition government with two socially conservative parties whose "democratic credentials" were "very much in doubt." *This* was a party led by a moderate "miner's daughter and avid reader."[39]

While the ruling parties that presided over the erosion of democracy in Hungary and Poland did not look much like populist parties elsewhere in Europe, neither did the economic and social conditions in those countries fit the stereotypes often associated with the "crisis of democracy" in contemporary Europe. In stark contrast to the familiar notion of economic and social stagnation pushing disgruntled masses into the arms of authoritarian leaders, these were among the more stable and prosperous places in Central and Eastern Europe. Despite some egregious mismanagement, the economy of Hungary (as measured by real GDP per capita) grew by 25% in the decade leading up to the election of Viktor Orbán in 2010. Poland's economy grew by a spectacular 45% in the decade leading up to the Law and Justice party's election in 2015. The "mildly authoritarian regimes" that emerged in these countries after 2010 were not products of widespread economic distress.

Some scholars of Western European politics have focused on the "hollowing out" of popular politics and civil society as a worrisome indicator of democratic decline. However, that line of analysis seems to be similarly unhelpful in accounting for developments in Hungary and Poland. Indeed, applying a

38. Lowell (1898); Stokes and Iversen (1962); Mueller (1973: chap. 9); Bartels (1998).

39. Albertazzi and Mueller (2013: 358–361). According to these authors, the League of Polish Families' youth wing "was staffed by large numbers of skinheads, quite open about their Nazi sympathies and responsible for attacks against gay and feminist groups, members of ethnic minorities and others," while Self-Defence had been organized in the early 1990s "as a militia aimed at defending farmers from debt collectors and it had not been a stranger to violence in the past." Adam Easton, "Poland Elections: Conservatives Secure Decisive Win," BBC News, 26 October 2015.

variety of indicators of "hollowing-out" to ten East Central European democracies in the first decade of the 21st century, Greskovits described Hungary as "a vibrant and mobilized civil society," the *least* "hollowed" among them. He concluded that "what really matters for the solidity or backsliding of democracy is not the vibrancy vs hollowness of the system, or the strength vs weakness of civil society per se. What seems to make the difference is the *liberal/democratic rather than illiberal/authoritarian ideology and purpose of the actors* who mobilize civil society organizations and their members for political participation." For example, the Catholic Church has been a key pillar of civil society in Hungary and Poland, and "a powerful influence" on both Fidesz and the Law and Justice party. However, the result has been that "both seek to preserve religious and traditional beliefs in what they view as an increasingly liberal and secular world."[40]

While Hungary and Poland were hardly "hollowed out" civil societies, it is true that citizens' trust in political leaders and institutions in these countries was quite low, and with good reason.[41] In Hungary, the rise of Fidesz to majority status was facilitated by Prime Minister Gyurcsány's remarkable 2006 admission of egregious deceit and bad faith. In Poland, governments of the center, left, and right successively got bogged down in major corruption scandals. But there is remarkably little evidence in the ESS data that political distrust *produced* support for Fidesz or for the Law and Justice party. Indeed, the statistical analyses reported in Tables 7.2 and 7.4 suggest that identification with both parties on the eve of their electoral breakthroughs was unrelated or, if anything, *negatively* related to political distrust. After these parties were in power, their supporters and the broader public became more trusting of parliament and politicians.

Nor is there much support for the notion that these democracies succumbed to ideological polarization. In a recent comparative analysis of democratic decline in Hungary, Turkey, and Venezuela, Robert Kaufman and Stephan Haggard argued that all three countries "experienced reinforcing cycles of democratic dysfunction, social polarization, and declining support

40. Mair (2013); Greskovits (2015: 32–35). Here, too, there is a strong parallel with Bermeo's (2003: 232) conclusion that democratic breakdowns in 20th-century Europe and Latin America often occurred "where civil society was relatively *dense*." Eatwell and Goodwin (2018: 142).

41. Analyzing the success of populist parties in 27 countries in Europe and the Americas, Castanho Silva (2019: 280) concluded that "elite collusion and corrupt governments are the most important factors behind the rise of populists."

for moderate, democratic political forces and institutions. These stresses on democratic rule were compounded by polarizing political appeals that cast competitors as enemies and even existential threats to the nation and the people. . . . Once in office, Orbán's effort to further polarize the electorate continued, with attacks on the EU, on outsiders such as George Soros, and a full-throated exploitation of the European migrant crisis to stoke racial and ethnic anxiety."[42]

While Orbán has indeed turned to "polarizing political appeals" to maintain himself in power, evidence from public opinion surveys provides rather little evidence that polarization was a key factor in his rise. In 2009, on the eve of the election that propelled him to power, ideological polarization in Hungary was higher than in most other European countries, but comparable to levels in France and Sweden, and significantly lower than in Czechia and Slovenia. Moreover, while the level of ideological polarization in Hungary has subsequently increased by about 11%, that increase mostly reflects shifts to the political left, not the right—hardly a testament to the potency of Orbán's "polarizing political appeals."[43] Similarly in Poland, ideological polarization was only moderately high on the eve of the Law and Justice party's election in 2015, though it subsequently increased (by about 7%, reflecting slight shifts to both the left and the right on the ideological spectrum).[44]

Finally, the electoral systems of Hungary and Poland provided opportunities for authoritarian consolidation of power that are absent in most of Europe. In the 2010 election that put Orbán in power in Hungary, Fidesz's 53.1% of the vote produced a two-thirds majority in the National Assembly, allowing the party to unilaterally amend the constitution. In the crucial 2015 election in Poland, Law and Justice's 37.6% of the vote produced an absolute majority of seats in the Sejm. As with the election of Donald Trump in the United States,

42. Kaufman and Haggard (2019: 419–420).

43. The standard deviation of left-right placements in Hungary increased from 2.29 in 2009 to 2.55 by 2019. The proportion of respondents placing themselves at 0, 1, or 2 on the zero-to-ten left-right scale increased from 8.7% to 13.4% (an estimated 4.7% increase with a standard error of 1.3), while the proportion placing themselves at 8, 9, or 10 *decreased* from 21.5% to 20.5% (an estimated 1.0% decrease with a standard error of 1.8).

44. The standard deviation of left-right placements in Poland increased from 2.32 in 2015 to 2.42 in 2016–2017 and 2.47 in 2018–2019. The proportion of respondents placing themselves at 0, 1, or 2 on the zero-to-ten scale increased from 7.9% to 9.3% (an estimated 1.4% increase with a standard error of 1.1), while the proportion placing themselves at 8, 9, or 10 increased from 24.3% to 25.5% (an estimated 1.2% increase with a standard error of 1.7).

these were instances in which popular support for authoritarian nationalism was greatly magnified in two distinct respects—first, by co-opting the existing support of established mainstream conservative parties, and second, by benefiting from significant disproportionality in the translation of electoral support into political authority. But unlike in the United States, with its famously fragmented system of government, modest election victories gave would-be autocrats in Hungary and Poland "overwhelming legislative power to infuse all the democratic institutions with authoritarian and illiberal 'checks and balances.'" There are few places in Europe where control over the levers of power is at once so complete and so accidental.[45]

Summary

In her historical survey of breakdowns of democracy, Nancy Bermeo argued that political elites rather than ordinary citizens are generally "the key actors" in precipitating transitions from democracy to dictatorship. She wrote,

> Even profound polarization—in both public and private space—is never, in itself, a sufficient condition for regime collapse. Democracies will only collapse if actors deliberately disassemble them, and the key actors in this disassembling process are political elites. . . . There were a few cases where anti-democratic movements became electorally successful political parties, but in the vast majority of our cases, voters did not choose dictatorship at the ballot box.[46]

So, too, in contemporary Hungary and Poland voters did not choose even "mildly authoritarian" regimes at the ballot box—at least not at first. Rather, they chose the only readily available alternatives to unsatisfactory incumbent governments, only to have their votes rather transparently trumped up by the winners into a "voting booth revolution" justifying "a new social contract" expanding the power of the ruling party at the expense of the courts, the media, and other political actors. As with the cases Bermeo examined, "the culpability for democracy's demise lay overwhelmingly with political elites."[47]

---

45. Lee (2020); Greskovits (2015: 34).
46. Bermeo (2003: 234, 222).
47. Bermeo (2003: 221).

There is a parallel here to political scientist Susan Stokes's account of "neo-liberalism by surprise" in late 20th-century Latin America.[48] However, in that context, avowedly left-wing governments faced significant economic and political pressures to pursue neoliberal policies once in office. The "illiberalism by surprise" pursued by Orbán in Hungary beginning in 2010 and by Kaczynski in Poland beginning in 2015 seems to have been much more a matter of choice than of duress. They engineered the dismantling of democratic checks and balances not in response to any overwhelming external or internal pressures, but simply because they could.

To attribute these developments to "populism" is a misunderstanding of the bases of popular support for Fidesz in Hungary and the Law and Justice party in Poland. But more broadly, and more profoundly, it is a misunderstanding of the role of ordinary citizens in democratic politics.

48. Stokes (2001).

8

Public Opinion and
Democratic Politics

WHY HAVE SO MANY WELL-INFORMED observers been so wrong about the basic contours of public opinion in contemporary Europe? Almost a century after Walter Lippmann wrote of "immense confusions in the current theory of democracy which frustrate and pervert its action," we are still struggling to learn to "think of public opinion as it is, and not as the fictitious power we have assumed it to be."[1]

Lippmann's observation regarding the "fictitious power" of public opinion in thinking about democracy was not new even in 1925, and it has been repeated periodically over the past century. Assessing the burgeoning scholarly subfield of public opinion research in the years after World War II, the eminent American political scientist V. O. Key Jr. regretted that, for all its "methodological virtuosity," this was research "whose relevance for the workings of the governmental system is not always apparent." Another leading midcentury American scholar, E. E. Schattschneider, complained that much writing about democratic politics was "essentially simplistic, based on a tremendously exaggerated notion of the immediacy and urgency of the connection of public opinion and events."[2]

The increasing ubiquity of opinion polls and the continuing "democratization" of popular political culture have only reinforced the centrality of public opinion in contemporary thinking about democracy, making it the pre-

---

1. Lippmann (1925: 200).
2. Lowell (1913); Key (1961: vii); Schattschneider (1960: 130).

sumptive cause of every observed effect.[3] If right-wing populist parties are gaining footholds in European parliaments, it must be because "'populist' sentiments are exploding." If immigration is "tearing Europe apart," it must be because anti-immigrant opinion is on the rise. If political elites are embroiled in squabbles about European integration, there must be "a backlash against the EU." And if democratic systems succumb to backsliding, it must be because "support for democracy as a system of government has weakened."

The evidence presented in this book casts considerable doubt on "the immediacy and urgency of the connection of public opinion and events" in contemporary Europe, to use Schattschneider's phrase. Significant developments are afoot—struggles to deal with momentous economic, environmental, public health, and security challenges, social frictions stemming from immigration, increased electoral support for populist parties in some countries, even disturbing erosion of democratic checks and balances. But none of these developments is immediately or urgently connected to shifts in public opinion, either in Europe as a whole or in specific countries.

Public Opinion as It Is

Table 8.1 provides a broad summary of shifts in European public opinion over the course of the 21st century. As in the more detailed analyses presented in earlier chapters, I distinguish three periods covered by the European Social Survey data: the pre-crisis period (2002–2007), the crisis period (2008–2013), and the post-crisis period (2014–2019). The final column shows the change in overall opinion between the pre-crisis and post-crisis periods.

Six of the ten indicators of public attitudes reported in the table are essentially unchanged from the pre-crisis period to the post-crisis period, with shifts in average opinion that are substantively small (less than 0.2 on each zero-to-ten scale) and statistically indistinguishable from zero. In two of these cases, satisfaction with the incumbent government and trust in parliament and politicians, opinion dipped during the economic crisis but then recovered completely. In other cases, including support for further European integration and satisfaction with democracy, public opinion was essentially stable even during the crisis.

---

3. On the power of popular sovereignty in thinking about democracy, see Achen and Bartels (2016: chaps. 1–3).

TABLE 8.1. Public Opinion in Europe before, during, and after the Economic Crisis

	2002–2007	2008–2013	2014–2019	Change
Conservative worldview	5.12	5.12	5.08	−.03
	(.03)	(.01)	(.02)	(.04)
Right-wing ideology	4.91	4.97	4.94	+.03
	(.03)	(.02)	(.03)	(.04)
Support for redistribution	6.99	7.13	7.19	+.20
	(.07)	(.04)	(.06)	(.10)
Support for immigration	5.16	5.34	5.54	+.39
	(.07)	(.06)	(.08)	(.11)
Support for European integration	5.16	5.17	5.21	+.05
	(.10)	(.07)	(.07)	(.12)
Satisfaction with national economy	4.34	3.98	4.90	+.56
	(.22)	(.13)	(.14)	(.26)
Satisfaction with incumbent government	4.03	3.88	4.17	+.13
	(.13)	(.09)	(.12)	(.17)
Trust in parliament and politicians	3.92	3.74	3.94	+.02
	(.08)	(.06)	(.07)	(.11)
Satisfaction with democracy	5.17	5.14	5.18	+.01
	(.08)	(.08)	(.07)	(.11)
Satisfaction with life as a whole	6.85	7.00	7.17	+.32
	(.05)	(.04)	(.03)	(.06)

Note: Ordinary least-squares regression parameter estimates (with standard errors clustered by country-round in parentheses). Fixed effects for countries included in the analyses but not shown.

Four other indicators record significant change in opinion. Average satisfaction with economic conditions was not only much higher in 2014–2019 than it had been during the Euro-crisis, but also more than half a point higher than it had been before the crisis began. Support for immigrants and immigration and for economic redistribution increased steadily through the crisis and after. Perhaps most remarkably of all, life satisfaction also increased steadily and substantially, by about one-third of a point on the zero-to-ten ESS scale. While Europeans, on average, seem to have been just as content with political life after the crisis as before, they seem to have been even more content with other aspects of their lives. It seems hard to avoid the conclusion that, whatever ails European democracy, it is not public opinion—or, if it is, the ailment is of such long standing that the notion of a "crisis" hardly seems apt.

In the most influential essay ever written about public opinion, political scientist Philip Converse claimed that "the broad contours of elite decisions over time can depend in a vital way upon currents in what is loosely called 'the history of ideas.' These decisions in turn have effects upon the mass of more common citizens. But, of any direct participation in this history of ideas and the behavior it shapes, the mass is remarkably innocent."[4] Converse's characterization of "belief systems in mass publics" has sometimes been criticized as belittling the democratic capacity of ordinary citizens. But when the currents of ideas in play involve anti-immigrant agitation and other manifestations of "populist" extremism, the word "innocent" has a rather different connotation.

Developments in Hungary and Poland underline another respect in which democratic theory has tended "to stereotype thought against the lessons of experience." Political scientist John Zaller has argued that public opinion "is capable of recognizing and focusing on its own conception of what matters."[5] But "what matters" to ordinary citizens may not be what matters to democratic theorists. Political scientists have frequently found citizens expressing allegiance to high-minded democratic values in the abstract but readily setting them aside in specific cases. Summarizing the implications of his comparative study of support for "the rules of the game" among political elites and masses, Herbert McClosky concluded that "it is the articulate classes rather than the public who serve as the major repositories of the public conscience and as the carriers of the [democratic] Creed." More than half a century later, Matthew Graham and Milan Svolik found that "only a small fraction of Americans prioritize democratic principles in their electoral choices," making public opinion a "strikingly limited" check on undemocratic behavior by elected officials. Turks and Venezuelans were similarly "reluctant to punish politicians for disregarding democratic principles when doing so requires abandoning one's favored party or policies."[6]

4. Converse (1964: 255).

5. Zaller interpreted President Bill Clinton's popularity in the wake of a major scandal as demonstrating "just how relentlessly the majority of voters can stay focused on the bottom line," meaning not just prosperity but, more broadly, "political substance." He noted that the public might not be "either wise or virtuous. For one thing, its sense of substance seems, in the aggregate, rather amoral—usually more like 'what have you done for me lately' than 'social justice'" Zaller (1998: 186).

6. McClosky (1964: 374); Prothro and Grigg (1960); Graham and Svolik (2020: 392); Bartels (2020). Svolik (2019: 26) focused primarily on ideological or partisan polarization as

In Hungary and Poland, public opinion has likewise proven to be a "strikingly limited" check on undemocratic behavior by leaders willing to flout the democratic "rules of the game." Indeed, citizens experiencing substantial improvements in subjective well-being under "mildly authoritarian" regimes have registered significant increases not only in political trust and approval, but also in satisfaction with "how democracy works." Their willingness to overlook some "cracking down on judges and the news media, refusing to take in migrants and lashing out at the European Union" in exchange for prosperity, order, and validation of their national identities may be egregious from the standpoint of democratic theory; but it is hardly surprising. When theory and political behavior collide, as Schattschneider wrote, "it is at least as likely that the ideal is wrong as it is that the reality is bad."[7]

One of the primary lessons of experience in democratic systems is that citizens care much more about outcomes than about procedures. When the corruption or incompetence of political leaders seems to impinge on their well-being, they will register their disapproval through whatever channels are most readily available to them. When they experience peace and prosperity, they will mostly be happy to let the people in charge carry on. If the results in either case amount to a "crisis of democracy," that is first and foremost a crisis of political leadership, not a crisis of public opinion.

Managing Political Extremism

In her comparative study of breakdowns of democracy in interwar Europe and late 20th-century Latin America, Nancy Bermeo emphasized the importance of "distancing capacity"—the ability and willingness of political elites, including party leaders, police, judges, and others, to condemn and control violence and lawlessness, even by current or potential political allies. Examining instances of successful maintenance of democracy in Finland, Czechoslovakia, and Venezuela, she noted, "In each of these cases, party elites exhibited a com-

---

a source of competing political values, but the same logic applies to trade-offs between democratic principles and other substantive values, including peace, prosperity, and social validation.

7. Palko Karasz, "Leaders of Hungary and Poland Chafe at E.U., but How Do Their People Feel?," *New York Times*, 6 September 2017. Gergely Szakacs, "Hungary Could Resume Anti-EU Campaigns, Says PM Orban," *Reuters*, 24 March 2019. Schattschneider (1960: 128).

mitment to democracy that led them to overcome interparty differences and form broad alliances against anti-democratic groups."[8]

The ability and willingness of mainstream political elites to "distance" themselves from political extremism is important even in times and places where that extremism does not rise to the level of violence and lawlessness. "Extreme" attitudes of various sorts are a ubiquitous feature of public opinion. Sometimes, they are not sufficiently visible to polite society to be broached in conventional opinion surveys. Sometimes they are so idiosyncratic and inconsistent that they are mistaken for mere "measurement error." But when political entrepreneurs manage to forge narratives that mobilize substantial constituencies, the ugly underside of public opinion comes to light, and mainstream politicians must decide how to respond. That is certainly the case in contemporary Europe, where, as Cas Mudde has observed, and as we saw in Chapter 6, "populist radical right attitudes" are "very widespread."[9]

It is easy to point to some clear failures of Europe's mainstream politicians to distance themselves from extremists. During Orbán's assault on checks and balances in Hungary, for example, "Leaders of Europe's conservative political parties—including Chancellor Angela Merkel of Germany—refrained from reining him in, largely because he was part of their coalition in Brussels, and because they thought they could control him." In 2018, leaders of the European Union's center-right European People's Party finally supported a resolution raising concerns "about the fairness of the courts, the independence of the news media and the freedom of academic institutions in Hungary." The following spring, they suspended Orbán's Fidesz party, but still refrained from expelling it so they could count its members as part of their parliamentary group.[10]

Recent history also provides some clear examples of well-meaning politicians botching efforts to defuse populist sentiment, with disastrous consequences. David Cameron's "calculated gamble, aimed at silencing the Eurosceptics in his

8. Bermeo (2003: 237–252).

9. Mudde (2007: 222). Broockman (2016) noted that many ordinary citizens express extreme policy preferences, but with so little ideological consistency that they are mistakenly classified as moderates.

10. Patrick Kingsley, "E.U.'s Leadership Seeks to Contain Hungary's Orban," *New York Times*, 11 September 2018. Patrick Kingsley and Steven Erlanger, "Hungary's Democracy Is in Danger, E.U. Parliament Decides," *New York Times*, 12 September 2018. Marc Santora and Steven Erlanger, "Top E.U. Coalition Suspends Party Led by Orban, Hungary's Leader," *New York Times*, 20 March 2019.

own party for a generation" by promising a national referendum on withdrawal from the European Union is a spectacular case in point. It is easy enough to fault the ordinary Britons who voted to leave the EU for being ill-informed and short-sighted, especially when subsequent polling suggested that many soon regretted their decision. But it was Cameron who tempted fate by putting Europe up for a vote.

In other cases, however, European political elites have demonstrated considerable skill in containing the ubiquitous populist currents in their societies. A striking example is Sweden, where, as we saw in Chapter 4, a long-standing policy of openness to immigrants nearly doubled the foreign-born population (from 11.3% to 19.5%) in less than two decades. Mainstream politicians have largely refrained from exploiting the social tensions generated by this transformation, contributing to Swedes' remarkably positive attitudes toward immigrants and immigration.

Mainstream politicians of all stripes have also skillfully limited the political impact of the Sweden Democrats, the right-wing populist party catering to people agitated by immigration and social change. Sweden Democrats crossed the 4% threshold for representation in the Riksdag in 2010, with 5.7% of the vote, then expanded its electoral support to 12.9% in 2014 and 17.5% in 2018. This was precisely the sort of development that has generated alarms in many parts of Europe over the past decade. Yet, the party has so far played virtually no role in national policymaking.

In the run-up to the 2014 election, Moderate Party Prime Minister Fredrik Reinfeldt called on the Swedish people to "show patience and open their hearts" in response to the increasing flow of refugees from war-torn Syria and Iraq. According to a *New York Times* report, Reinfeldt had "decided to gamble re-election on embracing the country's tradition of openness, in stark contrast to the anti-immigrant sentiment infusing politics across much of Europe." The report suggested that "the unity of the main political parties on this issue has helped to hold anti-immigrant feeling in check. Parties of left and right have erected a ring of sorts around the Sweden Democrats, treating them as political pariahs and refusing cooperation in Parliament." The leader of the Green Party said he was "proud to live in a country where a center-right party during an election campaign asks for solidarity when the world is burning."[11]

11. David Crouch, "Rift Emerges before Vote in Sweden as Immigration Tests a Tradition of Openness," *New York Times*, September 12, 2014.

Reinfeldt's Alliance for Sweden lost the election, as polls over the preceding year had consistently suggested it would. The Sweden Democrats' 12.9% of the vote earned the party 49 seats in the 349-seat Riksdag, potentially representing the balance of power between the center-right and left coalitions. However, the mainstream parties continued to treat the Sweden Democrats as "political pariahs," ruling them out as potential coalition partners. The result was a minority government pairing the largest single party, the Social Democrats, and the Green Party, sustained by the carefully calibrated sufferance of the mainstream center-right parties.[12]

In the 2018 election, the Sweden Democrats' 17.5% of the vote earned the party 62 seats in the new Riksdag, an even more imposing balance between the incumbent Red-Green coalition's 144 seats and the center-right Alliance's 143. Yet, once again, the party was successfully cordoned off from power. The result was a protracted series of failed attempts to form a governing coalition, first by incumbent Social Democratic Prime Minister Stefan Löfven and then by the new leader of the Alliance, Ulf Kristersson. Kristersson's effort failed when two of the smaller parties in the Alliance, the Centre Party and the Liberals, refused to form a government that would rely on the support of the Sweden Democrats. Finally, more than four months after the election, they agreed to support Löfven, resulting in a precarious but functional center-left coalition.[13]

The political isolation of the Sweden Democrats has required significant forbearance on the part of mainstream party leaders, even ceding control of government to their political rivals. That forbearance may not last indefinitely; indeed, the taboo on cooperating with the Sweden Democrats already seems to be eroding.[14] In the meantime, excluding the Sweden Democrats from power risks further alienating the party's already-alienated supporters. In the 2018–2019 ESS, conducted in the six months after the September 2018

12. Lars Bevanger, "Sweden Election: Social Democrats Rule Out Far-Right Pact," BBC News, September 15, 2014. Daniel Dickson and Johan Sennero, "Swedish Centre-Left Do Eight-Year Deal with Opposition to Avert Snap Election," Reuters, December 27, 2014.

13. Christina Anderson and Steven Erlanger, "Sweden's Centrists Prevail Even as Far Right Has Its Best Showing Ever," New York Times, 9 September 2018. Merrit Kennedy, "Swedish Politics in Chaos as Parliament Votes Out Prime Minister," NPR, 25 September 2018. Christina Anderson, "Sweden Forms a Government after 133 Days, but It's a Shaky One," New York Times, 18 January 2019. "Parties Take Up Positions after Government Collapse," Radio Sweden, 21 June 2021, https://sverigesradio.se/artikel/parties-take-up-positions-after-government-collapse.

14. Richard Milne, "Europopulism: Immigration Provides Opening for Sweden's Right Wing," Financial Times, 15 August 2018.

election, the drawn-out maneuvering to keep the Sweden Democrats out of government seems to have done just that. Among people who reported voting for or identifying with Sweden Democrats, satisfaction with the national government fell from an already low 3.2 on a zero-to-ten scale in 2018 to 2.0 in 2019, as it became increasingly clear that their party would once again be shut out of government; their satisfaction with the workings of democracy fell from 4.5 to 3.2.[15]

"For populist voters," as a *New York Times* report noted, this sort of maneuvering by mainstream politicians "feels like an establishment conspiracy to repress popular will, deepening outrage at a seemingly unresponsive system." Similarly, efforts to keep toxic issues off the political agenda may succeed in the short run but allow them to fester in the long run. "European integration, like immigration, was for long a taboo issue in European politics," Mudde wrote, "often consciously excluded from the political agenda by the political elites." Managing social conflicts inevitably involves balancing the short-term and long-term dangers of giving extremists what they want against the short-term and long-term dangers of *not* giving them what they want.[16]

Political Institutions and Democratic Stability

The political impact of "extreme" opinion clearly depends crucially on the responses to extremism of mainstream political elites. Those responses in turn are likely to be shaped, in significant part, by the strategic incentives and constraints created by political institutions, including electoral systems and "checks and balances" in the governmental process.

Multiparty proportional systems generally produce more votes for "extreme" parties, since there is little strategic incentive for voters drawn to these parties to make do with pale mainstream alternatives. However, there is no

---

15. In both cases, these declines were much too large to be plausibly attributed to sampling variability, despite the small number of Sweden Democrats supporters in the survey. The corresponding declines in satisfaction with the government and democracy among Swedes who were *not* Sweden Democrats supporters were much smaller, about one-fourth of a point on the zero-to-ten scales. Harteveld et al. (2021) documented a reciprocal tendency of right-wing populist supporters to report increased satisfaction with democracy when right-wing populist parties are included in coalition governments.

16. Max Fisher and Amanda Taub, "Western Populism May Be Entering an Awkward Adolescence," *New York Times*, 25 April 2017. Mudde (2013: 12).

proportional system in contemporary Europe where supporters of "extreme" parties number anything close to a majority of the electorate. Thus, their political impact depends crucially on coalition politics. In Sweden, as we have seen, right-wing populists have been effectively cordoned off from power. In Italy, where party politics is much more chaotic, post-election bargaining can produce virtually any outcome, from the "technocratic" government of the untested Mario Monti to the bizarre antiestablishment coalition of Lega and the Five Star Movement.

Mainstream parties face constant temptations to alter their own platforms in order to co-opt the supporters of right-wing populist parties. In many parts of Europe, parties have succumbed to those temptations by, for example, adopting increasingly harsh anti-immigrant policies and rhetoric. However, few have gone as far as they could in that direction. A detailed study of political behavior in Germany found that right-wing populists' "support for the AfD remains stable because other parties fail to meet their preferences on their most prioritized issue—immigration—not because they mistrust the political system altogether. Once we introduce the important counterfactual scenario in which other parties do adopt more restrictive immigration positions, up to half of the AfD's electorate leaves the party for more established alternatives." The reluctance of some mainstream parties to aggressively compete for right-wing populist votes may stem in part from principled commitments; but it may also reflect strategic concerns about potential backlash among their own supporters. The same study of German voters found that mainstream parties would "lose a large proportion of their own voters by becoming more restrictive on immigration, which, in the case of the SPD and CDU, more than offsets their gains from AfD voters."[17]

In majoritarian systems, the influence of right-wing populist parties is even less likely to stem directly from their parliamentary representation or role in government. Instead, like UKIP, they typically succeed to the extent that their concerns and convictions are absorbed by one of the major parties. As British political scientist Tim Bale observed, "The 'respectable' mainstream right and the unashamedly radical right often have far more in common than either of them care to admit. The UK Conservative Party's choices have been shaped by its relationship and rivalry with radical right-wing parties." "Conservative politicians flirted with populism," Bale observed,

17. Chou et al. (2021: 2228, 2250).

but rarely went further. Conservatives' squeamishness created a space for more radical right-wingers—populist politicians willing not just to stir the pot and keep it simmering but also to turn up the heat and see it boil over. These more radical politicians appealed to voters (and tabloid media) who wanted to go back to a society that was less inclusive, less insecure, less tolerant, less politically correct, less apologetic and, for some at least, whiter. These populist politicians were unlikely to make it into government. However, they could and did press their conservative counterparts to actually live up to their rhetoric.[18]

Flirting with populist extremism can be dangerous, as David Cameron's Brexit debacle demonstrated. But it is even more dangerous for a major political party to be captured outright by an extremist faction. As political scientist Frances Lee observed, by comparison with most of Europe, "the US system offers much less opportunity for organized populist *parties* but far more opportunity for populist *candidacies*." That is due principally to the nominating procedures employed by the major US parties, which rely heavily on relatively wide-open primary elections. This "democratization" of the parties' candidate selection processes makes them vulnerable to all sorts of popular impulses, including, sometimes, extremist factions.[19]

In her discussion of "distancing capacity" as a key factor in preventing breakdowns of democracy, Bermeo noted that the ability of mainstream politicians to resist potential encroachments on democracy often rests on "extremely hierarchical" party structures and personal prestige, not on active support for democracy from rank-and-file partisans. The insular, hierarchical party structures that American "reformers" have castigated as impediments to democracy have provided politicians in other times and places with crucial room to maneuver in their efforts to resist antidemocratic impulses.[20] Recent US experience seems to confirm this historical lesson by illustrating both the vulnerability of "democratic" candidate selection processes to capture and the impact of openness on the "distancing capacity" of party leaders who must decide whether to support or resist extremism.

18. Tim Bale, "Brexit Shows How a Tiny Party Can Have Big Consequences," *Washington Post*, 2 December 2019.

19. Lee (2020: 370); Polsby (1983); Bartels (1988). Christopher H. Achen and Larry M. Bartels, "The Presidential Primaries Are out of Control—And the Party Conventions Are Broken," *Los Angeles Times*, 2 May 2016.

20. Bermeo (2003: 237–252).

In 2016, the failure of Republican elites to unite around an acceptable alternative candidate allowed Donald Trump to parlay enthusiastic factional support into a string of primary victories that effectively ensured his nomination. Perhaps even more surprisingly, despite hedged support or even outright opposition from some of the party's most prominent leaders, Trump managed to ride the Republican Party brand to a narrow victory in November. While his success was a testament to the intensity of partisan polarization in contemporary US politics, it would be a mistake to interpret his 63 million votes as a specific mandate for Trumpism.[21]

In the White House, Trump's policy initiatives were mostly limited to traditional Republican priorities, including a major tax cut tilted toward corporations and the wealthy, economic and environmental deregulation, and fast-tracking conservative judicial appointments, including three Supreme Court appointments. Much of his time and energy were devoted, not to policymaking, but to skillful populist agitation and provocation, delivered via a constant barrage of tweets, old-fashioned rallies of the faithful, and fawning wall-to-wall coverage from Fox News. Democrats fumed, and the president's overall approval rating remained in negative territory throughout his term, despite a strong prepandemic economy. Nonetheless, his public support among Republicans was consolidated and even expanded.[22]

Some Republican elected officials were enthusiastic Trump supporters. Others attempted to rein in his worst impulses, but most lacked the political insulation necessary to "distance" themselves from the president, at least in ways that would be visible to the party rank-and-file. During the 2020 campaign, few pushed back against his incessant talk of rampant election fraud—though, when he floated the idea of postponing the election, prominent party figures quickly shot it down. Later, as he struggled to overturn the election outcome, his own attorney general told the Associated Press that he had "not seen fraud on a scale that could have effected a different outcome in the election." Dozens of judges and local election officials rejected appeals to invalidate ballots. "Repeatedly," one observer noted,

21. Larry Bartels, "2016 Was an Ordinary Election, Not a Realignment," *Washington Post*, 10 November 2016. Ezra Klein, "Why Did the 2016 Election Look So Much Like the 2012 Election?" *Vox*, 10 July 2017. Cohen et al. (2016); Sides, Tesler, and Vavreck (2018).

22. Larry Bartels, "The GOP Tax Bill Is Business as Usual in America's Unequal Democracy," *Washington Post*, 20 December 2017. Larry Bartels, "How Paul Ryan Lost the Republican Party," *Washington Post*, 15 April 2018. Bartels (2018).

"judges with ties to Trump have joined all the others in undermining his case."[23]

Rank-and-file Republicans were more supportive. Millions professed to believe that the election had been stolen, and hundreds engaged in a violent riot at the US Capitol protesting the certification of the outcome. Scores of Republicans in Congress paid homage to Trump's outrage by voting to throw out supposedly suspect electoral votes. Only ten in the House and seven in the Senate would vote to impeach or convict him for his role in inciting the riot.[24]

Even in his Twitter-less South Florida postelection exile, Trump remained a potent political force, peddling his "Big Lie" of a stolen election and demanding fealty from current and aspiring Republican officeholders. His leverage stemmed in significant part from the openness of American party organizations, which gives his enthusiastic supporters an outsized influence over the party's candidate selection processes. How far they will succeed in intimidating or replacing more traditional Republican leaders remains to be seen. Many Republican officeholders have shown little stomach for publicly challenging Trump. They have also demonstrated considerable willingness to engage in partisan fiddling with state election procedures. How many would be willing to take the next step, from tilting to decisively overturning an election result?[25]

"Under its separation of powers, bicameralism, and strong federalism," Lee argued, "governance in the United States requires leaders to obtain cooperation from an array of independent actors, all with their own bases of political power and formal authority." This fragmentation of power creates "formidable obstacles against authoritarianism, populist or otherwise. Albeit imperfect,

23. Maggie Haberman, Jonathan Martin, and Reid J. Epstein, "Trump Floats an Election Delay, and Republicans Shoot It Down," *New York Times*, 30 July 2020. Matt Zapotosky, Devlin Barrett, and Josh Dawsey, "Barr Says He Hasn't Seen Fraud That Could Affect the Election Outcome," *Washington Post*, 1 December 2020. Aaron Blake, "The Most Remarkable Rebukes of Trump's Legal Case: From the Judges He Hand-Picked," *Washington Post*, 14 December 2020.

24. Dan Barry, Mike McIntire, and Matthew Rosenberg, "'Our President Wants Us Here': The Mob That Stormed the Capitol," *New York Times*, 9 January 2021. Richard Cowan, David Morgan, and Makini Brice, "U.S. Senate Acquits Trump as Republicans Save Him in Impeachment Again," *Reuters*, 13 February 2021. Alison Durkee, "More Than Half of Republicans Believe Voter Fraud Claims and Most Still Support Trump, Poll Finds," *Forbes*, 5 April 2021.

25. Michael Kruse, "The Antipope of Mar-a-Lago," Politico, 29 January 2021. Thomas L. Friedman, "Trump's Big Lie Devoured the G.O.P. and Now Eyes Our Democracy," *New York Times*, 4 May 2021. Chris Cillizza, "How Believing the Big Lie Has Become Central to Being a Republican," CNN, 13 September 2021. Philip Elliott, "The Big Lie Has Been Proven False. Republicans Can't Shake It," *Time*, 1 November 2021.

these obstacles are likely to frustrate any but an overwhelmingly popular leader."[26]

Partisan polarization and the nationalization of elections have reduced the extent to which US elected officials are "independent actors, all with their own bases of political power." Nonetheless, their room to maneuver—and to resist encroachments on democratic procedures, should they be so inclined—is far from negligible. Consider, by way of comparison, the distribution of power in Orbán's Fidesz:

> In light of the formal rules, all power is concentrated in the party's National Presidium. . . . The party leadership dominates the relationship between national and local bodies by appointing electoral district presidents who enjoy considerable power within specific areas. This centralisation helps to bypass the party on the ground (local and middle-level leaders) and prevent the emergence of independent power centres. . . . Formally, the nomination [of parliamentary candidates] is managed by a national body, the Electoral Coordinating Committee (ECC), which is controlled and dominated by the National Presidency and the party leader due to personnel overlaps. The ECC can propose names for individual districts, country lists, and European Parliament lists. The room for modification is very limited: Local party units can only make comments on the proposed names. The National Board can only approve or reject the list but cannot suggest any modifications. Even in a case of rejection (which has never yet happened), the party leader has the right to override the decision and go forward with the original list. . . . It is also a telling fact that the nomination process for public offices like Prime ministership and presidency is not regulated in the party procedures, leaving more autonomy for the party leader to promote its favoured candidate (or themselves). . . . The result of personalisation and cartelisation is clear: The government, the party, and the leader are ultimately inseparable.[27]

As we saw in Chapter 7, the Hungarian electoral system compounded these centripetal tendencies by facilitating single-party control of government. Fidesz won the momentous 2010 election with just 53.1% of the vote; but that narrow majority in the electorate produced a two-thirds majority in the National Assembly. In a system where "the government, the party, and

---

26. Lee (2020: 381).
27. Metz and Várnagy (2021: 323–325).

the leader are ultimately inseparable," even a razor-thin supermajority gave Orbán broad power to amend the constitution, imposing "a new social contract," rolling back democratic checks and balances, and modifying electoral laws to further entrench Fidesz in power. Similarly, Poland's Law and Justice party won just 37.6% of the vote in the crucial 2015 election, but that was enough to secure an absolute majority of seats in the Sejm—a majority willing and able to reorganize the Constitutional Court, pack the National Council of the Judiciary, and put state radio and television under firm government control. These were instances in which democratic institutions proved highly vulnerable to encroachment, even by leaders with less-than-overwhelming popular support.

It is tempting to ask what political institutions are most conducive to democratic stability; but the impact of political institutions and political culture are complexly intertwined. In some circumstances, like those described by Bermeo, hierarchical party structures have bolstered party leaders seeking to resist encroachments on democracy. In other times and places, including contemporary Hungary, they have facilitated antidemocratic action. The key, it seems, is not the institutions themselves, but the character and values of the political leaders operating within and upon them.

A Crisis of Democratic Theory

Scholarship on democracy is shaped, more than an antiseptic caricature of the scientific process might suggest, by attitudes and concerns forged in the public events of the day. In the wake of fascism and world war, social scientists and historians struggled to understand the appeal of authoritarianism and the fragility of democratic institutions in putatively "advanced" European societies.[28] But through the second half of the 20th century, these so-called advanced democracies enjoyed a good deal of prosperity and political stability. The vanquishing of Soviet communism famously produced "the end of history," a supposedly permanent global ascendance of liberal democracy. Somewhat less famously, it corresponded with a vogue in scholarly studies of public opinion emphasizing "rationality," "reasoning," and the collective wisdom of the masses. The study of democratic breakdowns was

---

28. Adorno et al. (1950); Arendt (1951); Prothro and Grigg (1960); McClosky (1964). On the intellectual history of political studies in the postwar era, see Katznelson (2020).

largely relegated to scholars of Latin America and Africa, or left to historians.[29]

More recently, social scientists alarmed by contemporary political developments have scrambled to mine the histories of 20th century Europe and Latin America for lessons on "how democracies die," and to remind Americans of the "recurring crises" of democracy in their own political history. They have also worked to codify assessments of the quality of democratic performance and of the nature and magnitude of threats to democracy.[30] These efforts are immensely valuable; but their theoretical underpinnings can be no stronger than the theoretical underpinnings of democracy itself. Assessing threats to democracy requires us to agree, at least approximately, on what it is and how it works.

How far we are from such agreement is illustrated by the scholarly literature on populism. As the authors of an authoritative literature review noted, "Defining populism is anything but simple." However, "many scholars argue that, above and beyond its diverse manifestations, a defining attribute of populism is its reliance on leaders able to mobilize the masses and/or conduct their parties with the aim of enacting radical reforms." What is wrong with that? While "radical reforms" may be politically objectionable to some people, that in itself does not make them threatening to democracy. When, and how, populism as a political style or "thin ideology" is connected to the erosion of democratic institutions and procedures remains far from clear.[31]

In popular discourse, the term "populist" has been used both "to taint political opponents" and "to claim democratic credentials." Likewise, from a scholarly standpoint, populism "may constitute a threat to or a corrective for democracy," depending not only on the specific flavor of populism, but also on the specific brand of democracy one has in mind. If "those who adhere to populism tend to favour majoritarian and participatory conceptions of democracy, and are prone to disdain deliberative and liberal conceptions of democracy," assessing their actions would seem to require a clear understanding of

29. Fukuyama (1992); Popkin (1991); Sniderman, Brody, and Tetlock (1991); Page and Shapiro (1992); Lupia and McCubbins (1998); Linz and Stepan (1978); Mainwaring and Pérez-Liñán (2013).

30. Levitsky and Ziblatt (2018); Mettler and Lieberman (2020). On expert assessments of democracy, see the V-Dem project, https://v-dem.net/; and Bright Line Watch, https://brightlinewatch.org/.

31. Mudde and Kaltwasser (2014).

the intrinsic value and relationship among these alternative "conceptions of democracy." With no such understanding in sight, scholars are inevitably left to draw selectively upon one or another fragmentary notion of "democracy" to defend or castigate populist forces and their "radical reforms."[32]

Adam Przeworski has argued that "the 'anti-system' parties of today are not anti-democratic. While the label of 'fascist' is carelessly brandished to stigmatize these political forces, these parties do not advocate replacing elections by some other way of selecting rulers. They are ugly—most people view racism and xenophobia as ugly—but these parties campaign under the slogan of returning to 'the people' the power usurped by elites, which they see as strengthening democracy."[33]

Przeworski's emphasis on "replacing elections" as a hallmark of antidemocratic politics reflects the intellectual impact of the 20th-century economic historian Joseph Schumpeter, who threw a wrench in the gears of democratic theory by challenging what he called "the classical doctrine," in which democracy was understood as a political system "which realizes the common good by making the people itself decide issues through the election of individuals who are to assemble in order to carry out its will." In its place, Schumpeter offered a less heroic theory of democracy as an "institutional arrangement for arriving at political decisions in which individuals acquire the power to decide by means of a competitive struggle for the people's vote."[34]

By dispensing with the notion of "making the people itself decide issues," whether directly or indirectly, Schumpeter demoted public opinion to a more limited and, arguably, more realistic role in democratic politics. In that respect, his theory was, as some critics have called it, "minimalist." But it might more appropriately be thought of as a starting point for a reconstruction of democratic theory along different lines—a reconstruction that has unfortunately not proceeded very far in the decades since Schumpeter wrote.

Schumpeter's own remarks regarding the implications of his "theory of competitive leadership" have not been very influential. Nonetheless, they do suggest some of the issues that a reconstructed theory of democracy would have to address, ranging from the nature of political career paths to the building and maintenance of administrative capacity, the civic education of political elites, and even the limitations of democratic procedures "in troubled times"

---

32. Mudde and Kaltwasser (2014); Kaltwasser (2012).
33. Przeworski (2019: 134).
34. Schumpeter (1950: 250, 269).

when "allegiance to the structural principles of the existing society" and "tolerance for difference of opinion" are lacking.[35]

While these issues have certainly not been absent from the agenda of contemporary political science, they have seldom been considered within the framework of any explicit overarching theory of democracy. As a result, the "immense confusions in the current theory of democracy" that Lippmann identified nearly a century ago continue to loom large in our thinking.

Lippmann himself was clear about how much remained to be done. "I do not know," he wrote, "what the lessons will be when we have learned to think of public opinion as it is, and not as the fictitious power we have assumed it to be." Nor, a century later, do I. This book has offered no new theory of democracy, nor even a detailed description of the workings of contemporary European democracies. It is, essentially, a ground-clearing effort, not a construction project. Nonetheless, it does provide considerable support for Lippmann's conviction that "a false philosophy" of democracy "tends to stereotype thought against the lessons of experience," to the detriment of both political theory and political action.[36]

The Future before Us

In the concluding pages of another classic book on public opinion and democracy, Lippmann wrote,

> In politics the hero does not live happily ever after, or end his life perfectly. There is no concluding chapter, because the hero in politics has more future before him than there is recorded history behind him. The last chapter is merely a place where the writer imagines that the polite reader has begun to look furtively at his watch.[37]

While I have been busy reading, thinking, and writing about European democracy in the wake of the Euro-crisis, the political future of Europe has continued to unfold. Most remarkably, that once-in-a-lifetime crisis has already been superseded by an even more momentous crisis—a deadly global pandemic compounded by a disastrous economic slump as country after country

35. Schumpeter (1950: 284–302).
36. Lippmann (1925: 200).
37. Lippmann (1922: 411).

locked down in hopes of containing the transmission of Covid-19. According to one blistering assessment,

> The continent was overwhelmed. . . . Western Europe became an epicenter of the pandemic. Officials once boastful about their preparedness were frantically trying to secure protective gear and materials for tests, as death rates soared in Britain, France, Spain, Italy and Belgium. . . . Their pandemic plans were built on a litany of miscalculations and false assumptions. . . . Accountability mechanisms proved toothless. Thousands of pages of national pandemic planning turned out to be little more than exercises in bureaucratic busy work. Officials in some countries barely consulted their plans; in other countries, leaders ignored warnings about how quickly a virus could spread. European Union checks of each country's readiness had become rituals of self-congratulation. . . . Not every Western democracy stumbled. Germany, with a chancellor trained in physics and a sizable domestic biotech sector, managed it better than most. Greece, with fewer resources, has reported fewer than 200 deaths. But with several countries expected to conduct public inquests into what went wrong, Europe is grappling with how a continent considered among the most advanced failed so miserably.[38]

In response to the emergency, European leaders negotiated an €800 billion stimulus plan providing substantial assistance to countries hard hit by the pandemic. Crucially, the aid was financed with bonds backed by the European Union rather than individual countries—a dramatic departure from the self-imposed restrictions of the Euro-crisis. One journalist hailed it as "Europe's Hamiltonian moment," suggesting that "greater fiscal cooperation means that the odds of the EU lasting just went up. All that's left for Europe is a duel, a book by Ron Chernow and a musical by Lin-Manuel Miranda."[39]

Alas for Broadway, there were more challenges to come. Nine months after Europe's "Hamiltonian moment," an economic journalist wrote, "That money should eventually stimulate growth, but the process confronts the typically fractious politics of Europe. Finland, which tends toward frugality, has held

38. David D. Kirkpatrick, Matt Apuzzo, and Selam Gebrekidan, "Europe Said It Was Pandemic-Ready. Pride Was Its Downfall," *New York Times*, 20 July 2020.

39. Al Root, "Europe's Hamiltonian Moment," *Barron's*, 21 July 2020. Alex Ward, "What Alexander Hamilton Has to Do with the EU's $850 Billion Coronavirus Stimulus Plan," *Vox*, 21 July 2020.

up disbursement with demands for conditions on the use of the money. Further delays threaten to extend the downturn in southern European economies that are especially dependent on tourism, among them Greece, Italy, Spain and Portugal."[40]

A year into the pandemic, the IMF reported that "the United States has deployed extra public spending worth 25 percent of its national economic output toward pandemic-related stimulus and relief programs," while the corresponding figure in Germany was 10 percent and in France, Italy, and Spain, even less. The European Commission estimated that real GDP fell in 2020 by 6.5% in the 19-country Euro area, with the largest declines in countries that had already been devastated by the Euro-crisis—8.2% in Greece, 8.9% in Italy, and a wrenching 10.8% in Spain.[41]

The EU likewise "trailed the United States and Britain from the start" in the race to roll out the vaccines that would finally bring the pandemic under control. "The bloc was comparatively slow to negotiate contracts with drugmakers," the New York Times reported. "Its regulators were cautious and deliberative in approving some vaccines. Europe also bet on vaccines that did not pan out or, significantly, had supply disruptions. And national governments snarled local efforts in red tape." Perhaps most importantly, while the US "basically went into business with the drugmakers, spending much more heavily to accelerate vaccine development, testing and production," the EU "took a conservative, budget-conscious approach that left the open market largely untouched."[42]

However history may judge the EU's response to the coronavirus pandemic, the episode tends to reaffirm two important, contrasting lessons suggested by the Euro-crisis. First, as one observer put it, "In a crisis, it always becomes clear that the E.U. is not a country." When coordinated action is essential, a system in which Finland micromanages aid to Italy and Spain will inevitably be slower and less efficient than one with more centralized control. On the other hand, with every crisis it becomes clearer that the EU can and probably will continue to become more like a country. Having breached the

40. Peter S. Goodman, "Europe's Recession Contrasts Economic Fortunes of U.S. Expansion," New York Times, 30 April 2021.

41. International Monetary Fund Fiscal Monitor, April 2021, https://www.imf.org/en/Publications/FM/Issues/2021/03/29/fiscal-monitor-april-2021.

42. Matt Apuzzo, Selam Gebrekidan, and Monika Pronczuk, "Where Europe Went Wrong in Its Vaccine Rollout, and Why," New York Times, 20 March 2021.

long-standing constraint on direct EU borrowing in 2020, Europe will be better prepared for the next crisis, but also more likely to engage in further institutional innovation—a sporadic, often messy series of "Hamiltonian moments" resulting in gradual but substantial cumulative integration. One team of EU scholars colorfully described the process as "failing forward."[43]

Meanwhile, the impact of the Covid-19 pandemic on public attitudes toward the EU casts additional doubt on the notion that a "mounting popular backlash" will constrain "bold steps toward further integration." In the winter of 2021, as the pandemic continued to ravage Europe and observers castigated the EU's handling of the crisis, a Eurobarometer survey found a narrow plurality of Europeans dissatisfied with the EU's "measures taken to fight the coronavirus pandemic." Yet, they were even more dissatisfied with their national governments' handling of the pandemic, 59% said they trusted the EU "to make the right decisions in the future," and 84% agreed that "the EU should be given the means to better deal in the future with crises such as the coronavirus pandemic." More broadly, almost 60% agreed that "more decisions should be taken at EU level" (while just one-third disagreed), and overall trust in the EU reached its highest level in more than a decade. If, as political scientists Sara Hobolt and Catherine de Vries have argued, "the Union is increasingly reliant on public support for its continued legitimacy," that legitimacy seems, if anything, to have been bolstered by the Covid-19 crisis.[44]

The fallout from the pandemic also seems to have contributed to a development some observers claimed to discern even before it began—a decline in the popular appeal of right-wing populism, especially in central Europe. In Slovakia, the murder of a young investigative journalist spurred massive protests and forced the resignation of populist Prime Minister Robert Fico in 2018. A year later, political neophyte Zuzana Caputova was resoundingly elected Slovakia's first female president. "In a political climate where stridency is often rewarded and crudeness frequently seen as a marker of authenticity," one journalist wrote, Caputova "clung to the belief that decency is what voters want most," and her victory was "widely seen as a rebuke of

43. Jacob Kirkegaard of the German Marshall Fund, quoted by Apuzzo, Gebrekidan, and Pronczuk; Jones, Kelemen, and Meunier (2016).

44. Tooze (2018: 515). "The EU and the Coronavirus Pandemic," Standard Eurobarometer 94, Winter 2020–2021, https://europa.eu/eurobarometer/surveys/detail/2355. Hobolt and de Vries (2016: 414).

the illiberal and nativist strain of populism that has swept the European continent in recent years."[45]

A former State Department official cited the election of Caputova in Slovakia and liberal opposition candidates in local elections in Poland as evidence of "anti-populist trends" in central Europe. "The reigning orthodoxy is that it's only a matter of time until far-right populist parties begin winning elections in country after country," he wrote. "But the evidence from across Central Europe runs counter to that: Liberal leaders and activists have begun to push back against populism."[46]

In 2021, the *New York Times'* Warsaw bureau chief reported that the "right-wing populist wave in Eastern Europe . . . has collided with a serious obstacle: Its leaders are not very popular." Citing "public anger over their handling of the pandemic" and "growing fatigue with their divisive tactics," he quoted one observer suggesting that "the whole wave has lost its momentum." When Victor Orbán hosted a meeting of "like-minded leaders committed to creating a 'European renaissance based on Christian values,'" the report noted, "only two people showed up: Matteo Salvini, a fading far-right star in Italy who crashed out of government in 2019, and Poland's beleaguered prime minister, Mateusz Morawiecki."[47]

Do these developments mark the end of Europe's "crisis of democracy"? I suspect not. New political entrepreneurs will emerge to exploit the grievances that exist in every political system. While Salvini may be "a fading far-right star," we saw in Chapter 6 that an arguably even-more-radical figure, Giorgia Meloni, has risen as he has fallen. In a political system where anything can happen, bad things are bound to happen sometimes.

As for "anti-populist trends" in central Europe, even when the remarkable gains in subjective well-being that have reconciled many Hungarians and Poles to their "mildly authoritarian" governments reach an end, as they inevitably will, those governments have built institutional bulwarks against political accountability that will be difficult for liberal challengers to overcome. Eventually

45. Marc Santora, "Young Slovaks Buck a Trend, Protesting to Save Their Democracy," *New York Times*, 17 March 2018. Marc Santora, "In Slovakia, Unlikely Presidential Candidate Signals a Backlash against Populism," *New York Times*, 15 March 2019. Marc Santora, "Slovakia's First Female President, Zuzana Caputova, Takes Office in a Divided Country," *New York Times*, 15 June 2019.

46. Jeffrey A. Stacey, "Is a Tide Turning against Populism?," *New York Times*, 10 July 2019.

47. Andrew Higgins, "Populist Leaders in Eastern Europe Run Into a Little Problem: Unpopularity," *New York Times*, 21 June 2021.

the bulwarks will fall; but that will not be the end of the matter. In the US, the undemocratic political machines that governed many major cities in the 19th and early 20th centuries were periodically overthrown by "reformers." But as Jessica Trounstine's historical analysis of some of these cases demonstrated, changing leaders did not automatically reinstate the institutional status quo ante; "reformers" have their own methods and rationales for entrenching themselves in power. Like democracy itself, political accountability involves complex shades of gray, not just black and white, and contention over the mechanics of government is impossible to separate neatly from substantive political struggles.[48]

Politics, the American polymath Arthur Bentley wrote, is about "the adjustment or balance of interests" by means ranging "from battle and riot to abstract reasoning and sensitive morality." It is a difficult business, especially when political contention involves real or imagined threats to cherished social identities and values. The job of politicians is to manage the pressures arising from disagreement as efficiently as possible, and as much as possible on the basis of reasoning and sensitive morality rather than battle and riot. "We cannot analyze any bit of government very deeply," Bentley added, "without becoming aware that it is holding the balance between conflicting interests, that it is enforcing restraints on their activities in the political field, that it is standing between them and acting as mediator at the same time it is acting as ruler."[49]

In democratic politics, public opinion is a weighty manifestation of conflicting interests, though "not at all the most accurate," according to Bentley. It is also a resource to be organized and exploited by democratic leaders pursuing their own visions of the good. When they organize and exploit public opinion skillfully, for good ends—including the good end of safeguarding democracy itself—they deserve our gratitude and respect. When they fail, *that* is a crisis of democracy.

48. Trounstine (2008). Scheppele's (2018) discussion of "autocratic legalism" provides a helpful synthesis of mechanisms of entrenchment in Hungary, Poland, Turkey, and Venezuela.

49. Bentley (1908: 264, 259, 235, 453). Bentley's account remains the most penetrating, albeit often abstruse, analysis of politics "in terms of the various group pressures that form its substance."

APPENDIX

Data

MOST OF THE ANALYSES presented in the preceding pages are based on data from the European Social Survey (ESS), an academic project initiated in 2002 to track European's social and political views.[1] My analysis draws on 183 surveys conducted in nine biannual rounds in 23 countries from 2002 through 2019. (A tenth round of surveys, scheduled to begin in 2020, was postponed due to the Covid-19 pandemic.) The total sample includes 354,829 survey respondents.

Table A1 reports details of question wording and coding and descriptive statistics for 22 key variables derived from the ESS data. The sample sizes shown for each variable represent nonmissing data. A few questions were not asked in some rounds, and most of those that were asked in every round have some data missing due to scattered nonresponse or errors in survey administration. As a general matter, scattered missing data are replaced with neutral values (as indicated in footnotes in Table A1) when these variables are employed as explanatory variables in my analyses; however, I am not aware of any instances in which simply dropping cases with missing data would significantly alter the results. I always exclude cases for which dependent variables are missing data, which accounts for differences in the number of observations included in various analyses employing the same country-rounds.

I supplement the ESS data with a variety of country-level data on economic conditions, demographics, social spending, and immigration. Unless otherwise

1. Data, documentation, and background information appear on the ESS website, https://www.europeansocialsurvey.org/.

	Range	Mean	Standard deviation	Within-country standard deviation	N^a
Trust in parliament and politicians (2004–2019)	0 to 10	3.87	2.22	2.12	343,363[b]
	"Using this card, please tell me how much you personally trust each of the institutions I read out. Firstly, [country]'s parliament? . . . politicians?" (0—No trust at all, 10—Complete trust); responses averaged.				
Electoral support for right-wing populist parties (2014–2019)	0 to 1	.091	.288	.285	50,034 (16 countries; voters only)
	"Some people don't vote nowadays for one reason or another. Did you vote in the last [country] national election in [month/year]?" If yes: "Which party did you vote for in that election?"				
Identification with right-wing populist parties (2014–2019)	0 to 4	.150	.658	.653	80,535 (16 countries)
	"Is there a particular political party you feel closer to than all the other parties? Which one? How close do you feel to this party?" (Not at all close, not close, quite close, very close)				
Conservative ideology	0 to 10	4.94	2.14	2.11	311,087[c]
	"In politics people sometimes talk of 'left' and 'right'. Using this card, where would you place yourself on this scale, where 0 means the left and 10 means the right?"				
Satisfaction with life as a whole	0 to 10	7.01	2.19	2.13	353,269
	"All things considered, how satisfied are you with your life as a whole nowadays?" (0—Extremely dissatisfied, 10—Extremely satisfied)				
Satisfaction with the economy	0 to 10	4.42	2.42	2.25	347,233[d]
	"On the whole how satisfied are you with the present state of the economy in [country]?" (0—Extremely dissatisfied, 10—Extremely satisfied)				
Satisfaction with national government	0 to 10	4.03	2.39	2.32	341,858
	"Now thinking about the [country] government, how satisfied are you with the way it is doing its job?" (0—Extremely dissatisfied, 10—Extremely satisfied)				
Satisfaction with democracy	0 to 10	5.17	2.45	2.36	342,512[e]
	"And on the whole how satisfied are you with the way democracy works in [country]?" (0—Extremely dissatisfied, 10—Extremely satisfied)				

	Range	Mean	Standard deviation	Within-country standard deviation	N^a
Satisfaction with education	0 to 10	5.34	2.26	2.17	338,228
	"Now, using this card, please say what you think overall about the state of education in [country] nowadays?" (0—Extremely bad, 10—Extremely good)				
Satisfaction with health services	0 to 10	5.45	2.46	2.30	350,750
	"Still using this card, please say what you think overall about the state of health services in [country] nowadays?" (0—Extremely bad, 10—Extremely good)				
Support for redistribution	0 to 10	7.11	2.58	2.51	348,300
	"Using this card, please say to what extent you agree or disagree with each of the following statements. The government should take measures to reduce differences in income levels." (1—Agree strongly, 5—Disagree strongly); responses reversed and recoded to 0-to-10 scale.				
Support for European integration (2004–2019)	0 to 10	5.18	2.67	2.61	254,530[f]
	"Now thinking about the European Union, some say European unification should go further. Others say it has already gone too far. Using this card, what number on the scale best describes your position?" (0—Unification has already gone too far, 10—Unification should go further)				
Support for immigration	0 to 10	5.35	2.14	2.08	337,352[g]
	Six-item scale (see Table 4.1)				
Religious	0 to 1	.457	.307	.295	351,921[h]
	"Regardless of whether you belong to a particular religion, how religious would you say you are?" (0—Not at all religious, 10—Very religious)				
Conservative worldview	0 to 10	5.10	1.14	1.11	331,279[i]
	Ten-item scale (see Table 2.4)				
Foreign-born	0 to 1	.098	.297	.294	354,478[j]
Female	0 to 1	.516	.500	.500	354,829
Age (years)	15 to 99	46.9	18.8	18.8	353,371[k]

Continued on next page

	Range	Mean	Standard deviation	Within-country standard deviation	N[a]
Education (years)	0 to 20	12.35	3.90	3.78	350,883[l]

"About how many years of education have you completed, whether full-time or part-time? Please report these in fulltime-equivalents and include compulsory years of schooling."

	Range	Mean	Standard deviation	Within-country standard deviation	N[a]
Union member	0 to 1	.126	.332	.316	354,829

"Are you or have you ever been a member of a trade union or similar organization?" If yes: "Is that currently or previously?" (Only current union affiliations are counted.)

	Range	Mean	Standard deviation	Within-country standard deviation	N[a]
Income (percentile/100)	0 to 1	.500	.286	.286	270,181[m]

"Using this card, please tell me which letter describes your household's total income, after tax and compulsory deductions, from all sources? If you don't know the exact figure, please give an estimate." (Categorical responses are translated into percentiles within each country-round.)

	Range	Mean	Standard deviation	Within-country standard deviation	N[a]
Right-wing populist sentiment	0 to 10	4.95	1.28	1.25	274,955 (ESS rounds 2–4, 6–9)

Imputed based on conservative ideology, anti-immigrant sentiment, anti-EU sentiment, political distrust, dissatisfaction with democracy, conservative worldviews, and economic dissatisfaction (using averages of parameter estimates from Tables 6.1 and 6.2)

Note: ESS country-rounds weighted by adult population; data from 2002–2019 except where indicated.

[a] Nonmissing observations. When these variables are employed as explanatory variables, missing values are imputed as indicated.

[b] 11,466 missing values recoded to 5.01.

[c] 43,742 missing values recoded to 5.01.

[d] 7,596 missing values recoded to 5.01.

[e] 12,317 missing values recoded to 5.01.

[f] 100,299 missing values recoded to 5.01.

[g] 10,248 to 14,331 missing values for each of six survey items recoded to 5.01 (17,477 observations in total).

[h] Recoded from zero-to-ten scale; 2,908 missing values recoded to .49.

[i] 11,637 to 14,373 missing values for each of ten survey items recoded to 4.9 (23,550 observations in total).

[j] 351 missing values recoded to .10.

[k] 1,458 missing values recoded to 45.1; 23 values greater than 99 recoded to 99.

[l] 3,946 missing values recoded to 12.1; 7,887 values greater than 20 recoded to 20.

[m] 84,648 missing values imputed based on demographic variables.

TABLE A2. Key Variables from OECD

	Range	Mean	Standard deviation	Within-country standard deviation	N
ln(GDP per capita)	9.54 to 11.34	10.55	.25	.09	437
	Annual National Accounts: GDP per head, US $, constant prices, constant purchasing power parity, reference year 2015				
Δ(GDP per capita) (%)	−14.26 to 24.02	1.21	2.38	2.17	437
	Annual percentage change in real GDP per capita				
Unemployment rate (%)	2.0 to 27.5	8.71	4.52	3.18	422
	Annual Labor Force Statistics: Rate of unemployment as % of labor force				
ln(social expenditures per capita)	7.62 to 9.66	9.10	.34	.10	391 (2001–2017)
	Social Expenditure Database: Total public expenditure per head, at constant prices (2015) and constant PPPs (2015), in US dollars				
Population over age 64 (%)	10.8 to 22.7	17.72	2.37	1.30	414 (2001–2018)
	Population Statistics: Historical population data: Share of 65 and over—elderly				
Population under age 15 (%)	13.2 to 21.5	15.95	1.94	.62	414 (2001–2018)
	Population Statistics: Historical population data: Share of under 15—children				
Immigrants (per 1,000 population)	.45 to 27.51	6.93	4.78	3.06	393
	International Migration Database: Inflows of foreign population by nationality				
Asylum-seekers (per 1,000 population)	.005 to 17.72	1.00	1.48	1.31	418
	International Migration Database: Inflows of asylum seekers by nationality				

Note: Country-years weighted by adult population; data from 2001–2019 except where indicated.

indicated, these data were compiled and harmonized by the OECD.[2] The key OECD data are summarized in Table A2.

Weighting Survey Data by Population

The populations of the countries included in my analyses range from just over one million in Estonia to more than 70 million in Germany. To provide a trustworthy summary of public opinion in Europe as a whole, I weight the data from each country in each round of the survey in proportion to its adult population (age 15 and older). The resulting weights for each country in each ESS round, expressed as percentages of the total weighted sample, appear in Table A3. Germany accounts for 20% of the weighted sample, while the six most populous countries (Germany, France, Great Britain, Italy, Spain, and Poland) combined account for 74%.

The substantive implications of weighting country-rounds by population are summarized in Table A4, which compares estimated changes in public opinion from 2002–2007 to 2014–2019 with and without population-weighting.[3] The tabulations based on population-weighted data, in the first column of the table, show significantly higher levels of satisfaction with the economy, support for immigration, and satisfaction with life as a whole after the Euro-crisis than before it began, and (possibly) a modest increase in satisfaction with national governments. Trust in parliament and politicians, conservative ideology, satisfaction with democracy, and support for European integration were all essentially unchanged. The estimates derived from weighting each ESS respondent equally (aside from survey weights within country-rounds), in the second column of the table, likewise show significant increases in satisfaction with the economy, support for immigration, and satisfaction with life as a whole, though these increases are about 30% smaller in magnitude, on average. Again, there is a more modest (and statistically uncertain) estimated increase in satisfaction with national government. The

2. For data and documentation, see the OECD.Stat website, https://stats.oecd.org/. Some series are updated periodically; the data analyzed here were the most recent available as of the spring of 2021.

3. In both cases, the analyses incorporate weights provided by the ESS staff to reflect features of the sampling design in specific country-rounds as well as post-stratification based on differences in nonresponse by age-group, gender, education, and region. To mitigate sensitivity of the results to extreme weights, I truncate values greater than 2.5 times the average value for the country-round (about 2% of all observations).

TABLE A3. Population-Weighted European Social Survey Data, 2002–2019

	1	2	3	4	5	6	7	8	9	Total
Austria (AT)	0.21	0.21	0.21	—	—	—	0.23	0.23	0.24	1.33
Belgium (BE)	0.26	0.26	0.26	0.27	0.27	0.28	0.28	0.28	0.29	2.46
Czechia (CZ)	0.26	0.27	—	0.28	0.28	0.28	0.28	0.28	0.27	2.20
Denmark (DK)	0.13	0.13	0.13	0.13	0.14	0.14	0.14	—	—	0.94
Estonia (EE)	—	0.04	0.04	0.04	0.03	0.03	0.03	0.03	0.03	0.28
Finland (FI)	0.13	0.13	0.13	0.13	0.14	0.14	0.14	0.14	0.14	1.22
France (FR)	1.48	1.51	1.54	1.55	1.57	1.58	1.60	1.62	1.64	14.09
Germany (DE)	2.17	2.20	2.22	2.23	2.24	2.20	2.23	2.26	2.26	20.01
Great Britain (GB)	1.44	1.46	1.50	1.53	1.55	1.58	1.60	1.62	1.63	13.91
Greece (GR)	0.28	0.29	—	0.29	0.30	—	—	—	—	1.16
Hungary (HU)	0.26	0.26	0.26	0.26	0.27	0.26	0.26	0.26	0.26	2.37
Ireland (IE)	0.09	0.09	0.10	0.10	0.10	0.10	0.10	0.11	0.11	0.91
Italy (IT)	1.53	—	—	—	—	1.61	—	1.65	1.66	6.45
Lithuania (LT)	—	—	—	—	0.08	0.08	0.08	0.08	0.07	0.39
Netherlands (NL)	0.39	0.39	0.40	0.41	0.41	0.42	0.43	0.43	0.44	3.73
Norway (NO)	0.11	0.11	0.11	0.11	0.12	0.12	0.13	0.13	0.13	1.06
Poland (PL)	0.94	0.96	0.98	1.00	1.01	1.01	1.02	1.01	1.01	8.94
Portugal (PT)	0.27	0.27	0.27	0.28	0.28	0.28	0.28	0.28	0.28	2.48
Slovakia (SK)	—	0.13	0.14	0.14	0.14	0.14	—	—	0.14	0.84
Slovenia (SI)	0.05	0.05	0.05	0.05	0.06	0.06	0.05	0.05	0.05	0.49
Spain (ES)	1.11	1.14	1.18	1.22	1.23	1.23	1.22	1.22	1.24	10.79
Sweden (SE)	0.22	0.22	0.23	0.23	0.24	0.24	0.24	0.25	0.25	2.12
Switzerland (CH)	0.18	0.19	0.19	0.20	0.21	0.21	0.22	0.22	0.22	1.85
Total	11.49	10.32	9.95	10.47	10.66	12.00	10.56	12.17	12.38	100%

Note: Share of weighted sample (%) by country and ESS round.

TABLE A.4. Estimated Shifts in European Public Opinion, Comparing Population-Weighted and Unweighted Samples

	Country-rounds weighted by population	Survey design and post-stratification weights only
Trust in parliament and politicians	+.02	+.10
	(.11)	(.07)
Conservative ideology	+.03	−.00
	(.04)	(.03)
Satisfaction with life as a whole	+.32	+.24
	(.06)	(.04)
Satisfaction with the economy	+.56	+.41
	(.26)	(.16)
Satisfaction with incumbent government	+.13	+.13
	(.17)	(.12)
Satisfaction with democracy	+.01	+.07
	(.11)	(.08)
Support for European integration	+.05	−.15
	(.12)	(.08)
Support for immigration	+.39	+.24
	(.11)	(.07)

Note: Estimated changes from 2002–2007 to 2014–2019 (with standard errors clustered by country-round in parentheses). Fixed effects for countries are included but not shown.

tabulations also show a modest decline in support for European integration and (perhaps) a small increase in political trust, neither of which appear in the population-weighted tabulations.[4] In general, however, the results based on the unweighted data are consistent with those based on population-weighted data in providing no evidence of significant deterioration, and some instances of improvement, in these measures of public opinion in the wake of the Euro-crisis.

4. The estimates in the second column are somewhat more precise, reflecting the greater statistical efficiency of less extreme weighting of the raw data. The standard deviation of the weights reflecting variation in design factors and post-stratification only is .51; the standard deviation of the weights incorporating differences in population as well is 1.28.

Discrepancies between Reported
and Actual Electoral Support

In Chapter 6, I analyze the bases of support for 16 right-wing populist parties. As I note there, the ESS data significantly underestimate electoral support for these parties. This systematic underrepresentation of right-wing populist supporters presumably reflects some combination of biases in sampling, differential response rates, and reluctance on the part of some survey respondents to report voting for parties that may be viewed as unconventional or even disreputable.

Figure A1 shows the relationship between election outcomes and survey reports for all 93 surveys in which these 16 parties (or clear predecessors) were included as response options in ESS vote questions. In a substantial majority of cases—78 of 93—the surveys underestimated the actual vote totals. On average, the underestimates amount to 3 percentage points, or 20% of the actual right-wing populist vote in these elections. This underestimate exactly matches the 20% underestimate of support for "radical right parties" in surveys conducted as part of the Comparative Study of Electoral Systems, another large-scale cross-national collaborative academic survey.[5]

The underreports of support for right-wing populist parties are generally roughly proportional to their actual vote shares. Thus, despite the underreporting, the correlation between reported and actual support across parties and elections is reassuringly high, .90. However, the relative magnitude of underestimation of right-wing populist support has increased by about 1% per year over the course of the ESS project, perhaps due to the increasing difficulty of conducting representative opinion surveys.[6] The dashed line in the figure

---

5. For all 93 surveys, the average ESS reported right-wing populist vote is 11.6% and the actual right-wing populist vote share is 14.5%. In the 42 surveys conducted after 2013, the average ESS reported vote (11.6%) is 78% of the average actual vote (14.9%). Regressing reported vote shares on actual vote shares (with no constant) produces a parameter estimate of .813 (with a country-clustered standard error of .057) for all 93 surveys, and .760 (with a country-clustered standard error of .037) for the 42 surveys conducted after 2013. For the corresponding underestimate in CSES data, see Valentim (2021: Table A1).

6. For all 93 surveys, the share of actual support reflected in the surveys decreased by about 1.5% per year (a regression parameter estimate of −.015 with a country-clustered standard error of .005). However, part of that apparent trend reflects an *overestimation* of support for the Slovenian Democratic Party in early ESS rounds. Omitting the 8 cases from Slovenia produces a parameter estimate of −.009 (with a country-clustered standard error of .006). Hooghe and

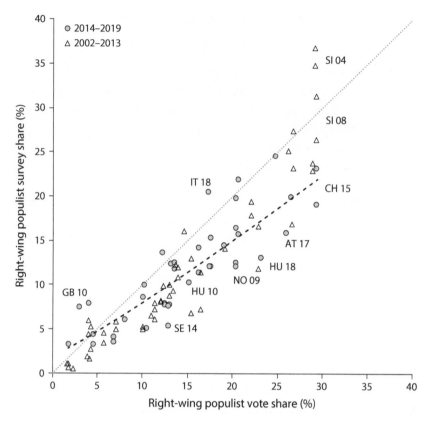

FIGURE A1. Underreporting of Right-Wing Populist Support in ESS

shows the quadratic relationship between actual and reported vote shares for the 42 post-crisis surveys—the cases I focus on in Chapter 6.

Aside from this temporal trend, there is little evident pattern in the discrepancies between survey results and election outcomes. For example, large and small vote shares for right-wing populist parties were roughly

Reeskens's (2007: Table 4) detailed comparison of actual and reported support for right-wing populist parties in the first two ESS rounds suggested that underreporting was strongly related to low survey response rates, as well as low election turnout rates and low aggregate levels of political trust. However, they found only negligible relationships between underreporting and the size and age of right-wing populist parties, aggregate levels of ethnocentrism and political interest, and the time interval between elections and surveys.

similarly underestimated in proportional terms. Sudden gains in electoral support were sometimes significantly understated in the ESS data (for True Finns in 2011, UKIP in Great Britain in 2015, and Germany's AfD in 2017), but sometimes not (for France's National Front in 2012 and Lega in Italy in 2018). Two of the largest underestimates were for one of the most venerable and consistently successful right-wing populist parties in Europe, the Swiss People's Party.

In some cases, the survey reports seem to have been colored by shifts in sentiment since the last election. For example, 15.8% of 2018–2019 ESS respondents in Austria reported having voted for the Freedom Party in October 2017, far less than the party's actual vote share, 26.0%; in the next election eight months later, the party tallied 16.2%. In Hungary, reported support for Jobbik in the April 2014 election fell from 19.7% in mid-2015 to 11.9% in mid-2017; public polls showed contemporaneous support for Jobbik falling by about the same amount over that period.[7] Overall, however, there is no systematic relationship between the timing of surveys and the extent of underreporting of right-wing populist sentiment, or even the absolute magnitude of discrepancies between actual and reported votes.[8]

While the ESS data generally understate electoral support for right-wing populist parties, they consistently *overstate* support for Fidesz in Hungary and the Law and Justice party in Poland. It may be tempting to suppose that survey respondents in those countries felt pressure to express support for increasingly authoritarian ruling parties. However, in both cases, the exaggeration of support predated the party's rise to power, increasing only marginally thereafter. Moreover, in Poland, electoral support for the main opposition party, Civic Platform, was also exaggerated in the ESS data, even after 2015. On average,

7. According to Politico's "poll of polls" compilation, https://www.politico.eu/europe-poll -of-polls/hungary/, support for Jobbik fell from 26% in May 2015 to 19% in June 2017.

8. For all 93 surveys, the share of actual support reflected in the surveys decreased by about 2.5% for every year between the election and the survey (a regression parameter estimate of −.025 with a country-clustered standard error of .017). However, this apparent relationship is entirely due to the 8 cases from Slovenia; in the other 85 cases, the gap between the election and the survey had no effect at all on underreporting (a parameter estimate of +.003 with a country-clustered standard error of .014). Overall, the (root mean squared) discrepancy between actual votes and survey reports was 4.59 percentage points in the 46 surveys conducted in the election year or the year after, and 4.63 percentage points in the 47 surveys conducted in the second, third, or (rarely) fourth year following the election.

electoral support for both major parties in both countries was exaggerated by 15%, at the expense of a variety of smaller parties. Nonetheless, as with right-wing populist parties, the variation in support for these parties across countries and elections is reflected with considerable fidelity in the ESS data; the overall correlation between actual vote shares and estimated vote shares in the surveys is .92.[9]

9. The average vote share for the four major parties in these two countries—Fidesz and MSZP in Hungary (2002–2018) and Law and Justice and Civic Platform in Poland (2005–2015)—was 35.0; the corresponding average ESS reported vote share was 40.2. Regressing ESS reported vote shares on actual vote shares (with no constant) produces a parameter estimate of 1.150 (with a standard error of .035) for all 18 cases (two major parties in each of five elections in Hungary and four in Poland). The corresponding parameter estimate for the nine winning parties in these elections is 1.180 (with a standard error of .049).

ACKNOWLEDGMENTS

THIS BOOK BEGAN, as all projects should, with a visit to Paris. My thinking about democracy in Europe was stimulated by participating in a roundtable at Sciences Po in May 2017 on the political consequences of the Euro-crisis. I am grateful to Nonna Mayer for inspiring that event, and to her colleagues for including me in it. The tentative findings I presented at Sciences Po appeared in a brief report posted on the *Washington Post*'s Monkey Cage blog. A few years later, I presented a broader summary of the argument (alas, remotely) at a conference in Athens marking the 2,500th anniversary of the Battle of Salamis.[1]

Having spent most of my career studying American politics, I have benefited even more in this project than in others from the help of knowledgeable colleagues and friends. Nancy Bermeo has been a patient and authoritative tutor in the field of comparative politics, as well as an influential model of engaged scholarship on democracy. As always, Chris Achen provided wise advice and constructive criticism. Hanspeter Kriesi generously shared his data on protests and a prepublication version of his analysis of those data. Sheri Berman, Kaitlen Cassell, Kathy Cramer, Marc Hetherington, Frances Lee, Benjamin Page, Wendy Rahn, Bryn Rosenfeld, and John Sides contributed helpful discussions, some explicitly related to the arguments presented here and others less so. John Zaller has been an unfailing source of perspective and encouragement.

Vanderbilt University has generously supported my work, both collegially and materially. Participants in the Vanderbilt political science department's faculty workshop offered valuable feedback at various stages of the project. Shannon Meldon-Corney, program coordinator for the Center for the Study of Democratic Institutions, expertly and graciously smoothed the occasional rough edges of my professional life. Kaitlen Cassell provided splendid research

---

1. Larry Bartels, "The 'Wave' of Right-Wing Populist Sentiment Is a Myth," *Washington Post*, 21 June 2017. Bartels (2022).

assistance, gathering and digesting a great deal of relevant material, including much that I didn't know enough to know I wanted. Vanderbilt's May Werthan Shayne Chair provided financial support for her work, while a semester leave in the spring of 2021 provided me with concentrated time to produce a complete draft of the manuscript.

For extensive feedback on that draft, I am grateful to Achen, Berman, Cramer, Hetherington, Kriesi, Mayer, Zaller, Allison Anoll, André Blais, Carles Boix, Rafaela Dancygier, Anna Grzymala-Busse, Dan Hopkins, Lane Kenworthy, Mikael Persson, Markus Prior, Bob Putnam, Wouter Schakel, Sue Stokes, two anonymous reviewers, and my editor at Princeton University Press, Bridget Flannery-McCoy. While I have not succeeded in incorporating all of their good advice, I owe many significant improvements to their generous assistance.

Most of the research and writing of this book was done during the Covid-19 pandemic. My ability to work through that trying time, largely insulated from the hardships that afflicted so many people, bespeaks a life of great privilege. I am especially grateful for the love and support of my wife, Denise. Through more than four decades of marriage, I often imagined that there was no one in the world I would rather spend a year alone with. Happily, for me and for this book, that turned out to be true.

REFERENCES

Aassve, Arnstein, Gianmarco Daniele, and Marco Le Moglie (2019). "Never Forget the First Time: The Persistent Effect of Corruption and the Rise of Populism in Italy." Unpublished manuscript. https://www.aeaweb.org/conference/2020/preliminary/paper/QNi4Rb4b.

Abts, Koen, and Stefan Rummens (2007). "Populism versus Democracy." *Political Studies* 55, 405–424.

Achen, Christopher H., and Larry M. Bartels (2016). *Democracy for Realists: Why Elections Do Not Produce Responsive Government*. Princeton, NJ: Princeton University Press.

Adorno, T. W., Else Frenkel-Brunswik, Daniel J. Levinson, and R. Nevitt Sanford (1950). *The Authoritarian Personality*. New York: Harper & Row.

Albertazzi, Daniele, and Sean Mueller (2013). "Populism and Liberal Democracy: Populists in Government in Austria, Italy, Poland and Switzerland." *Government and Opposition* 48, 343–371.

Alesina, Alberto, and Edward L. Glaeser (2004). *Fighting Poverty in the US and Europe: A World of Difference*. New York: Oxford University Press.

Almond, Gabriel A., and Sidney Verba (1963). *The Civic Culture: Political Attitudes and Democracy in Five Nations*. Princeton, NJ: Princeton University Press.

Anderson, Christopher J., and Jason D. Hecht (2014). "Crisis of Confidence? The Dynamics of Economic Opinions during the Great Recession." In Nancy Bermeo and Larry M. Bartels, eds., *Mass Politics in Tough Times: Opinions, Votes, and Protest in the Great Recession*, 40–71. New York: Oxford University Press.

Arendt, Hannah (1951). *The Origins of Totalitarianism*. New York: Harcourt, Brace and Company.

Armingeon, Klaus, and Kai Guthmann (2014). "Democracy in Crisis? The Declining Support for National Democracy in European Countries, 2007–2011." *European Journal of Political Research* 53, 423–442.

Arzheimer, Kai, and Carl C. Berning (2019). "How the Alternative for Germany (AfD) and Their Voters Veered to the Radical Right, 2013–2017." *Electoral Studies* 60, 102040.

Bartels, Larry M. (1988). *Presidential Primaries and the Dynamics of Public Choice*. Princeton, NJ: Princeton University Press.

Bartels, Larry M. (1998). "Electoral Continuity and Change, 1868–1996." *Electoral Studies* 17, 301–326.

Bartels, Larry M. (2013a). "Political Effects of the Great Recession." *ANNALS of the American Academy of Political and Social Science* 650: 47–76.

Bartels, Larry M. (2013b). "Party Systems and Political Change in Europe." Presented at the Annual Meeting of the American Political Science Association. https://my.vanderbilt.edu /larrybartels/files/2011/12/europe1.pdf.

Bartels, Larry M. (2014). "Ideology and Retrospection in Electoral Responses to the Great Recession." In Nancy Bermeo and Larry M. Bartels, eds., *Mass Politics in Tough Times: Opinions, Votes, and Protest in the Great Recession*, 185–223. New York: Oxford University Press.

Bartels, Larry M. (2017). "Political Inequality in Affluent Democracies: The Social Welfare Deficit." Presented at the 4th Conference in Political Economy & Political Science, Toulouse, https://www.vanderbilt.edu/csdi/includes/Working_Paper_5_2017.pdf.

Bartels, Larry M. (2018). "Partisanship in the Trump Era." *Journal of Politics* 80, 1483–1494.

Bartels, Larry M. (2020). "Ethnic Antagonism Erodes Republicans' Commitment to Democracy." *Proceedings of the National Academy of Sciences* 117, 22752–22759.

Bartels, Larry M. (2022). "Democracy Erodes from the Top: Public Opinion and Democratic 'Backsliding' in Europe." In Emmanouil M. L. Economou, Nicholas C. Kyriazis, and Athanasios Platias, eds., *Democracy in Times of Crises: Challenges, Problems and Policy Proposals*, 41–67. Cham, Switzerland: Springer.

Bentley, Arthur F. (1908). *The Process of Government: A Study of Social Pressures*. New Brunswick, NJ: Transaction, 2008.

Berman, Sheri (2019). *Democracy and Dictatorship in Europe: From the Ancien Régime to the Present Day*. New York: Oxford University Press.

Bermeo, Nancy (2003). *Ordinary People in Extraordinary Times: The Citizenry and the Breakdown of Democracy*. Princeton, NJ: Princeton University Press.

Bermeo, Nancy, and Larry M. Bartels (2014). "Mass Politics in Tough Times." In Bermeo and Bartels, eds., *Mass Politics in Tough Times: Opinions, Votes, and Protest in the Great Recession*, 1–39. New York: Oxford University Press.

Bermeo, Nancy, and Jonas Pontusson (2012). *Coping with Crisis: Government Reactions to the Great Recession*. New York: Russell Sage Foundation.

Blinder, Alan S. (2013). *After the Music Stopped: The Financial Crisis, the Response, and the Work Ahead*. New York: Penguin Press.

Boswell, Christina, and Andrew Geddes (2011). *Migration and Mobility in the European Union*. New York: Palgrave Macmillan.

Breton, Charles, and Gregory Eady (2022). "Does International Terrorism Affect Public Attitudes toward Refugees? Evidence from a Large-Scale Natural Experiment." *Journal of Politics* 84, 554–559.

Broockman, David E. 2016. "Approaches to Studying Policy Representation." *Legislative Studies Quarterly* 41, 181–215.

Brooks, Clem, and Jeff Manza (2007). *Why Welfare States Persist: The Importance of Public Opinion in Democracies*. Chicago: University of Chicago Press.

Bull, Martin J., and Gianfranco Pasquino (2018). "Italian Politics in an Era of Recession: The End of Bipolarism?" *South European Society and Politics* 23, 1–12.

Cantat, Céline, and Prem Kumar Rajaram (2019). "The Politics of the Refugee Crisis in Hungary: Bordering and Ordering the Nation and Its Others." In Cecilia Menjívar, Marie Ruiz, and Immanuel Ness, eds., *The Oxford Handbook of Migration Crises*, 181–195. New York: Oxford University Press.

Castanho Silva, Bruno (2019). "Populist Success: A Qualitative Comparative Analysis." In Kirk A. Hawkins, Ryan E. Carlin, Levente Littvay, and Cristóbal Rovira Kaltwasser, eds., *The Ideational Approach to Populism: Concept, Theory, and Analysis*, 279–293. New York: Routledge.

Castles, Francis G. (2004). *The Future of the Welfare State: Crisis Myths and Crisis Realities*. New York: Oxford University Press.

Cavaille, Charlotte, and John Marshall (2019). "Education and Anti-Immigration Attitudes: Evidence from Compulsory Schooling Reforms across Western Europe." *American Political Science Review* 113, 254–263.

Chou, Winston, Rafaela Dancygier, Naoki Egami, and Amaney A. Jamal (2021). "Competing for Loyalists? How Party Positioning Affects Populist Radical Right Voting." *Comparative Political Studies* 54, 2226–2260.

Citrin, Jack (1974). "Comment: The Political Relevance of Trust in Government." *American Political Science Review* 68, 973–988.

Claassen, Christopher (2020). "Does Public Support Help Democracy Survive?" *American Journal of Political Science* 64, 118–134.

Cohen, Marty, David Karol, Hans Noel, and John Zaller (2016). "Party versus Faction in the Reformed Presidential Nominating System." *PS: Political Science & Politics* 49, 701–708.

Converse, Philip E. (1964). "The Nature of Belief Systems in Mass Publics." In David E. Apter, ed., *Ideology and Discontent*, 206–261. New York: Free Press.

Copelovitch, Mark, Jeffry Frieden, and Stefanie Walter (2016). "The Political Economy of the Euro Crisis." *Comparative Political Studies* 49, 811–840.

Crozier, Michel, Samuel P. Huntington, and Joji Watanuki (1975). *The Crisis of Democracy: Report on the Governability of Democracies to the Trilateral Commission*. New York: New York University Press.

Dancygier, Rafaela M. (2010). *Immigration and Conflict in Europe*. New York: Cambridge University Press.

Dancygier, Rafaela, and Michael Donnelly (2014). "Attitudes toward Immigration in Good Times and Bad." In Nancy Bermeo and Larry M. Bartels, eds., *Mass Politics in Tough Times: Opinions, Votes, and Protest in the Great Recession*, 148–184. New York: Oxford University Press.

Day, Michael (2015). *Being Berlusconi: The Rise and Fall from Cosa Nostra to Bunga Bunga*. New York: St. Martin's Press.

De Jonge, Léonie (2020). "The Curious Case of Belgium: Why Is There No Right-Wing Populism in Wallonia?" *Government and Opposition*. https://doi.org/10.1017/gov.2020.8.

Dennison, James, and Andrew Geddes (2019). "A Rising Tide? The Salience of Immigration and the Rise of Anti-Immigration Political Parties in Western Europe." *Political Quarterly* 90, 107–116.

Drozdiak, William (2017). *Fractured Continent: Europe's Crises and the Fate of the West*. New York: W. W. Norton & Company.

Dukelow, Fiona, and Mairéad Considine (2014). "Outlier or Model of Austerity in Europe? The Case of Irish Social Protection Reform." *Social Policy and Administration* 48, 413–429.

Dukelow, Fiona, and Patricia Kennett (2018). "Discipline, Debt and Coercive Commodification: Post-Crisis Neoliberalism and the Welfare State in Ireland, the UK and the USA." *Critical Social Policy* 38, 482–504.

Eatwell, Roger, and Matthew Goodwin (2018). *National Populism: The Revolt against Liberal Democracy*. London: Pelican Books.

Eichengreen, Barry (2015). *Hall of Mirrors: The Great Depression, the Great Recession, and the Uses—and Misuses—of History*. New York: Oxford University Press.

Elsässer, Lea, and Armin Schäfer (2018). "Unequal Representation and the Populist Vote in Europe." Unpublished paper prepared for the workshop "Political Equality in Unequal Societies," Villa Vigoni. https://www.democratic-anxieties.eu/wordpress/wp-content/uploads/2018/05/Elsa%CC%88sser-Scha%CC%88fer-VV18.pdf.

Erlingsson, Gissur Ó., Karl Loxbo, and Richard Öhrvall (2012). "Anti-Immigrant Parties, Local Presence and Electoral Success." *Local Government Studies* 38, 817–839.

Esping-Andersen, Gøsta (1990). *The Three Worlds of Welfare Capitalism*. Princeton, NJ: Princeton University Press.

Esping-Andersen, Gøsta (1996). "After the Golden Age? Welfare State Dilemmas in a Global Economy." In Esping-Andersen, ed., *Welfare States in Transition: National Adaptations in Global Economies*, 1–31. Thousand Oaks, CA: Sage Publications.

Feldman, Stanley, and Karen Stenner (1997). "Perceived Threat and Authoritarianism." *Political Psychology* 18, 741–770.

Fitzgerald, Jennifer (2018). *Close to Home: Local Ties and Voting Radical Right in Europe*. New York: Cambridge University Press.

Foa, Roberto Stefan, and Yascha Mounk (2016). "The Democratic Disconnect." *Journal of Democracy* 27, 5–17.

Fomina, Joanna, and Jacek Kucharczyk (2016). "Populism and Protest in Poland." *Journal of Democracy* 27, 58–68.

Ford, Robert, and Matthew Goodwin (2014). *Revolt on the Right: Explaining Support for the Radical Right in Britain*. New York: Routledge.

Frey, Arun (2020). "'Cologne Changed Everything'—The Effect of Threatening Events on the Frequency and Distribution of Intergroup Conflict in Germany." *European Sociological Review* 36, 684–699.

Fukuyama, Francis (1992). *The End of History and the Last Man*. New York: Free Press.

Gabel, Matthew J. (1998). *Interests and Integration: Market Liberalization, Public Opinion, and European Union*. Ann Arbor: University of Michigan Press.

Geithner, Timothy F. (2014). *Stress Test: Reflections on Financial Crises*. New York: Broadway Books.

Ghodsee, Kristen, and Mitchell A. Orenstein (2021). *Taking Stock of Shock: Social Consequences of the 1989 Revolutions*. New York: Oxford University Press.

Graham, Matthew H., and Milan W. Svolik (2020). "Democracy in America? Partisanship, Polarization, and the Robustness of Support for Democracy in the United States." *American Political Science Review* 114, 392–409.

Greskovits, Béla (2015). "The Hollowing and Backsliding of Democracy in East Central Europe." *Global Policy* 6, 28–37.

Guvenen, Fatih, Serdar Ozkan, and Jae Song (2014). "The Nature of Countercyclical Income Risk." *Journal of Political Economy* 122, 621–660.

Harteveld, Eelco, Andrej Kokkonen, Jonas Linde, and Stefan Dahlberg (2021). "A Tough Trade-Off? The Asymmetrical Impact of Populist Radical Right Inclusion on Satisfaction with Democracy and Government." *European Political Science Review* 13, 113–133.

Hetherington, Marc J., and Jonathan D. Weiler (2009). *Authoritarianism and Polarization in American Politics*. New York: Cambridge University Press.

Hetherington, Marc, and Jonathan Weiler (2018). *Prius or Pickup? How the Answers to Four Simple Questions Explain America's Great Divide*. Boston: Houghton Mifflin Harcourt.

Hibbing, John R., and Elizabeth Theiss-Morse (2002). *Stealth Democracy: Americans' Beliefs about How Government Should Work*. New York: Cambridge University Press.

Hobolt, Sara B., and Catherine E. de Vries (2016). "Public Support for European Integration." *Annual Review of Political Science* 19, 413–432.

Hobolt, Sara B., and James Tilley (2016). "Fleeing the Centre: The Rise of Challenger Parties in the Aftermath of the Euro Crisis." *West European Politics* 39, 971–991.

Hooghe, Marc, and Tim Reeskens (2007). "Are Cross-National Surveys the Best Way to Study the Extreme-Right Vote in Europe?" *Patterns of Prejudice* 41, 177–196.

Inglehart, Ronald F., and Pippa Norris (2016). "Trump, Brexit, and the Rise of Populism: Economic Have-Nots and Cultural Backlash." HKS Faculty Research Working Paper RWP16-026, John F. Kennedy School of Government, Harvard University.

Irwin, Neil (2013). *The Alchemists: Three Central Bankers and a World on Fire*. New York: The Penguin Press.

Ivarsflaten, Elisabeth (2008). "What Unites Right-Wing Populists in Western Europe? Re-Examining Grievance Mobilization Models in Seven Successful Cases." *Comparative Political Studies* 41, 3–23.

Jones, Erik, R. Daniel Kelemen, and Sophie Meunier (2016). "Failing Forward? The Euro Crisis and the Incomplete Nature of European Integration." *Comparative Political Studies* 49, 1010–1034.

Judis, John B. (2016). *The Populist Explosion: How the Great Recession Transformed American and European Politics*. New York: Columbia Global Reports.

Kahneman, Daniel, and Angus Deaton (2010). "High Income Improves Evaluation of Life but Not Emotional Well-Being." *Proceedings of the National Academy of Sciences* 107, 16489–16493.

Katznelson, Ira (2020). *Desolation and Enlightenment: Political Knowledge after Total War, Totalitarianism, and the Holocaust*. New York: Columbia University Press.

Kaufman, Robert R., and Stephan Haggard (2019). "Democratic Decline in the United States: What Can We Learn from Middle-Income Backsliding?" *Perspectives on Politics* 17, 417–432.

Kavanagh, Nolan M., Antil Menon, and Justin E. Heinze (2021). "Does Health Vulnerability Predict Voting for Right-Wing Populist Parties in Europe?" *American Political Science Review* 115, 1104–1109.

Kenworthy, Lane (2009). "The Effect of Public Opinion on Social Policy Generosity," *Socio-Economic Review* 7, 727–740.

Kenworthy, Lane (2019). *Social Democratic Capitalism*. New York: Oxford University Press.

Kenworthy, Lane, and Lindsay A. Owens (2011). "The Surprisingly Weak Effect of Recessions on Public Opinion." In David B. Grusky, Bruce Western, and Christopher Wimer, eds., *The Great Recession*, 196–291. New York: Russell Sage Foundation.

Key, V. O., Jr. (1949). *Southern Politics in State and Nation*. New York: Alfred A. Knopf.

Key, V. O., Jr. (1961). *Public Opinion and American Democracy*. New York: Knopf.

Kinder, Donald R., and Nathan P. Kalmoe (2017). *Neither Liberal nor Conservative: Ideological Innocence in the American Public*. Chicago: University of Chicago Press.

Knutsen, Oddbjørn (1995). "Value Orientations, Political Conflicts and Left-Right Identification: A Comparative Study." *European Journal of Political Research* 28, 63–93.

Kriesi, Hanspeter (2014). "The Political Consequences of the Economic Crisis in Europe: Electoral Punishment and Popular Protest." In Nancy Bermeo and Larry M. Bartels, eds., *Mass Politics in Tough Times: Opinions, Votes, and Protest in the Great Recession*, 297–333. New York: Oxford University Press.

Kriesi, Hanspeter (2020). "Overall Trends of Protest in the Great Recession." In Hanspeter Kriesi, Jasmine Lorenzini, Bruno Wüest, and Silja Häusermann, eds., *Contention in Times of Crisis: Recession and Political Protest in Thirty European Countries*, 77–103. New York: Cambridge University Press.

Kriesi, Hanspeter, Edgar Grande, Martin Dolezal, Marc Helbling, Dominic Höglinger, Swen Hutter, and Brunot Wüest (2012). *Political Conflict in Western Europe*. New York: Cambridge University Press.

Kriesi, Hanspeter, Jasmine Lorenzini, Bruno Wüest, and Silja Häusermann, eds. (2020). *Contention in Times of Crisis: Recession and Political Protest in Thirty European Countries*. New York: Cambridge University Press.

Kustov, Alexander, Dillon Laaker, and Cassidy Reller (2021). "The Stability of Immigration Attitudes: Evidence and Implications." *Journal of Politics* 83, 1478–1494.

Lachat, Romain (2018). "Which Way from Left to Right? On the Relation between Voters' Issue Preferences and Left-Right Orientation in West European Democracies." *International Political Science Review* 39, 419–435.

Lee, Frances E. (2020). "Populism and the American Party System: Opportunities and Constraints." *Perspectives on Politics* 18, 370–388.

Lenz, Gabriel S. (2012). *Follow the Leader? How Voters Respond to Politicians' Policies and Performance*. Chicago: University of Chicago Press.

Lerman, Amy E. (2019). *Good Enough for Government Work: The Public Reputation Crisis in America (And What We Can Do to Fix It)*. Chicago: University of Chicago Press.

Levitsky, Steven, and Daniel Ziblatt (2018). *How Democracies Die*. New York: Crown.

Lewis-Beck, Michael (1988). *Economics and Elections: The Major Western Democracies*. Ann Arbor: University of Michigan Press.

Linz, Juan J., and Alfred Stepan, eds. (1978). *The Breakdown of Democratic Regimes* (4 vols.). Baltimore: Johns Hopkins University Press.

Lippmann, Walter (1922). *Public Opinion*. New York: The Macmillan Company.

Lippmann, Walter (1925). *The Phantom Public*. New York: Harcourt, Brace and Company.

Lopez-Valcarcel, Beatriz G., and Patricia Barber (2017). "Economic Crisis, Austerity Policies, Health and Fairness: Lessons Learned in Spain." *Applied Health Economics and Health Policy* 15, 13–21.

Lowell, A. Lawrence (1898). "Oscillations in Politics." *Annals of the American Academy of Political and Social Science* 12, 69–97.

Lowell, A. Lawrence (1913). *Public Opinion and Popular Government*. New York: Longmans, Green.

Lowell, A. Lawrence (1934). "The Present Crisis in Democracy." *Foreign Affairs* 12, 183–192.

Loxbo, Karl, and Niklas Bolin (2016). "Party Organizational Development and the Electoral Performance of the Radical Right: Exploring the Role of Local Candidates in the Breakthrough

Elections of the Sweden Democrats 2002–2014." *Journal of Elections, Public Opinion and Parties* 26, 170–190.

Lupia, Arthur, and Mathew D. McCubbins (1998). *The Democratic Dilemma: Can Citizens Learn What They Need to Know?* New York: Cambridge University Press.

Maarse, Hans, and Aggie Paulus (2011). "The Politics of Health-Care Reform in the Netherlands since 2006." *Health Economics, Policy and Law* 6, 125–134.

Mader, Matthias, and Harald Schoen (2019). "The European Refugee Crisis, Party Competition, and Voters' Responses in Germany." *West European Politics* 42, 67–90.

Mainwaring, Scott, and Aníbal Pérez-Liñán (2013). *Democracies and Dictatorships in Latin America: Emergence, Survival, and Fall.* New York: Cambridge University Press.

Mair, Peter (2013). *Ruling the Void: The Hollowing-Out of Western Democracy.* New York: Verso.

Martinsson, Johan, and Ulrika Andersson, eds. (2021). *Swedish Trends: 1986–2020.* Gothenburg: SOM Institute.

McClosky, Herbert (1964). "Consensus and Ideology in American Politics." *American Political Science Review* 58, 361–382.

McCoy, Jennifer, Tahmina Rahman, and Murat Somer (2018). "Polarization and the Global Crisis of Democracy: Common Patterns, Dynamics, and Pernicious Consequences for Democratic Polities." *American Behavioral Scientist* 62, 16–42.

Messina, Anthony M. (2007). *The Logics and Politics of Post-WWII Migration to Western Europe.* New York: Cambridge University Press.

Mettler, Suzanne, and Robert C. Lieberman (2020). *Four Threats: The Recurring Crises of American Democracy.* New York: St. Martin's Press.

Metz, Rudolf, and Réka Várnagy (2021). "'Mass,' 'Movement,' 'Personal,' or 'Cartel' Party? Fidesz's Hybrid Organisational Strategy." *Politics and Governance* 9, 317–328.

Mody, Ashoka (2018). *EuroTragedy: A Drama in Nine Acts.* New York: Oxford University Press.

Moffitt, Benjamin (2016). *The Global Rise of Populism: Performance, Political Style, and Representation.* Stanford, CA: Stanford University Press.

Moffitt, Benjamin (2020). *Populism.* New York: John Wiley & Sons.

Mounk, Yascha (2018). *The People vs. Democracy: Why Our Freedom Is in Danger and How to Save It.* Cambridge, MA: Harvard University Press.

Mudde, Cas (2004). "The Populist Zeitgeist." *Government and Opposition* 39, 541–563.

Mudde, Cas (2007). *Populist Radical Right Parties in Europe.* New York: Cambridge University Press.

Mudde, Cas (2013). "Three Decades of Populist Radical Right Parties in Western Europe: So What?" *European Journal of Political Research* 52, 1–19.

Mudde, Cas (2016). *On Extremism and Democracy in Europe.* New York: Routledge.

Mudde, Cas, and Cristóbal Rovira Kaltwasser (2014). "Populism and Political Leadership." In R. A. W. Rhodes and Paul t'Hart, eds., *The Oxford Handbook of Political Leadership*, 376–388. New York: Oxford University Press.

Mueller, John E. (1973). *War, Presidents and Public Opinion.* New York: John Wiley & Sons.

Muliro, Arthur (2017). "Editorial: The Crisis of Democracy." *Development* 60, 145–148.

Müller, Jan-Werner (2016). *What Is Populism?* Philadelphia: University of Pennsylvania Press.

Murphy, Justin, and Daniel Devine (2020). "Does Media Coverage Drive Public Support for UKIP or Does Public Support for UKIP Drive Media Coverage?" *British Journal of Political Science* 50, 893–910.

Norris, Pippa, and Ronald Inglehart (2019). *Cultural Backlash: Trump, Brexit, and Authoritarian Populism.* New York: Cambridge University Press.

Oliver, J. Eric, and Wendy M. Rahn (2016). "Rise of the *Trumpenvolk*: Populism in the 2016 Election." *ANNALS of the American Academy of Political and Social Science* 667, 189–206.

Page, Benjamin I., and Robert Y. Shapiro (1992). *The Rational Public: Fifty Years of Trends in Americans' Policy Preferences.* Chicago: University of Chicago Press.

Pap, András L. (2018). *Democratic Decline in Hungary: Law and Society in an Illiberal Democracy.* New York: Routledge.

Pierson, Paul (1994). *Dismantling the Welfare State? Reagan, Thatcher, and the Politics of Retrenchment.* New York: Cambridge University Press.

Polsby, Nelson W. (1983). *Consequences of Party Reform.* New York: Oxford University Press.

Popkin, Samuel L. (1991). *The Reasoning Voter: Communication and Persuasion in Presidential Campaigns.* Chicago: University of Chicago Press.

Prothro, James W., and Charles M. Grigg (1960). "Fundamental Principles of Democracy: Bases of Agreement and Disagreement." *Journal of Politics* 22, 276–294.

Przeworski, Adam (2019). *Crises of Democracy.* New York: Cambridge University Press.

Putnam, Robert D., with Robert Leonardi and Raffaella Y. Nanetti (1993). *Making Democracy Work: Civic Traditions in Modern Italy.* Princeton, NJ: Princeton University Press.

Radcliff, Benjamin (2013). *The Political Economy of Human Happiness: How Voters' Choices Determine the Quality of Life.* New York: Cambridge University Press.

Rahn, Wendy M., and Howard Lavine (2018). "Representation Gaps and Recent Presidential Elections." Paper prepared for presentation at the inaugural conference of the Citrin Center: Trust and Populism in the Age of Trump, Institute for Governmental Studies, University of California, Berkeley.

Roche, William K., Philip J. O'Connell, and Andrea Prothero (2017). "'Poster Child' or 'Beautiful Freak'? Austerity and Recovery in Ireland." In Roche, O'Connell, and Prothero, eds., *Austerity and Recovery in Ireland: Europe's Poster Child and the Great Recession*, 1–22. New York: Oxford University Press.

Roiser, Martin, and Carla Willig (2002). "The Strange Death of the Authoritarian Personality: 50 Years of Psychological and Political Debate." *History of the Human Sciences* 15, 71–96.

Rosenfeld, Bryn (2021). *The Autocratic Middle Class: How State Dependency Reduces the Demand for Democracy.* Princeton, NJ: Princeton University Press.

Rovira Kaltwasser, Cristóbal (2012). "The Ambivalence of Populism: Threat and Corrective for Democracy." *Democratization* 19, 184–208.

Rueda, David (2012). "West European Welfare States in Times of Crisis." In Nancy Bermeo and Jonas Pontusson, eds., *Coping with Crisis: Government Reactions to the Great Recession*, 361–398. New York: Russell Sage Foundation.

Schäfer, Armin (2013). "Liberalization, Inequality and Democracy's Discontent." In Armin Schäfer and Wolfgang Streeck, eds., *Politics in the Age of Austerity*, 169–195. Cambridge, UK: Polity Press.

Schäfer, Armin, and Wolfgang Streeck (2013). "Introduction: Politics in the Age of Austerity." In Armin Schäfer and Wolfgang Streeck, eds., *Politics in the Age of Austerity*, 169–195. Cambridge, UK: Polity Press.

Scharpf, Fritz W. (2013). "Monetary Union, Fiscal Crisis and the Disabling of Democratic Accountability." In Armin Schäfer and Wolfgang Streeck, eds., *Politics in the Age of Austerity*, 108–142. Cambridge, UK: Polity Press.

Schattschneider, E. E. (1960). *The Semisovereign People: A Realist's View of Democracy in America*. New York: Holt, Rinehart and Winston.

Scheppele, Kim Lane (2018). "Autocratic Legalism." *University of Chicago Law Review* 85, 545–584.

Schlozman, Kay Lehman, and Sidney Verba (1979). *Injury to Insult: Unemployment, Class, and Political Response*. Cambridge, MA: Harvard University Press.

Schumpeter, Joseph A. (1950). *Capitalism, Socialism and Democracy*, 3rd ed. New York: Harper & Row.

Schut, Frederik T., and Wynand van de Ven (2011). "Effects of Purchaser Competition in the Dutch Health Care System: Is the Glass Half Full or Half Empty?" *Health Economics, Policy and Law* 6, 109–123.

Sides, John, and Jack Citrin (2007). "European Opinion about Immigration: The Role of Identities, Interests, and Information." *British Journal of Political Science* 37, 477–504.

Sides, John, Michael Tesler, and Lynn Vavreck (2018). *Identity Crisis: The 2016 Presidential Campaign and the Battle for the Meaning of America*. Princeton, NJ: Princeton University Press.

Simonsen, Kristina Bakkær (2020). "Immigration and Immigrant Integration Policy: Public Opinion or Party Politics?" In Peter Munk Cristiansen, Jørgen Elklit, and Peter Nedergaard, eds., *The Oxford Handbook of Danish Politics*, 609–626. New York: Oxford University Press.

Sniderman, Paul M., Richard A. Brody, and Philip E. Tetlock (1991). *Reasoning and Choice: Explorations in Political Psychology*. New York: Cambridge University Press.

Sniderman, Paul M., Louk Hagendoorn, and Markus Prior (2004). "Predisposing Factors and Situational Triggers: Exclusionary Reactions to Immigrant Minorities." *American Political Science Review* 98, 35–49.

Stenner, Karen (2005). *The Authoritarian Dynamic*. New York: Cambridge University Press.

Stimson, James A. (2015). *Tides of Consent: How Public Opinion Shapes American Politics*, 2nd ed. New York: Cambridge University Press.

Stokes, Donald E., and Gudmund R. Iversen (1962). "On the Existence of Forces Restoring Party Competition." *Public Opinion Quarterly* 26, 159–171.

Stokes, Susan C. (2001). *Mandates and Democracy: Neoliberalism by Surprise in Latin America*. New York: Cambridge University Press.

Svolik, Milan W. (2019). "Polarization versus Democracy." *Journal of Democracy* 30, 20–32.

Tarchi, Marco (2018). "Voters without a Party: The 'Long Decade' of the Italian Centre-Right and Its Uncertain Future." *South European Society and Politics* 23, 147–162.

Tillman, Erik R. (2013). "Authoritarianism and Citizen Attitudes towards European Integration." *European Union Politics* 14, 566–589.

Tillman, Erik R. (2021). *Authoritarianism and the Evolution of West European Electoral Politics*. New York: Oxford University Press.

Tooze, Adam (2018). *Crashed: How a Decade of Financial Crises Changed the World*. New York: Viking.

Treas, Judith (2010). "The Great American Recession: Sociological Insights on Blame and Pain." *Sociological Perspectives* 53, 3–17.

Trounstine, Jessica (2008). *Political Monopolies in American Cities: The Rise and Fall of Bosses and Reformers*. Chicago: University of Chicago Press.

Turnbull-Dugarte, Stuart J., José Rama, and Andrés Santana (2020). "The Baskerville Dog Suddenly Started Barking: Voting for VOX in the 2019 Spanish General Elections." *Political Research Exchange* 2. https://www.tandfonline.com/doi/full/10.1080/2474736X.2020.1781543.

Valentim, Vicente (2021). "Parliamentary Representation and the Normalization of Radical Right Support." *Comparative Political Studies* 54, 2475–2511.

Van de Ven, Wynand, and Frederik T. Schut (2008). "Universal Mandatory Health Insurance in the Netherlands: A Model for the United States?" *Health Affairs* 27, 771–781.

Van der Brug, Wouter, Meindert Fennema, and Jean Tillie (2005). "Why Some Anti-Immigrant Parties Fail and Others Succeed: A Two-Step Model of Aggregate Electoral Support." *Comparative Political Studies* 38, 537–573.

Van der Meer, Tom W. G. (2017). "Political Trust and the 'Crisis of Democracy.'" *Oxford Research Encyclopedia, Politics*. https://doi.org/10.1093/acrefore/9780190228637.013.77.

Van Hauwaert, Steven M., and Stijn Van Kessel (2018). "Beyond Protest and Discontent: A Cross-National Analysis of the Effect of Populist Attitudes and Issue Positions on Populist Party Support." *European Journal of Political Research* 57, 68–92.

Varoufakis, Yanis (2016). *And the Weak Suffer What They Must? Europe's Crisis and America's Economic Future*. New York: Nation Books.

Varoufakis, Yanis (2017). *Adults in the Room: My Battle with the European and American Deep Establishment*. New York: Farrar, Straus and Giroux.

Walker, Jack L. (1966). "A Reply to 'Further Reflections on the Elitist Theory of Democracy.'" *American Political Science Review* 60, 391–392.

Wettstein, Martin, Anne Schulz, Marco Steenbergen, Christian Schemer, Philipp Muller, Dominique S. Wirz, and Werner Wirth (2020). "Measuring Populism across Nations: Testing for Measurement Invariance of an Inventory of Populist Attitudes." *International Journal of Public Opinion Research* 32, 284–305.

Zaller, John (1998). "Monica Lewinsky's Contribution to Political Science." *PS: Political Science and Politics* 31, 182–189.

INDEX

Note: Page numbers in *italic* type refer to figures or tables.

Ingram Content Group UK Ltd.
Milton Keynes UK
UKHW040239160323
418396UK00006B/6/J